CRUSADE
Against the GRAIL

CRUSADE
Against the GRAIL

THE STRUGGLE BETWEEN THE CATHARS, THE TEMPLARS, AND THE CHURCH OF ROME

OTTO RAHN

TRANSLATED AND ANNOTATED BY CHRISTOPHER JONES

Inner Traditions
Rochester, Vermont

Inner Traditions
One Park Street
Rochester, Vermont 05767
www.InnerTraditions.com

Originally published in German in 1933 under the title *Kreuzzug gegen den Gral*
by Urban Verlag
First U.S. edition published in 2006 by Inner Traditions

Library of Congress Cataloging-in-Publication Data
Rahn, Otto, 1904–1939.
  [Kreuzzug gegen den Gral. English]
  Crusade against the Grail : the struggle between the Cathars, the Templars, and
the Church of Rome / Otto Rahn ; translated and annotated by Christopher Jones.
— 1st U.S. ed.
    p. cm.
  Summary: "The first English translation of the book that reveals the Cathar
stronghold at Montsegur to be the repository of the Holy Grail"—Provided by
publisher.
  Includes bibliographical references and index.
  ISBN-13: 978-1-59477-135-4
  ISBN-10: 1-59477-135-9
  1. Grail. 2. Albigenses. I. Title.
  BX4891.R313 2006
  272'.3—dc22
                                                                    2006021691

Printed and bound in the United States by Lake Book Manufacturing

10 9 8 7 6 5 4 3 2 1

Text design and layout by Priscilla Baker
This book was typeset in Sabon, with Trajan and Charlemagne used as display
typefaces

To send correspondence to the author of this book, mail a first-class letter to the
author c/o Inner Traditions • Bear & Company, One Park Street, Rochester, VT
05767, and we will forward the communication.

CONTENTS

Translator's Foreword   vii
Map of Southern France   xvi
Prologue   xix

PART ONE

Parsifal   3

PART TWO

The Grail   43
The Golden Fleece   53
Gwion's Cup   59
How the Bard Taliesin Came to the World   67
The Legend of the Bard Cervorix   68
The "Pure Ones" and Their Doctrine   70
The Caves of Trevrizent Close to the Fountain
    Called La Salvaesche   93
Monmur, the Enchanted Castle of Oberon   101
Muntsalvaesche and Montségur   104
Repanse de Schoye   108

PART THREE

The Crusade   115

PART FOUR

The Apotheosis of the Grail   157

Appendix: Observations on the Theoretical Part   190
Notes   193
Bibliography   211
Index   224

TRANSLATOR'S FOREWORD

————◆————

WHEN URBAN VERLAG IN FREIBURG published the first edition of *Crusade Against the Grail* [*Kreuzzug gegen den Gral*] in 1933, the book was not an immediate bestseller. But its eloquence deeply moved those who read it. One so moved was Albert H. Rausch, the 1933 Georg Büchner prize-winner who published under the pseudonym Henry Benrath. Rausch wrote an introduction for the book called *Kreuz und Gral* [*Cross and Grail*], which eventually appeared in the *Baseler Nachrichten* later in the year.[1]

Perhaps this was why Hans E. Günther Verlag in Stuttgart decided to republish the work in 1964 under the supervision of Karl Rittersbacher, a disciple of Rudolf Steiner's Theosophical Society. Rittersbacher's edition coincided with the twenty-fifth anniversary of Otto Rahn's death in the Tyrolean Mountains. Over the years, some very successful books have named *Crusade* as a key source, although, oddly, it was never translated into English.[2] Now, seventy-three years after its initial publication, we owe this first English language edition to Verlag Zeitenwende in Dresden and Inner Traditions in Vermont—and my wife's indulgence.

The book's author, Otto Rahn, was twenty-eight at the time of its publication. Anchoring his work in the poetry of the troubadours, he hoped to resolve the legend of the Grail and surpass Heinrich Schliemann, the celebrated nineteenth century German archeologist who had used Homer's *Iliad* to locate ancient Troy. "To open the gates of Lucifer's kingdom," Rahn would write, "you must equip yourself with a *Dietrich* [skeleton key] . . . I carry the key with me."

Rahn was convinced that Wolfram von Eschenbach's thirteenth

century epic *Parsifal* provided him with the key that would unlock the mysteries of the medieval Cathars and their heretical, dualistic form of Christianity, which venerated something called the *Mani*. According to Rahn, the characters described by Wolfram were not the products of an old troubadour's imagination; they were clearly identifiable as Albigensian Cathars, and their story would guide him to their lost treasure—the Grâl (Grail).

Skillfully blending legends and tales, oral history, religion, art, and colorful depictions of one of the most beautiful parts of Europe—the region of southern France that is still known as "the land of the Cathars" *[le pays des Cathares]*—Rahn describes the brutality of the Papal crusade against southern France and the repression of the Albigensian sect by the Inquisition. The Vatican and Royal Paris combined to destroy Occitan civilization in the first genocide of modern history because the Cathars had worshipped the Mani or Grail and rejected the cross. According to some estimates, this crusade killed nearly a million people.

As his translator, I have tried to be as faithful as possible to Rahn's text. Whenever possible, personal names appear in their original Provençal form. Respecting Rahn's desire for academic scholarship, I have restored and reedited his notes, adding new sources along the way that either correct or reinforce his assertions. When necessary, I have checked my own Middle German translations with Professor A. T. Hatto's wonderful version of *Parzival*.[3] The result may be unconventional for mainstream medievalists, but it should be remembered that this daring work is based on solid research in France's prestigious Bibliothèque Nationale, and that early editions included a thorough bibliography.

To the best of my knowledge, this is also the first time that parts of Nikolaus Lenau's melancholic poem *Die Albigenser* (1842) have appeared in English. Lenau, considered Austria's chief lyric poet, was a pseudonym for Nikolaus Niembsch Edler von Strehlenau (1802–1850), an Austrian aristocrat who was born in Hungary. Basing his verses on historical research, Lenau wrote in a letter that "the subject fascinates me," and "my courage is great . . . for all, I hope that God looks benevolently on this work." According to Lenau's biographer Anastasius Grün, the task was easily completed, although the poet's mind failed in 1844. He died in an asylum.

In other important passages, Rahn calls upon the prophetic thoughts of Goethe (1749–1832) and Novalis (1772–1801) to help us understand the moral and political confrontation between the Cathars and Roman Catholicism. This clash marked the end of an era of individual spiritual experimentation and the beginning of an epoch of pious strangulation, which is personified in *Crusade* by the vicious thirteenth century Dominican Inquisitor Bernard Gui.

Gui's famous handbook for interrogators is an important if highly flawed source of the little knowledge we have of the Albigensian sects. Like the Italian semiotician Umberto Eco, who used the sadistic character of Gui many years later in his book *The Name of the Rose* (1984), Rahn contrasts Cathar spiritual freedom with the Inquisition's cruel techniques as a bizarre symbol of "the gloss of stifling authority."[4] Just recently, Gui's book, *Le Livre des sentences de l'Inquisiteur Bernard Gui* (1308–1323)—better known as *The Inquisitor's Manual*—was republished in French under the supervision of Annette Palès-Gobillard, although, perhaps as a sign of the times, an English translation is not planned.[5]

The Romantic period of the 1840s, which saw revolutions sweep across Europe in 1848, coincided with the 600th anniversary of the fall of the Cathar fortress of Montségur. Many republican revolutionaries saw the Cathars as the forerunners of the anticlerical radicals who stormed the Bastille in 1789. Momentarily freed from the censorship of reactionary Catholicism, many academics took a fresh look at the Cathars' tragic story, and this renewed interest in the Albigensian crusade provided Rahn with several important cornerstones for his book.

Prominent among these works are the monumental five volumes of *L'Histoire des Albigeois* (1870–1881) by Napoléon Peyrat (1809–1881).[6] An authentic Romantic historian in the tradition of Michelet, the Ariège-born Peyrat became a Protestant pastor in 1831, and was close to the anticlerical poet Béranger. His first major work, *Les Pasteurs du désert* (1842), deals with the revolt of the Protestant *camisards* and *cévenols* in the seventeenth century. Curiously, just like Otto Rahn, Peyrat was convinced that he was descended from Cathar heretics. This obsession led him to spend forty years researching and writing the history of the Cathars (the last volume of *L'Histoire des Albigeois* was published posthumously). Although Peyrat certainly popularized the fortress of Montségur as the symbol of Cathar resistance, his works, like

Rahn's book, are well supported by solid research in the archives of the Inquisition that are still kept in Carcassonne.

Rahn's theological ideas were greatly influenced by Ernest Renan (1823–1892). The beliefs he expressed in his series, *L'Histoire des Origines du Chrétianisme [The History of the Origins of Christianity]*, which included his most famous work, *La Vie de Jésus* (1863), were quite close to the liberal Protestant school (David Friedrich Strauss and others). A tremendous success, *La Vie de Jésus* sold nearly 5,000 copies per week. But Catholics were enraged: between 1863 and 1864, an incredible 300 books and booklets were published denouncing his "blasphemy" and "mistakes." But the book was published again and again; today, forty-five different editions have come out, with the most recent appearing in 2005.

Another important source from this period was *Beiträge zur Sektengeschichte des Mittlealters [Essays on the History of Sects in the Middle Ages]* (1890) by the Bavarian theologian Ignaz von Döllinger (1799–1890). The son of a medical professor, Döllinger was elected in 1848 to the liberal National Assembly in Frankfurt, where he defended the separation of church and state. Vehemently opposed to the doctrine of Papal infallibility, he took part in the first Vatican Council in 1869–1870. Although the Pope excommunicated Döllinger on April 17, 1871, he was named rector of the Munich University in 1872. Today, he is remembered as a pioneer of the German ecumenical movement.

Otto Wilhelm Rahn was born in 1904 in Michelstadt in the German state of Hesse, an area brimming with tales of medieval chivalry. Rahn's father Karl introduced his son to the legends of Parzival, Lohengrin, and naturally Siegfried and the *Nibelungenlied* during their walks in the Odenwald forest. Rahn later explained, "My ancestors were pagans, and my grandparents were heretics." His family's home was not far from Marburg am Lahn, where the insidious Inquisitor Konrad had terrorized the court of the Landgrave of Thüringia in the thirteenth century. Rahn long considered writing a historical novel about the "magister," who was responsible for (among other things) beating the Landgrave's wife (later Saint) Elizabeth of Hungary to death and burning hundreds of German Cathars at the stake before a group of knights killed him.

Rahn's favorite professor, Baron von Gall, a lecturer in theology at the University of Giessen, greatly impressed him with his descriptions of the tragedy of Catharism. Rahn wrote, "It was a subject that completely captivated me." After obtaining his bachelor's degree in 1922 and pursuing further studies at the Universities of Heidelberg, Giessen, and Freiburg, Rahn was ready to begin his travels abroad. When a French family invited him to visit Geneva in 1931, he gravitated to the French Pyrenees to begin his own investigations.

Before leaving for the south of France, Rahn asked a Swiss friend, Paul-Aléxis Ladame (1909–2000), to accompany him because Ladame had some experience in speleology and mountaineering. He was also descended from an old Cathar family (the name was originally La Dama) that escaped from Béziers to Switzerland during the crusade. We owe a lot to him. Long after his friend's death, Ladame wrote down his vital recollections of Rahn and their Pyrenean explorations in several entertaining works. His last work, *Quand le Laurier Reverdira,* recalled a Cathar adage: "In 700 years, when the laurel grows green again" *[al cap de set cent ans, lo laurel verdejara]*—the final words of the last Cathar *Perfectus,* Guilhem de Bélibaste, before he was burned alive.[7]

Accompanied at times by Rahn's friend and mentor, Antonin Gadal, they conducted extensive explorations of the Montségur area. In the grottoes of the Sabarthès they were thunderstruck when they visited a huge cavern called "the Cathedral" by the locals. In it were a large stalagmite called "The Altar" and another known as "The Tomb of Hercules." The forest around the legendary castle of Muntsalvaesche was called Briciljan. Near Montségur is a small forest called the Priscilien Wood. As evidence accumulated, the Wagnerian mists cleared: Wolfram had based his story on fact. Rahn confidently proclaimed that the fortress castle of Montségur in the French Pyrenees was the Temple of the Grail, and that mystical Cathar Christianity, based on the veneration of the Holy Spirit as symbolized by the Mani, was the Church of the Holy Grail. The gates of Lucifer's kingdom had been thrown open; the result was *Crusade Against the Grail.*

Soon the book came to the attention of the leaders of the Third Reich. According to Ladame, Rahn explained that he had received a mysterious telegram while he was in Paris. As usual, he was depressed because he was having difficulty finding backers for a French translation of *Crusade.* The person who wrote the telegram did not give his name, but offered Rahn 1,000 Reichsmarks per month to write a sequel to the book. A little later, money was wired to Paris so that he could settle his affairs in France and return to Germany to a specific address in Berlin: 7, Prinz Albrechtstrasse. When Rahn finally turned up, he was shocked to learn that the telegram's sender was none other than Heinrich Himmler! The head of the SS welcomed him personally and invited the young author to join the SS as a civilian historian and archeologist. Rahn later told Ladame, "What was I supposed to do? Turn him down?"

In an effort aimed at reinforcing National Socialist ideology, the SS was organizing expeditions all over the globe to trace the origins of the Indo-Europeans. Dr. Ernst Schäfer led a famous German-Himalayan expedition to prove that Tibet was the cradle of the Arya, and to investigate the legend of the "Abominable Snowman." Another expedition visited the South Pole and studded the polar cap with small swastika flags. An elderly colonel in the former Austro-Hungarian army, Karl Maria Wiligut, better known as "Weisthor," became Himmler's esoteric "lord" of runology. At Wiligut's insistence, Rahn participated in a German expedition to Iceland to research the origin of the Eddas and the birthplace of Stalde Snorri Sturluson—despite the fact that he was becoming disaffected with the Nazi elite.

Thanks to his position as Himmler's archaeologist specializing in the legend of the Grail, Rahn had become a sort of Nazi shooting star, giving lectures and radio talks about his explorations. But gradually, almost imperceptibly, he began to move in circles that were openly opposed to the regime. This came to the attention of Adolf Hitler at least once, when Rahn invited regime opponents like the post-Romantic composer Hans Pfiztner to the 1938 inauguration of the *Haus der deutsche Kunst* in Munich. Rahn's friendship with Adolf Frisé must have also come to Himmler's attention; Frisé, whose real name was Adolf Altengartner, was the publisher of Robert Musil's famous novel *A Man Without Qualities*. The author was living in exile in Switzerland, bitterly opposed to the Nazis and Hitler's *Anschluss* that had incorporated their Austrian homeland into the Nazi Reich.

Rahn's second book, *Luzifers Hofgesind, eine Reise zu den guten Geistern Europas [Lucifer's Court, a Journey to Europe's Good Spirits]*, appeared in Leipzig in 1937; it remains controversial to this day. The intinerary of his European journey included Bingen, Paris, Toulouse, Marseille, Milan, Rome, Verona, Brixen, Geneva, Worms, Michelstadt,

Burg Wildenberg near Amorbach, Giessen Marburg Goslar, Cologne, Berlin, Warnemünde, Edinburgh, Reykyavik, and Reykholt. In the book, Rahn does not identify Lucifer with the Devil; for him, Lucifer was the Pyrenean Abellio or the Greek God Apollo—all bearers of light.

Nevertheless, the book contains at least one passage that is openly anti-Semitic, which led Paul Ladame to conclude that the Nazis had tampered with the final draft of the manuscript. Many years later he was quoted as saying, "Otto Rahn would never have written that." Apparently, Rahn dictated much of the book to his secretary, who was keeping an eye on his activities for Himmler.

More and more, Rahn yearned for a golden renaissance of traditional values based on the unity of France and Germany under neo-Cathar beliefs, and opposed the pernicious policies that were leading Europe to war. He was convinced that the intolerance inherent in the Old Testament was essentially responsible for the constant cycles of ethnic and genocidal violence throughout history. In fact, there is a strange symmetry between Hitler's war, which resulted in the Holocaust, and the Papal crusade against the Cathars, which obliterated Occitan civilization. After apparently quarreling with Himmler (which led to a tour of duty as a camp guard as punishment), amid accusations of homosexuality and possible Jewish heritage, he resigned from his post early in 1939. He wrote, "There is much sorrow in my country. Impossible for a tolerant, liberal man like me to live in the nation that my native country has become."

Trapped and overpowered by a malicious culture, Otto Wilhelm Rahn died in the snow of the Wilderkaiser on March 13, 1939, almost the anniversary of the fall of Montségur. An apparent suicide, he ended his life in the style of the ritual Cathar *endura*. When he learned of Rahn's death, Antonin Gadal wrote, "Otto Rahn's suffering was over." Rahn was buried in 1940 in Darmstadt. As Karl Rittersbacher concluded, "the transit of this soul, in eternal search for a new and desired spirituality that he could not find on Earth, reminds me as if a benevolent angel of death had brought him the *consolamentum*."

As he explains in his prologue to *Crusade*, Otto Rahn did not wish to point an accusing finger. For multiple reasons he wanted to chart a new path toward the future—and come to terms with human destiny. By addressing such problems as our own mortality, so essential to the human condition, *Crusade* contains a powerful message for our greedy and narcissistic society. "For some time now, I have resided in the mountains of the Tabor. Often, deeply moved, I have wandered through the crystal halls and marble crypts of the caves of the heretics, moving aside the bones of 'Pure Ones' and knights fallen in 'the fight for the spirit,' my steps echoing on the wet floor in the emptiness. Then I stop—listening—half expecting a troubadour to sing a sonnet in honor of the supreme *Minne,* that sublime love that converted men into gods."

Perhaps it shouldn't come as a surprise, but Rahn's medieval world resembled that of his time, and our own, in its moral hypocrisy. With a remarkable sense of drama, he shows how the Cathars' genuine values were totally irrelevant to the despotic Pope and his power-hungry henchmen. He constantly contrasts the depravity of the Holy See and Saint Dominic's instrument for repression—the Inquisition—with the symbolic purity of the Grail. And yet, throughout the book, the mystery of the Cathar Mani or "Grâl" lacks a single, sharply defined description. What was it?[8]

In *Parzival,* Wolfram describes how a Kabbalistic astronomer named Flegetanis described the Grâl as a "stone from the stars" to another Minnesinger named Kyot who in turn related the story to Wolfram. Frequently, I have deliberately left the spelling of "Grail" in its middle German equivalent to emphasize that we are dealing with the legend of a "grail," and not the Holy Grail, the chalice that Joseph of Arimathea used to catch the blood of Jesus when he died on the cross. Like many others, Rahn was convinced that the founders of the church simply Christianized a pagan symbol. In *Crusade,* Rahn develops the Grail into an icon for the survival of the human soul. In this way, he is able to convey its dazzling yet indefinable power over the Cathars. Robert Graves wrote, "Symbolism or allegory is 'truer' than realism in that the former allows more possibilities or interpretations. And more possibilities—implying greater freedom and less context dependence—translate to a greater truth. Accordingly, it has been said, 'The more numerous the poetic meanings that could be concentrated in a sacred name; the greater was its power.'" In this way, the Grâl is perhaps the most powerful symbol of all for a simple reason: nobody has ever seen it.

Finally, in an age when we all have a stake in overcoming the scourge of extremism, I am hoping that the publication of Rahn's book may provide an important contribution. The English-language publication of *Crusade Against the Grail* would not have been possible without the help of many people who encouraged me to undertake this project.

In France, I would to thank French philosopher, author and magazine editor Alain de Benoist, and author and medievalist André Douzet, who is the driving force behind the Société Pérrillos for their help. As always I must thank the world's foremost experts in the art and wisdom of the Catalan surrealist Salvador Dali, Robert and Nicolas Descharnes, who always do their best to steer me in the right direction.

In the Anglo-Saxon publishing world, there were very few voices of encouragement, which of course makes these acknowledgments even more poignant: Barnaby Rogerson of Eland Publishing in London, Gilles Tremlett at *The Guardian*'s bureau in Madrid, and Michael Moynihan, the publisher and editor of Dominion Books, deserve special recognition. Finally, special thanks are reserved for Sven Henkler at Verlag Zeitenwende in Dresden, Jon Graham of Inner Traditions, Ronald Hilton, Professor Emeritus at Stanford University, and Anne Dillon, my editor at Inner Traditions for her patient dedication. And most important of all, without the understanding and patient support of my wife Eva Maria, my own quest to see this book published would never have succeeded.

CHRISTOPHER JONES

Christopher Jones is a historical scholar, translator, editor, and documentary producer. A contributing scholar to Scribner's *Encyclopedia of Europe,* he is a member of Ronald Hilton's WAIS historical discussion forum at Stanford University, the editor of White Star publishers' *Adventure Classics* 2006 reissue of William Bligh's *Mutiny on the Bounty,* and the editor and translator of Robert Descharnes' *Dali: The Hard and the Soft* and Descharnes' memoir, *Dali: The Infernal Heritage.*

During the translation of *Crusade Against the Grail,* Jones retraced Otto Rahn's footsteps in the Pyrenees, exploring the caves and grottoes of the Cathars just as Rahn had done. Jones is also a translating Otto Rahn's second book, *Lucifer's Court: A Journey in Search of Europe's Good Spirits.*

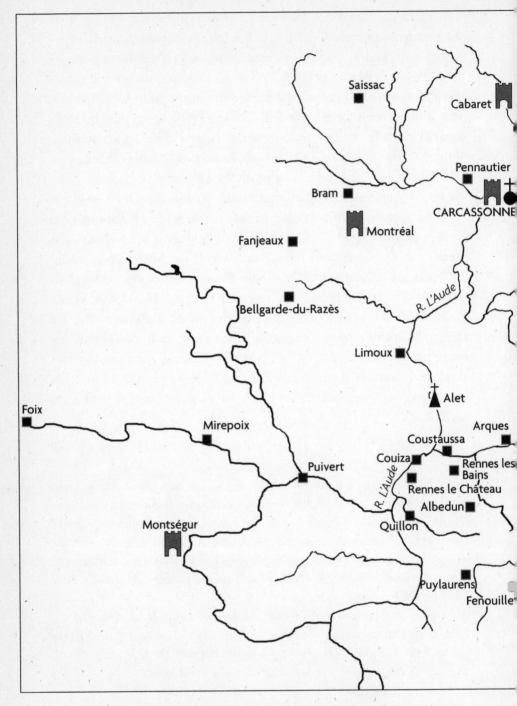

Key Cathar cities, towns, and strongholds in
Southern France possibly related to the Holy Grail

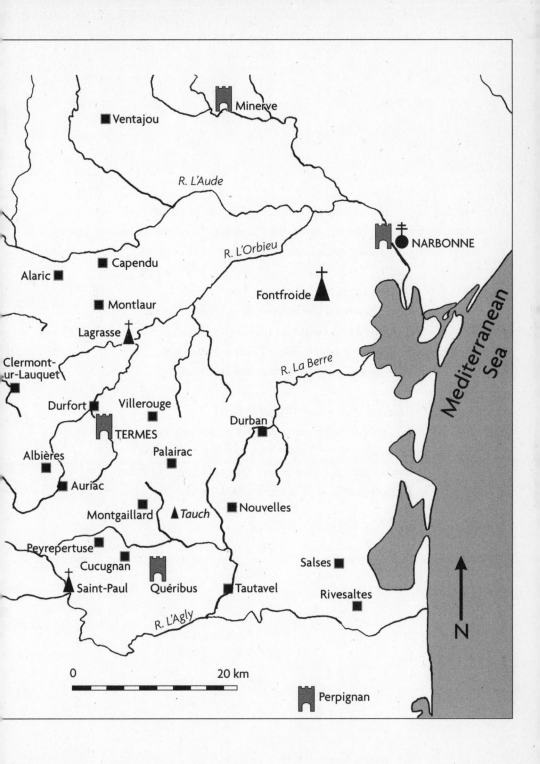

Ventajou

Minerve

R. L'Aude

Capendu

Alaric

R. L'Orbieu

NARBONNE

Montlaur

Fontfroide

Lagrasse

Clermont-
ur-Lauquet

R. La Berre

Durfort

Villerouge

Durban

TERMES

Albières

Palairac

Auriac

Montgaillard

▲*Tauch*

Nouvelles

Peyrepertuse

Cucugnan

Salses

Saint-Paul

Quéribus

Tautavel

Rivesaltes

R. L'Agly

N

0   20 km

Mediterranean Sea

Perpignan

In the Sabarthès, among the numerous signs, drawings, and names that can be found in the caves of the "cathedral" is the following poetry, written by an anonymous hand in the year 1850:

Dédie aux prêtres! Qu'est-ce dieu?
Loin de rien décider de cet être suprême,
Gardons en l'adorant un silence profond.
Le mystère est immense et l'esprit si confond,
Pour dire ce qu'il est, il faut être lui (même)

[Dedicated to priests! What is God?
Far from deciding anything of this supreme being,
Let us keep a profound silence while adoring him,
The mystery is immense and the spirit so confounded,
To say what he is, it is neccesary to be him (self)]

If Master Chrestien de Troyes has done wrong by this story,
Kyot, who sent us the authentic tale, has good cause to be angry.
The authentic tale with the conclusion to the romance has been sent to
The German lands for us from Provence.
I, Wolfram von Eschenbach, intend to speak no more of it
Than what the master uttered over there.[1]

PROLOGUE

———◆———

WOLFRAM VON ESCHENBACH INFORMS US that Kyot, "the famous Master," brought the true legend of the Grail from Provence to German soil, and that Chrétien de Troyes (the author of *Perceval le gaullois ou le conte du graal*) changed it. While it is true that no epic poem about the Grail by "Kyot" exists, we do know that by the end of the twelfth century a French poet from Provence named Guyot toured the most renowned courts of the north and south of France, and that among his poems was a "Bible" in which he caricatured his contemporaries. It seems possible to attribute a version of *Parsifal* that has never reached us to this Guyot. The first part of Wolfram's *Parzival* is strongly influenced by Chrétien's unfinished *Perceval le gaullois,* and is an obvious imitation of it. But starting with the ninth book, Wolfram embarks on an entirely new formulation of the tale of the Holy Grail. If this were inspired by Guyot, his contribution would have affected only the last, most important part, which refers to the Grail.

Why did Guyot's original version never reach us?[2]

Many theories have been put forward, but in my mind the real reason has never been discussed. We have never fully recognized that the crusades of 1209 to 1229 against Provence and Languedoc, and above all the Inquisition in the south of France, destroyed a large portion of

Provençal literature. The censorship applied by the members of the "Crusade against the Albigenses" and the Inquisition was very efficient. Every book suspected of heresy was subjected to a "trial by fire," thrown into a bonfire. Only those books considered non-heretical were left intact and held aloft. With the use of such methods, it is easy to understand why precious little remained.

Walter Map, a cleric in the court of England's Henry II and perhaps the author of the *Grand Saint Graal* (written circa 1189), relates that while there were no "heretics" in Brittany, by contrast there were many in Anjou, and that they were numerous in Burgundy and Aquitania (and consequently in Provence and Languedoc).[3] Caesarius von Heisterbach explains that the "Albigensian heresy" spread with such intensity that it had converts in almost a thousand towns, and if it had not been obliterated with blood and fire, it would have taken over all of Europe.[4] A historian belonging to the order of the Minorites cites it, together with Jews, pagans, Muslims, and German emperors, as the five great enemies of Rome.

Regarding their doctrine, the "Albigenses" (who shared only their name with Albi, a town in southern France) belonged to two different heretical sects. The best known were the Waldenses (founded by a merchant from Lyon named Peter Waldo), who spread throughout Western Europe in an incredibly short period of time. The second were the Cathars (from the Greek *katharos* = pure, and the origin of the German word *ketzer* or heretic). They could easily be called the Mahatma Gandhis of the West in the Middle Ages. Bent over their looms, they pondered whether "the spirit of the world weaves the living suit of divinity in the creaking loom of time." This explains why they were also called the "weavers."

Considering that this book does not pretend to describe the histories of all these sects, I will only refer to the Waldenses when they appear within the framework of my investigations. My work is centered on the study of the Cathars and their mysteries.

To this day, we know very little about the Cathars because almost all of their literary works were destroyed. We will not waste time trying to value the confessions that some Cathars made in the torture chambers of the Inquisition. Apart from a few technical works of a historical or theological character (of which only a few get close to reality), practically nothing has been written about them. Moreover, for reasons that became evident during my work, their purity and the unheard-of courage of their declarations of faith have been silenced.

Maurice Magre, the amiable prophet of Hindu wisdom to whom I would like to express my sincere thanks for his recommendations regarding his native region in southern France, dedicated a chapter in his book *Magiciens et illuminés* to the mystery of the Albigenses: "Le maître inconnue des Albigeois [The unknown master of the Albigenses]."[5] His hypothesis that the Cathars were Western Buddhists has a lot of adherents, and it is defended by some very respectable historians, for example Jean Guiraud in his *Cartullaire de Notre Dame de Prouille* (1907). Further on, we will deal with this in greater detail. Nevertheless, as fascinating as it appears, Magre's theory that a Tibetan wise man brought the Hindu doctrine of metempsychosis and Nirvana to the southern regions of France does not withstand even the most benevolent scrutiny.

When I decided to spend an extended period in one of the most beautiful (and at the same time savage and inhospitable) parts of the Pyrenees, it was not, as some French newspapers asserted, to prove the theories of my friend Maurice Magre.[6] Rather I wished to place in situ a subject that had captured my imagination.

In the Bibliothèque Nationale de France, as I was reexamining and appraising the results of my investigations in the Pyrenees, an opuscule entitled *Le secret des troubadours [The Secret of the Troubadours]* by Joséphin Péladan fell into my hands.[7] The author suspected that the Cathar and Templar troubadours, the legend of Montsalvat, and the ruins of the castle of Mont Ségur (the last Cathar stronghold to fall during the crusade against the Albigenses), were secretly linked.

I was lucky enough to have already discovered in Pyrenean caves the last traces of certain distinct periods, unknown until then, in the heretics' tragic history. Corroborated by local legends, they led me to conclude that without a doubt, far more than an etymological relation existed between Montsalvat *(mons salvatus)* and Mont Ségur *(mons securus)*.

Catharism was a heresy, and only theology provides us with the key to deciphering its mysticism and its secrets. Only a historian of civilizations is capable of describing the birth and decline of Occitan culture with dignity. Only an expert in literary subjects can get a grip on the epic poems of King Arthur, Parsifal, Galahad, and Titurel. The caves—which were my most important documents, and very difficult and dangerous ones at that—require a speleologist and an expert in prehistory. And only an artist can supply the "open sesame" that permits access to the mystical and mythical circle of the Grail.

I must ask the reader for his indulgence if I lack some of these requirements. My desire was nothing more than to guide the men of my time to a hitherto unknown world that I had uncovered with a rope, my miner's lamp, and a lot of effort, and at the same time tell my contemporaries the story of the martyrdom of the Templar heretics.

I would like to conclude my prologue with the words of Franz Kampers, words that together with my lamp helped me at times to illuminate the dark labyrinths of the caves of the Grail. "The word 'Grâl' was obscure from the beginning. The lack of clarity of the name itself and its origin indicates precisely how sacred was a moment in history when a Majesty existed, known and understood, that was called Grâl."[8]

OTTO RAHN, 1933

PART ONE

Parsifal

———◆———

In Provence and Languedoc, eyes accustomed to Northern light feel blinded by the constant luminosity of the colorful landscape, where normally the sun always shines and the sky is always blue. Blue sky, a sea even more blue, a purple rocky coastline, golden yellow mimosas, black pines, green laurel bushes, and mountains where the snow never vanishes from their peaks.

When night falls, titillating stars sparkle larger than life and seem so close that you could grab them with your hand. And the southern moon is not the northern moon; it is her twin sister, only more beautiful and seductive.

The sun and moon in the South generate love and songs. When the sun shines, songs blossom; no longer locked away by the silence of winter fog, they reawaken and rise into the sky in pursuit of larks. And when the moon rises over the sea, sonnets are heard in the wind competing with the songs of nightingales—to woo gracious women.

Between Alpine glaciers and the sun-baked Pyrenees, from the vineyards of the Loire Valley to the paradisal terraced gardens of the Côte d'Azûr and the Côte Vermeille, a brilliant civilization developed at the beginning of our millennium, genteel and filled with spirit, where poetry and the *Minne* (the ideal love, sublime love) were law. It is said that these laws, *las leys d'amors* [the laws of the Minne] were given to the first troubadour by a hawk that sat on a branch of a golden oak tree.[2]

The leys d'amors contained thirty-one statutes. The oddity was that they established as a basic principle that the Minne should exclude carnal love or marriage. It was the union between souls and between

3

hearts—marriage is the union of two physical bodies. With marriage, Minne and poetry die. Love by itself is only passion that disappears with sensual pleasure. He who keeps the authentic Minne in his heart does not desire the body of his loved one, only her heart. The real Minne is pure love without embodiment. The Minne is not simply love; Eros is not sex.

Guilhelm Montanhagol, a troubadour from Toulouse, wrote: "Those who love should have a pure heart, and think about nothing other than the Minne, because the Minne is not sin, but virtue that turns the bad into the good and makes the good even better: *E d'amor mou castitatz* [The Minne makes chaste]."[3] In reality, the troubadours established the *leys d'amors*. In so-called "courts of love," ladies judged those knights and troubadours who had infringed upon the laws of the Minne.

The troubadours called the *Minnedienst* or "devotion to love" (an homage rendered to grace and beauty) *domnei* (from domina = lady). Domnei provoked in the *domnejaire* [servant of the Minne] the *joy d'amor*: desire, energy, and impetuousness that led the poet to create the Minne. The poet who composed the most beautiful *Minnelieder* (love sonnets) was the winner. Once the cantor had rendered homage to his lady, she would receive him as a vassal paying tribute. From then on, she could dispose of him as if he were a serf. On his knees, the troubadour would swear eternal fidelity to his lady as if she were a feudal lord. As a token of her love, she would give her paladin-poet a golden ring, and as he stood up, a kiss on his forehead. This was always the first kiss and many times, the only one. *E d'amor mou castitatz.* . . .

There were Provençal priests who blessed these mystic unions by invoking the Virgin Mary.

In the north of France, even more so in Italy, and above all in Germany, a knight knew no other home than the armory, the tournament, and the field of battle. In these countries, knighthood was inconceivable without nobility. Only a noble who could leave for war on his steed, and his armed horsemen, were considered true knights.

By contrast, chivalry in Occitania was at home in the mountains and forests. Any burgher or peasant could become a knight [*chavalièr*] if he was valiant and loyal or knew how to compose poetry. The attributes of Occitan knighthood—accessible to anyone—were nothing other than the sword, the word, and the harp. A peasant who dominated the spoken word was raised to the category of noble, and the artisan-poet was consecrated a knight.

Troubadour Arnaut de Mareulh came from a modest family. He was first a scribe and later a poet in the court of the Viscount of Carcassonne and Béziers. He once wrote:

A well born man should be an excellent warrior, and a generous host; he should attach great importance to good armor, chosen elegance, and courtesy. The more virtues a noble possesses, a better knight he will be. But also burghers can aspire to chivalrous virtues. Although they may not be nobles by birth, they can become so, nevertheless through their behavior. At any rate, there is a virtue that all nobles, and burghers should possess: *loyalty*.

Who is poor can supplement his lack of economic means with courteous language and gallantry. But he who knows nothing of doing, and saying, does not merit any consideration, and is not worthy of my verses.

Whether of high birth or modest parentage, anyone could aspire to become a knight under the condition that he be a valiant and loyal or a poet and servant of the Minne. Cowards and the foul-mouthed were unworthy of chivalry. Their palfrey was their burden.

Troubadour Amaniu des Escas wrote the following recommendation:

Stay away from foolish men, and avoid evil-sounding conversations. If you wish to travel in the world, be magnanimous, frank, intrepid, and always ready to answer courtly questions. If you do not have sufficient money for splendid garments, at the very least try to make sure that all is very clean, above all your shoes, belt, and dagger. This is what pleases, and offers a more palatine aspect. He who desires to obtain something in the devotion of ladies should be an expert in everything so that his lady should never discover a single defect in him. In the same way, try to please the acquaintances of your lady so that only good things are told to her about you. This is a big influence on the heart. If your lady should receive you, do not embarrass her by confessing that she has robbed your heart. If she accedes to your desires, do not tell anyone. Better lament to all that you have achieved nothing, because ladies cannot stand indiscreet fools. Now you know how to open your path in life and how to please the ladies.[4]

The troubadours led a happy but raucous life. When they were taken with a comely face outside of their "pure" dedication to their patrons, and entertained throughout the night without ever arriving at the castle where they were to dine, it was noticed. The weather in the South is very pleasant; fruit can be found on any tree and the water from the springs tastes as good as the sweet wine from the Roussillon.

The leys d'amors required that a troubadour be as pure as a prayer, but hot blood circulated in the veins of the men of the South, and before becoming old, the troubadours were also young, and the ladies with years no longer needed or found admirers.

Poetry was the melodious voice of chivalry; its gracious language, Provençal, is the primogenitor among neo-Latin languages, interwoven like a colorful carpet with Iberian, Greek, Celt, Gothic, and Arab touches.[5]

From France, Italy, Catalonia, Aragon, and Portugal, the troubadours headed for Montpellier, Toulouse, Carcassonne, and Foix to learn new rhymes and to compete with poet-kings and princes like Richard the Lionheart, Alfonso of Aragon, and Raimundo of Toulouse.

Who hasn't heard of the intrepid Bertran de Born, a combative troubadour whom Dante had decapitated in Hell, or the eternally in love Arnaut Daniel, who "tearfully sings, and contemplates past insensitivities" in Purgatory while begging the great Florentine to keep him always in his thoughts? And all the rest, some scatterbrained, others full of talent, such as Bernart de Ventadorn, Gaucelm Faidit, Peire Vidal, Marcabru, Peire Cardenal, Raimon de Miravalh, and the melancholic Arnaut de Mareulh, chosen disciple of Arnaut Daniel and the unfortunate admirer of the Countess of Carcassonne.[6]

Michel de La Tour, an eyewitness who was better informed than anybody about these "rhymers," described how the Occitan troubadours lived, loved, laughed, and cried. I am going to make a free translation of some of his descriptions:

A native of the area around Carcassonne, Raimon de Miravalh was a knight of modest birth; owing to his poetry and excellent diction, he dominated the art of the Minne, and his devotion to ladies was renowned.[7] He was very respected and appreciated by the Count of Toulouse, who gave him horses, garments, and arms. He was a vassal of the Count as well as of King Pedro of Aragon, the Viscount of Béziers, Lord Bertran de Sassac, and all the great barons of that area; there was no distinguished lady who did not covet his love, or at least his deep friendship. He knew better than anybody how to celebrate and honor them. All had the honor of his friendship. One especially attracted his satisfaction. Her love inspired him in many beautiful sonnets; but all the world knew that he never had the *ben* of any lady, *ben* to which he had a right in the Minne. All of them cheated him.

> *A double task torments me;*
> *Carnal love or sublime love,*
> *In which should I confide?*
> *Shall I sing or not sing to the ladies*
> *While my existence lasts?*
> *I have many reasons, and weighty,*
> *To no longer sing again.*
> *But I continue, because my appetite for love, and youth*
> *Instructs me, incites me, captivates me*

Intelligent, agreeable, handsome, and very cultivated, Peire de Auvergne [or Peire d'Alvernha], the son of a burgher, was a native of the bishopric of Clermont. An excellent versifier and cantor, he was the country's first well-known troubadour. The best rhymes are found in his poetry:

> *When the day is short and the night long*
> *And the firmament gray and drab*
> *It is then, when my muse awakens*
> *Flowering and seasoning my moans*

Extolled and praised by all the ladies, barons, and distinguished lords, Peire was considered the greatest troubadour until the day Giraut de Bornelh began to act. Peire said of himself:

The voice of Peire de Auvergne resonates
Like the croaking of frogs in the lake.
He boasts of his melodies.
Having almost too much talent
It is difficult to understand him,
Happy I discovered this little sonnet
With the light of the torches of Poivert.

The dauphin of Auvergne, in whose lands Peire came into this world, told Michel de La Tour that the troubadour lived to an old age and that at the end of his days, he repented.

Guilhem de Cabestanh came from the Roussillon, a region that borders with Catalonia and includes the area around Narbonne. He had a distinguished bearing and was well-versed in weapons, chivalry, and pleasing the ladies. In his homeland, there was a lady named Donna Seremonda, who was young, happy, noble, and quite beautiful. She was the wife of Raimundo del Castell Roselló, a powerful, evil, violent, rich, and proud lord. Guilhem de Cabestanh was crazily in love with her, and this rumor finally came to the attention of Raimundo. An irate and jealous man, he had his wife watched day and night. One day, when he met Guilhem de Cabestanh alone, he killed him, tore out his heart, and chopped off his head. He then ordered his servants to roast the heart, prepare it in pepper sauce, and serve it to his wife. After the meal, he asked, "Do you know what you have just eaten?" She replied, "No, but it was delicious." Then he told her that she had just eaten the heart of Guilhem, and as proof, he showed her the troubadour's head. When she saw it, she fainted. When she regained consciousness, she said, "The meat that you prepared for me was so excellent, lord, that I will never eat anything again." Then she ran to the balcony and threw herself to her death.

The news of the miserable deaths of Guilhem de Cabestanh and Donna Seremonda, and the story that Raimundo del Castell Roselló had given the heart to his wife to eat, spread like wildfire through Catalonia and the Roussillon. Mourning and grief spread everywhere. Complaints were lodged with the King of Aragon, Raimundo's lord. The King hurried to Perpignan where he summoned Raimundo, arrested him on the spot, confiscated all his goods, and threw him into his deepest dungeon.

The bodies of Guilhem and his lady were brought to Perpignan and buried before the main door of the church. It is possible to read about their unhappy end on the gravestone. All knights and their ladies of the County of Roussillon were ordered to make a pilgrimage once a year to this place to celebrate the funeral.

> When I saw you so haughty, sublime and beautiful
> And I heard that you joked with gracious charm
> I believed that for me calm had settled.
> But since then, I have never found it
> I love you my Lady, something bad must have happened to me
> If to other ladies I would give my affect
> My Lady! Will the hour never come to me?
> When you tell me that I am your friend?[8]

Raimon Jordan, Viscount of Saint-Antoine in the parish of Cahors, loved a noble woman who was married to the lord of the Pena in the region of Albi. Beautiful and accomplished, she enjoyed great esteem and distinction. He was cultivated, generous, gallant, well versed with arms, elegant, agreeable, and a good poet. The love that they professed was immense. But as it happened, the Viscount suffered such grave wounds in a bloody battle that his enemies left him for dead. So great was the grief of the Viscountess that she decided to enter the heretical order. God ordained that the Viscount should regain good health. Nobody dared to tell him that the Viscountess had become a heretic. Once cured, the Viscount returned to Saint-Antoine, where he learned that his lady, distraught by his death, had entered into religion. The news meant that the jokes, smiles, and happiness disappeared from his life, replaced by groans, wails, and affliction. He gave up his horse and lived in isolation for a year. All the charitable souls of the region were very saddened by it, so much so that Alix de Montfort, a young, amiable, and good-looking lady, told him to be happy, because in compensation for the loss he suffered, she offered him her person and her love. This was the genteel message that she sent: "I ask and implore you to come and see me."

When the Viscount received this honor, an immeasurable sweetness began to flood his heart. He started to feel happier, and he began again to walk among people, dress properly, and engage his retinue. He decked himself out appropriately and rode to see Alix, who received him with pleasure for the honor that he had just bestowed on her. He also felt content and happy for the honor that she had accorded him. Charmed by his generosity and virtues, she did not regret promising him her love. He knew how to conquer her and he told her that he had her engraved forever in his heart. She accepted him as her knight, received his homage, embraced and kissed him, and gave him a ring from one of her fingers as a pledge, guaranty, and security. Viscount Raimon, satisfied and radiant, left his lady, returning to his sonnets and happy ways, finally composing the famous song: "Before you, entreating, I prostrate myself, before you who I love . . ."[9]

Among the countless dynasties in the Pyrenean mountain chain, two stood out above the others.

The House of Aragon reigned on the Spanish side; its origins are lost in the mists of early Basque history. It counted among its ancestors Lupo, the Basque leader who appears to have defeated Roland at Roncevalles.

Alfonso I (1104–1134) freed Saragossa from Moorish domination in 1118 and established the capital of Aragon there. His brother Ramiro II had a daughter named Petronila who married Raimón Berenguer, the Count of Barcelona, in 1137. Their eldest son, Alfonso II (1162–1196), who was called "the Chaste," brought Catalonia and Aragon together under his scepter. His power extended over Aragon, Catalonia, Valencia, and the Balearic Islands, over part of Provence to the south of the Durance, the Counties of Urgell and Cerdagne, both bordering on Andorra, and the Roussillon, the part between the Mediterranean and the County of Toulouse.

Alfonso the Chaste was a prominent patron of the *gai savoir* (the noble art of poetry) and one of the troubadours who composed in the Provençal language. The poet Guyot de Provins, who was a native of the north of France, speaks of this *rois d'Arragon* as his magnanimous protector, and celebrated his poetic talent and his chivalrous virtues with admiration. Alfonso the Chaste competed with another troubadour, Arnaut de Mareulh, for the favors of Adélaide de Burlath, daughter of Raimundo V, Count of Toulouse, and wife of Roger-Tailhefer, Viscount of Carcassonne.

The powerful Counts of Toulouse dominated the north of the Pyrenees. Hursio, a Gothic prince, was their forefather. When Alaric II, King of the Visigoths, lost his residence in Toulouse to the Frankish King Clovis in 507, Hursio was obliged to remain as marquis of the city. Little by little, Hursio's descendants became lords over the entire region between the Alps, the Durance, the Dordogne, and the Pyrenees as far as Gascony.

Raimundo de Saint-Gilles, the fourteenth descendant of Hursio, left for the Holy Land in the First Crusade (1096–1099) at the head of a huge army of Occitan pilgrims. Although he failed in his attempt to wrest the crown of Jerusalem from Geoffrey de Bouillon, he founded the County of Tripoli in Lebanon. The Syrian cities of Tripoli, Arado, Porfyre, Sidon, and Tyre were converted into the Toulouse, Carcassonne, Albi, Lavaur, and Foix of Asia Minor. Tripoli, their capital city, was in a forest of palm, orange, and pomegranate trees, and the wind played songs in the cedars of Lebanon, on the snows of Sannin, and the temples of Baalbek. The Count of Toulouse no longer missed his homeland; he sighed for his Oriental paradise.[10]

Melisenda of Tripoli was the great-granddaughter of Raimundo; her exquisite beauty and her fabulous properties exercised such an attraction on Jaufre Rudel that the unfortunate troubadour, as Petrarca sings in his *Trionfo d'Amore*, "used sail and oar to search for his death."

Raimundo de Saint-Gilles' sons divided their paternal inheritance between them. Bertran, who was born in Toulouse, took the County of Tripoli. Alfonso, born in Tripoli, left for Toulouse, where he took the titles of Count of Toulouse, Marquis of Provence, and Duke of Narbonne. The powerful counts and Viscounts of Carcassonne, Béziers, Montpellier, and Foix recognized him as the supreme feudal lord.

Alfonso was forty-five years old when Bernard, the Abbot of Clairvaux, preached the Second Crusade (1147–1148). He took up the cross in Vezelay together with Louis VII of France, and died—poisoned— just after he disembarked in Caesarea. Baldwin III, the King of Jerusalem, was accused of having masterminded his assassination. It would appear that the motive of the crime was the fear that Alfonso could take Baldwin's crown from him.

Princess India of Toulouse, who accompanied her father to the Holy Land, buried Alfonso next to his parents, Raimundo de Saint-Gilles and

Elvira of Castile, on Pilgrim Mount in Lebanon. During the course of the crusade, India was made prisoner by the infidels and taken to the harem of Sultan Nur ad-Din in Aleppo. The enslaved India eventually became his wife and reigned over the empire of the Seljuqs after his death.

Alfonso's son Raimundo was only ten years old when his father left for Palestine. After Alfonso's death, the Kings of France, England, and Aragon and their most powerful neighbors contested his inheritance. Louis VII of France, as a descendant of Clovis and Charlemagne, believed that he could claim Toulouse. Henry II of England, as the husband of Eleonore of Poitiers (who was related to the Counts of Toulouse), believed his wife had rights to it. For his part, the King of Aragon insisted that he was the successor of the legendary Basque leader Lupo. Raimundo followed the only path left open for him: He allied himself with one of the kings against the other two, "rendered homage to the King of France, and married Louis' sister, Constance, widow of the Count of Boulogne."

The resulting marriage was a dismal failure. Constance was a cold woman, quarrelsome, and to top it off, older than her husband. It also appears that she didn't take conjugal loyalty very seriously, something that Raimundo could also be reproached for. He didn't behave any better, and the monk-historiographer Pierre de Vaux-Cernay even claimed that he was a homosexual.[11] Whatever he was, the Castel Narbonnais, the palace where the Counts of Toulouse resided, was filled with their rancor.

Raimundo locked Constance in a tower before declaring war against the King of Aragon, with whom he disputed the sovereignty of Provence. She managed to flee to her brother in Paris, who was obviously not convinced that she was right because he refused to break with his brother-in-law.

The House of Anjou had reigned in England since 1154. The name Plantagenet comes from the branch of the furze (planta geneta) that adorned its coat of arms. Henry II, the son of Geoffrey of Anjou and the English Princess Mathilde, dominated England, Anjou, Tourraine, and since 1106, Normandy. In addition, his marriage to Eleonore de Poitiers (1152) brought him Aquitania, Poitou, Auvergne, Périgord, and Limousin, which is to say a quarter of France.

Henry II, called Curtmantle (for having introduced to England the fashion of short capes), undertook a campaign against the Count of Toulouse in 1159; but Louis of France invaded the territories he had gained through marriage to Eleonore of Aquitania, Poitou, Limousin, Auvergne, and Périgord, which pressured him to break off his campaign.

The peace of the House of Anjou-Plantagenet was also disturbed by conjugal problems. Eleonore had all the reason in the world to be jealous of her husband. A precious lady, with the even more precious name of Rosamonde, had stolen his heart. Eleonore decided to poison her rival and incite Prince Henry, the inheritor of the throne, to rebel against his father. Henry had her imprisoned, a measure that served Raimundo as a pretext to resist the English invasion.

In 1173, Prince Henry rebelled, starting a war against Henry II. The King of France and Raimundo of Toulouse supported Prince Henry with all their vassals and troubadours. Troubadour Bertran de Born composed the "Call" of the campaign.

Bertran de Born was none other than the Viscount of Hautefort, near Périgueux.

There is a period manuscript with a miniature image of this bellicose rhymer. He appears resplendent in armor, mounted on a black steed with crimson livery and a green saddle, galloping toward an enemy knight.

> *Please me happy Easter time,*
> *Which brings leaves and flowers,*
> *And it pleases me to hear how*
> *The birds make their songs*
> *Resonate in the forests.*
>
> *But also I like to see rise on the fields*
> *Tents and pavilions,*
> *And they fill me with happiness*
> *When I contemplate, ready for combat,*
> *Knights, and armed knights.*
>
> *I tell you that eating, drinking and sleeping*
> *Doesn't please me as much*
> *To hear the shouts: "At them! Attack!*
> *Help! Help! Help!"*

Listen to me barons: pillage
Castles, villas and cities
Before others make war on you.

And you Papiol, choose:
Yes or no "Wake up! Don't sleep!
The moment to choose has arrived:
Yes or no! One, two and three . . ."

FROM A QUATRAIN OF BERTRAN DE BORN[12]

Bertran called the English prince Richard the Lionheart, "Papiol."[13] The nickname has no translation; it can mean "little father" as well as "cork head."

"Papiol" said, "Yes."

In another quatrain, Bertran lists those princes who participated in the campaign against England: the Counts of Toulouse, Béarn, Barcelona (as a consequence, the King of Aragon), Périgord, and Limoges, and all the viscounts, barons, and consuls from the Rhône to the ocean.

Had it not been for the defection of the King of Aragon, who marched on Toulouse, the allies would have sided with the King of England. At the last minute, Raimundo succeeded in repelling Prince Henry and stepped up pressure for an alliance with the English King. Indignant, Bertran de Born composed a quatrain about the King of Aragon's shameful betrayal of the Occitan cause. In it, Bertran wrote that the King of Aragon could never be a descendant of Lupo, the hero of the Pyrenees; the troubadour declared him the vassal of a serf from the rabble: "Aragon, Catalonia, and Urgell are ashamed of their cowardly king, who magnifies himself in his own songs, and who puts money above his personal honor."

Then Richard the Lionheart said "No!" for once and reconciled himself with his father. A short time later in the Limousin, his brother Prince Henry, whom Bertran had named in his songs *"lo rei joven,"* died unexpectedly in the castle of Martel. The sudden death of Bertran's favorite hero shocked him. He wept over the young prince in a *planh*.[14]

Bertran would have been pleased to see the war prosecuted, but unfortunately for him, the Aquitanian barons gathered around Henry of England, their feudal lord, and together they went to Hautefort, Bertran's castle. Henry had sworn to seek revenge. When Alfonso of

Aragon, Bertran's most irreconcilable enemy, joined Henry's siege, the situation became critical, but the poet did not lose his courage. To mock Alfonso, and to let the besiegers know that his castle was very well provisioned, he sent him an ox, asking him to appease the ire of the English king.

The castle at Hautefort fell to the siege. Bertran was taken prisoner and led before King Henry.

"Bertran, you boasted that you needed only half of your talent. I am afraid that even both halves together are not enough to save you."

"Yes, Sire," answered Bertran calmly. "Quite so I said, and told the truth."

"But Bertran, have you ever had talent?"

"Yes, Sire, but I lost it when your son Henry died."

Then Bertran de Born sang his elegy dedicated to the death of Henry, the young prince. The old King cried bitterly, and said, "Bertran, my son loved you more than anybody in the world. For the love of my son, I pardon your life. I leave you your lands and your castle. I wish to compensate the damages that you have suffered with these five hundred silver marks. Bertran, Bertran. . . . I felt the breeze of your genius pass by!"[15]

Bertran fell to the feet of the King, but got up more triumphant than ever.

Shortly thereafter (1186), King Henry died and was succeeded by Richard the Lionheart. Bertran, still unsatisfied with the royal "yes and no" that he had addressed to Richard in his quatrain, incited Richard's brother Geoffrey to rise up against him. Geoffrey was defeated and sought refuge at the court of the King of France, where he died, trampled to death under horses' hooves during a tournament.

Three years later, the Third Crusade was preached.[16] Sultan Saladin had reconquered Jerusalem and replaced the cross in the Church of the Holy Sepulcher with the Star and Crescent. He offered the Christians of Jerusalem a choice: remaining within the walls of the Holy City without being disturbed, or withdrawing to the coastal cities of Tyre, Tripoli, or Akkon.

Quite possibly, Princess India of Toulouse contributed to Saladin's generosity. After Nur ad-Din's death, Saladin married her to become the lord over the Seljuq Empire. Whatever the cause, the fact remains that Saladin did not drench the Holy Land in blood as the crusaders had eighty-six years earlier during the First Crusade when, as Torcuato Tasso wrote, they "filled the city and the temple with corpses."

Saladin's victory sowed fury and panic throughout the Western world. Rome preached another crusade. The clergy's sermons were accompanied by the harps of the troubadours. The most renowned poets, such as Bertran de Born, Peire Vidal, Guiraut de Bornelh, and Peire Cardenal, called on the faithful to take part in the holy war. What really motivated the troubadours was not nostalgia for the holy places of Palestine, rather the desire to visit foreign lands and sing about their adventures in ballads and quatrains before ladies, desolate at having been left at home. How many feminine tears must have flowed when rhymers and knights departed their native lands with the cross on the armor and shields!

The other day I found seated on a carpet of grass and white flowers, close to the fountain of an orchard in whose fruit trees the birds sang, a noble lady, the daughter of the lord of the castle. I thought that she had come to bask in the springtime, the green foliage, and the songs of the birds; but it was not so.

With profound sighs, she complained saying: "Jesus, for You, I suffer such pain. Why do you want the most valiant of this world to cross the sea, and go to serve you! My friend, his graces so genteel and valiant, has gone. And I stay here alone with my desire, my tears, and my affliction."

Upon hearing such lament, I approached the brook of crystal water, and told her: "Sweet lady, tears cloud your beauty. You should not lose hope. God who lets the trees flower can also give you back your happiness."

"Sir," she answered, "I believe that one day in another life God will have mercy with me and other sinners. But why take it from me in this life? He who was my happiness and now who is so far from me."

TROUBADOUR MARCABRU

It was extraordinarily difficult for the poet Peirol to tear himself away from Donna Sail de Claustra, who groaned and rebuked him:

When my love saw that my heart no longer thought about her, she began her reproaches. You will see some: "Friend Peirol, it is not right on your part that you leave me in the lurch. If your thoughts no longer belong to me alone, and if you no longer sing, of what use are you?"

—My love, for so much time I have served you, and you no longer sympathize with me. You know perfectly well how little you think of me.

—But Peirol, have you already forgotten the beautiful and noble lady who received you with such mercy and Minne? Nobody would have suspected such a frivolous heart in your songs and verses. You appeared so happy and in love!

—My love, I loved you from the first day, and I continue loving you. But the hour has come when more than one man who—if Saladin didn't exist—would be lucky to stay with his lady, has no other recourse than, even with tears, to separate himself from her.

—Peirol, your participation in the crusade will hardly contribute to the liberation of the city of David from the Turks and Arabs that occupy it. Listen to my well-thought-out advice: love, versify, and let the crusade follow its course. Look at the Kings who, instead of going there, are fighting amongst themselves; take the barons for an example, who are trying to avoid taking up the cross under the vain pretexts of quarrels.

—My love, I have always loyally served you. You know it yourself. But today, I am obliged to deny you my obedience. The crusade has delayed too much, and it should have already gone to the aid of the pious Marquis of Montferrat.[17]

This "Marquis of Montferrat" was Conrad, Prince of Tyre who, surrounded by Saladin, pleaded for help from the West. Bertran de Born answered him in the following terms: "Lord Conrad: Seek divine protection! Had it not been for the vacillations of counts, princes, and kings, which induced me to stay where I am, I would already be there with you, and for quite some time. In addition, after seeing again my charming blond lady, I have no desire to go."

At the beginning of the crusade, Bertran de Born was one of its most enthusiastic heralds, but he remained on his estates, preferring to love beautiful ladies, compose verses, and proclaim:

"God wishes that Philip of France and Richard of England fall into Saladin's hands!"

His greatest happiness would have come if the King of Aragon had also taken up the cross and all three never returned.

Frederick Barbarossa, together with his forces, was the first to leave his German homeland. En route, he had to break the resistance of the distrustful Greek emperor Issac Angelos. Only the occupation of Adrianopolis allowed him to continue his march and sail to Asia Minor. One year later, King Philip of France embarked from Marseille, and Richard the Lionheart from Genoa. They had agreed that their fleets would gather in Messina, where they would wait until the spring.

At the time, a famous hermit named Joachim of Flora, who possessed the gift of prophecy, lived in Sicily.[18] Following the model of the monasteries of Mount Athos, Lebanon, and the Sinai, he established convents in the mountains of Calabria, along the straits of Messina, and on the Lipari Islands off Sicily. Among his contemporaries, he was known as the best author of commentary on the Apocalypse of Saint John. Richard the Lionheart went to visit the illustrious monk and beseeched him to explain chapter twelve of the Apocalypse to him.

"The woman dressed as the sun, with a moon under her feet, and a crown of twelve stars on her head is the church," said the hermit. "The large red snake with seven heads and seven diadems is the devil. The seven heads are the seven great persecutors of the Gospel: Herod, Nero, Constantine (who emptied the treasury of the Church of Rome) Mohammed, Melsemut, Saladin, and the Antichrist. The first five are dead. Saladin lives, and uses his power. The Antichrist will come soon. Saladin still triumphs, but he will lose Jerusalem and the Holy Land."

"When will it happen?" asked Richard the Lionheart.

"Seven years after taking Jerusalem."

"So, have we come too early?"

"Your coming was necessary, King Richard. God will give you victory over your enemies, and will make your name glorious. Regarding the Antichrist, he is among us, and soon he will sit on the throne of Peter."

Richard the Lionheart never liberated Jerusalem. Saladin triumphed for a long period. And as for the Antichrist: Who can say that Joachim's Antichrist was not Innocent III?

Philip and Richard left Sicily in the springtime. On Cyprus, Richard married off his favorite troubadour, Peire Vidal of Toulouse, to a Greek captive of high birth. Thanks to Michel de la Tour's biography, we know just how much royal grace influenced the life of Peire.

The Crusade was a disaster. Frederick Barbarossa drowned in the Saleph, the same river where Alexander the Great was almost killed. Although Philip and Richard the Lionheart managed to take the city of Akkon in July 1191 after a siege that lasted almost two years, disagreements regarding the sharing of the booty, jealousy of Richard's popularity, and a supposed illness induced the King of France to return to Europe after the city's fall. For the crusaders who remained, Philip's departure was tantamount to desertion, and the troubadours' satires accompanied him across the sea.

A year later, Richard learned that Philip was trying to take Normandy and Anjou, and that his brother was set on taking the crown of England from him. With no time to lose, he decided to start negotiating with Saladin in order to return as soon as possible to his country. He agreed with the sultan that his sister Joan should marry the emir Malek-Adel, Saladin's brother, and that together they should reign over Jerusalem and the Holy Land. The Roman prelates were able to thwart this plan, which would have put an end to the bloodshed in Palestine. The two rulers were only able to sign a cessation of hostilities for three years, three months, and three days. For such an auspicious occasion, Saladin and Richard organized grandiose festivities. Both monarchs and their troops fought bloodless competitions with lance and harp.

Saladin also brought with him his court poets because from the

Bosphorus to the Persian Gulf, the Arab ruwahs composed "as many verses as there are grains of sand in the desert, and as many ghasels [poems] as gazelles exist." The troubadours sang of how Rudel and Melisende died of love; the ruwahs, the no less sad story of Hinda and Abdallah. Let's listen to it:

> Abdallah, the son of an illustrious and rich family, had married Hinda, the rose of her tribe. Because their marriage was sterile, Abdallah, in a stupor, repudiated poor Hinda, who fled to her father's tent. Shortly thereafter, she married a man from the Amirides tribe. Abdallah sang with his harp about his unhappy love and its loss. He left his tribe to look for Hinda. He found her crying at the mouth of a well. And the happiness of seeing each other again broke their hearts. . . .

Once the festivities were over, Richard left the Holy Land. It is not necessary for us to recount how the Austrian duke Leopold VI, whom he gravely offended one day at Akkon, imprisoned him in the castle of Dürrnstein, or later when the emperor Heinrich VI locked him up in Trifels, and how he recovered his liberty.

For quite some time, Richard the Lionheart was the darling of the Mediterranean world, Aquitania, and England. In the Orient, the ruwahs celebrate the "Melek-rik." In Occitania and Aquitania, the troubadours sang with enthusiasm of his heroic prowess; they described how the *joglar* [juggler] Blondel had freed him, and lauded him as the first knight of the Round Table, another King Arthur.[19]

When Richard arrived back in England in 1194, he was confronted with the fact that his younger brother John had allied himself with Philip to dethrone him. John fled to Paris and Richard was able to reconquer his provinces of Normandy and Anjou, which Philip had usurped from him. Only then, after nearly a four-year absence, could he head toward Toulouse.

"Bertran de Born was very happy," related a chronicler.

When Bertran learned that King Philip had secretly hurried back from the Holy Land, he easily guessed the French King's plans for Richard's possessions in Aquitania, and the troubadour never doubted for an instant that the French monarch's real aim was to extend his frontiers all the way to the Pyrenees. Bertran, who had until then been Richard's adversary, openly declared in his favor. He managed to persuade Pedro of Aragon, who had recently been crowned King, and the Count of Toulouse to forget their profane quarrels and get the crown prince of Toulouse to ask Richard for the hand of his sister Joan as a symbol of reconciliation between the Plantagenet and Toulouse families. In this way, the differences between Aquitania and Languedoc were overcome and Aquitania recovered the image that it had in the tenth century when the counts—the "Heads of Burlap"—and Raimundo-Pons of Toulouse reigned fraternally, side by side, from Occitania to the Rhône.

From Toulouse, Bertran went to visit the most important woman of Occitania, Adélaide de Burlats. A widow, she was the daughter of Raimundo V of Toulouse and Constance of France. She lived in Carcassonne, which was by far the most elegant city of the Languedoc, and from which she governed the territories of the House of Trencavel during the minority of her son Raimon-Roger. From Carcassonne, Bertran traveled to the summer residence of the Counts of Toulouse at Beaucaire on the Rhône. There, all the princes and lords of Provence, Languedoc, Aquitania, the Pyrenees (from Perpignan to Bayonne), and Aragon, as well as the consuls of all the free cities of the Midi, and all the troubadours and joglars of Occitania had come to witness the reconciliation of the three monarchs and attend the marriage of Raimundo de Toulouse and Joan Plantagenet. A chronicler of the time, the Prior de Vigeois, describes for us how the festivities at Beaucaire were celebrated.

> Ten thousand knights flowed to Beaucaire. Through the mediation of the seneschal of Agoût, Count Raimundo divided one thousand gold pieces among those knights who were lacking resources. Twelve yokes of oxen plowed the spot where they were going to celebrate the tournaments, and the Count planted three thousand silver and gold coins in small ditches, so the people could also have their share of happiness after the tournaments. A baron who was lodging four hundred knights in his castle had goats and oxen roasted on spits. A countess from the House of Provence placed on the head of the joglar Iveta, who was proclaimed king of the troubadours, a crown made from forty thousand silver and gold coins.[20]

To symbolize the end of the fratricidal war between Aquitania, Languedoc, and Aragon, a knight had his thirty warhorses burned in a gigantic pyre.

Two decades later, Occitania would see other pyres blaze under very different circumstances, as ordered by Pope Innocent III. . . .

After the festivities at Beaucaire, the Count of Toulouse declared war on France, but the death of Richard the Lionheart put a quick end to the conflict.

It was said at the time that the outbreak of hostilities in the Occitan states, the marriage of Raimundo to Joan, and Toulouse's declaration of war on Paris were all the work of Bertran de Born.

In the meantime, Saladin had died. Before his last breath, he gave the order that the shroud that would cover his corpse, woven with purple and gold, was to be paraded through the streets of Jerusalem as a herald proclaimed, "This is all that the sovereign of the world, Jussuf Mansor Saladin, took with him."

His seventeen sons and his brother, Emir Malek-Adel, divided his immense Muslim empire amongst themselves. Pope Innocent III, who had been crowned on February 22, 1198, believed that the moment to launch a new crusade in Palestine had arrived. He entrusted Fulk of Neuilly-sur-Marne with the recruitment campaign for this Holy War. The first monarch Fulk visited was Richard the Lionheart.

But Richard had learned to say no. He knew Greece and the Orient well. Saladin had become his friend. As we have seen, he wanted to marry his sister to Malek-Adel in order to establish a Christian-Muslim kingdom of Jerusalem. Together with the King of France, he had taken up the cross in Rome's favor. But now he had become Rome's adversary and irreconcilable enemy. He didn't want to hear any more of "crusades." Fulk became irritated:

"Sire, in the name of God the Almighty, I implore you to marry off your three corrupt daughters if you wish to escape condemnation!"

"You lie! I don't have a single daughter!" shouted the King.

"You have three. Their names are Arrogance, Greed, and Lust!"

"Very well, I will give 'Arrogance' to the Templars, 'Greed' to the Cistercian monks, and 'Lust' to the prelates of the Catholic Church."[21]

The Roman Curia excommunicated the King of England.

For some time, Bertran had buried his anger with Richard over the king's "yes and no" instead of "yes or no." An intimate friendship united the Sovereign of England and Aquitania with the Provençal poet of the "Guerra me plai."

Bertran was without any doubt the most important troubadour of Occitania. The influence of his songs and the sounds of his harp evoked the fables recounted by the poets of antiquity. One day, Richard the Lionheart found himself with his troops on the sandy dunes of the Poitou, not far from the Sables-d'Olonne. Hunger had decimated both men and beasts: no bread for the soldiers and no grass for the horses. Bertran picked up his harp and sang a romanza about Princess Laina Plantagenet, Richard's sister, later the duchess of Saxony. It is said that the barons and knights forgot their hunger, their thirst, and the storm that came in from the sea, whipping their faces with hailstones.

In 1199, Richard laid siege to the Castle of Châlus-Charbrol that belonged to his vassal, the Viscount Améric de Limoges. A treasure was kept inside Châlus' walls, which Richard claimed was his as feudal lord.

He wanted to unite the useful and the agreeable. Améric de Limoges had sided with France. The King of England hoped to simultaneously get the treasure and punish a disloyal vassal. But while he was indicating to his soldiers the spot where they should scale the castle walls, an arrow from an archer's bow pierced his shoulder, near his heart. Mortally wounded, Richard fell into the arms of Bertran de Born.

The furious assailants took the castle; the garrison's throats were cut, and the able archer, who was none other than the lord of the castle, was lynched.[22] The treasure that was found paid for the king's funeral.

All his vassals and troubadours, including Bertran, King of the Poets, escorted the Poet-King to Fontevrault, where the mausoleum of the Plantagenets is located, where that eternally restless King found his eternal rest. Perhaps it shouldn't surprise us that Richard the Lionheart was lowered into his tomb without prayers, holy water, or the blessings of the Church. The King of England, Ireland, Anjou, Arles, and Cyprus remained excluded from the community of the Catholic Church.

All the harps, from the North to the South, wailed over the loss of this Alexander, this Charlemagne, this King Arthur. All the troubadours intoned their elegies of Richard's death—except for one.

The most tears were those of the poet Gaucelm Faidit, who had accompanied the monarch to the Holy Land. From his elegy:

Descendants remote in time,
How could you understand?
My bitter pain, my acute suffering
That I will never forget!
Know at least
That Richard the Lionheart
King of England
Is already dead!
So cruel was the hand of God!
Richard is already dead![23]

Bertran de Born did not intone any elegy. His capacity to love was as large as his ability to hate. His pain at losing his friend was too strong. This time, his songs were silenced. One afternoon, he knocked at the door of the Convent of Grammont, a door that closed behind him forever. Bertran turns up only once more, in Hell, where the great Florentine poet Dante Alighieri places him: "Bertran is condemned to carry his head separate from the trunk, because he separated what was united." Decapitated, the troubadour of the castle of Hautefort carries his own head in front of him to illuminate the pathways of Hell.

According to an Occitan legend that is still very much alive among the common folk, Bertran, distraught by the curse that hangs over his homeland, remains frozen in a block of ice in the glacier of the Maldetta mountain range.

The story of Richard the Lionheart and Bertran de Born forced us to neglect another, no less important, hero of those lands: Raimundo V, the Count of Toulouse. Not only was he the most powerful sovereign of the Occitan world and one of the most influential chiefs of state of the Western world, but his capital Toulouse was also the metropolis of Occitan civilization and culture.

The possessions of Hursio's powerful descendant were more extensive than those of the French crown; as its most important vassal, the Count of Toulouse enjoyed a semi-independent status. Along with the County of Toulouse, the Duchy of Narbonne belonged to him, a dignity that made him the first noble of France. He was the feudal lord over fourteen counts, and the troubadours compared him to an emperor:

Car il val tan qu'en soa valor
Auri' assatz ad un emperador[24]
["Because he was worth in his value
as much as an emperor"]

They called him "the good Count Raimundo," because like them, he was a troubadour, always attentive to their worries and needs.

A singular fact: Raimundo of Toulouse never wanted to go to the Holy Land, not even to visit Toulouse's Tripoli. He was the only one among the great Christian princes of the twelfth century who did not participate in the overseas crusades. Did he foresee that, shortly after his death in 1194, Occitania would become the theater of the most horrible crusade of all? Raimundo was not interested in seeing the Holy Sepulcher or Golgotha. Did he suspect that Occitania under his successor Raimundo VI would live its own Golgotha and have its own Holy Sepulcher? Raimundo V performed considerable services for Occitan civilization, practicing *le gai savoir,* the spirit of chivalry, and irreproachable politics. One thing he disregarded: He remained estranged from Occitan Catharism. It proposed a "Pure Doctrine" that the rest of the Christian world called a heresy. And yet the "Gospel of the Consoling Paraclete" needed his support. As we will see further on, in all these aspects his son-in-law and grandson, who belonged to the House of Trencavel de Carcassonne, were to guard the mystical Round Table, whose unifying link was constituted by its "desire for Paradise."

Upon a green achmardi,
She bore the consummation of heart's desire
To its roots and blossoming:
A thing called the Grâl[25]

In his quatrain to his poet-friends, the troubadour Raimon de Miravalh indicates the protectors of the "noble art" who will provide a good welcome, recognition, and presents:

In the first place, head for Carcassonne whose barons I will not list, because I would need forty quatrains for it. Accept their presents, and leave. I still don't know exactly in which direction you should gallop, but greet Senyor Raimon Drut for me, who almost certainly will have you leaving on a horse if you arrived on foot.

Afterwards, go in search of Peire Roger de Mirepoix. If you cannot find him, I promise to double your reward.

On to Baron Bertran de Saissac: sing to him quatrains—or better still—*canzones*. If Lord Bertran is not in the humor to give gifts, he will not deny you an old nag.

Then ride to the lord Améric de Montréal, who will remove your worries with a good horse, livery, and a cape.

In very remote times, oak trees—the sacred trees of the Druids—rose on a rocky hill in the heart of the city of Carcassonne; the etymology of the name Carcassonne refers to it: ker = rock, casser = oak.[26] Alaric, the King of the Visigoths, had such an imposing belt of towers and walls constructed around the city that King Clovis of France and Emperor Charlemagne besieged it in vain. The Emperor only entered when the city wanted to open its doors.

At the eastern side of the city, where the hill drops off above the Aude river, rises the majestic castle of the Viscounts of Carcassonne and Béziers, who were called the "Trencavel" (those who cut well).

From Carcassonne, the Trencavel dominated the rich cities of Albi, Castres, and Béziers. All the lands bordered by the Tarn River, the Mediterranean, and the eastern Pyrenees were theirs. They were related to the most noble princes of the Western world: the Capetians of France, the Plantagenet in England and Anjou, the Hohenstauffen in Swabia, Aragon in Catalonia, and the descendants of Hursio in Toulouse.

Influenced by his uncle King Alfonso of Aragon and the King of England, Viscount Raimon de Trencavel took part in the war against the young Count Raimundo V of Tolouse, which provoked the count's subjects to rebel against the civil war that was being imposed on them. During the hostilities, a burgher from Béziers fought with a knight. The barons asked Raimon Trencavel to hand over the burgher, who had to suffer an ignominious punishment, the details of which we know nothing.

With the war over, the burghers of Béziers demanded reparations from the viscount for the treatment of one of their own. He answered that he would submit to the arbitration of the barons and the notables. On October 15, 1167, Trencavel, accompanied by the bishop, appeared in the Church of the Magdalene in Béziers, where the burghers, armed with clubs and wearing chain mail vests under their garments, were waiting for him.

The burgher who was at the center of the altercation advanced toward the viscount with a somber face.

"My Lord," he said, "I am the unfortunate one who cannot support your disgrace. Do you promise to give the burghers of Béziers satisfaction for the affront that was done to me?"

"I am ready," replied the prince, "to submit to arbitration by barons and notables."

"This is no satisfaction. Our ignominy can only be washed clean with your blood!"

As these words were pronounced, the conspirators drew their daggers. The viscount, his youngest son, the barons, and the bishop were assassinated before the altar.

Forty years later, the Church of the Magdalene and its major altar would witness another, even more horrible massacre. The house of God would explode like a volcano, burying under it the charcoaled bodies of all the burghers of Béziers.

The consuls were left as lords over the city. For two years, they refused to hear or speak about the bishop or the viscount. They sneered at the fury of the nobles and excommunication by the Vatican. So arrogant and untamed was the independence of the Occitan city republics! This haughty independence recalls Gothic feudalism, Roman consuls, and the Iberian patriarchs, from whom they could have descended.

In the year 1050, Toulouse, Barcelona, Saragossa, Narbonne, Béziers, Carcassonne, Montpellier, Nîmes, Avignon, Arles, Marseille, and Nice were virtually independent republics. All had a capitulum (council of citizens) elected by the citizenry, under the fictitious presidency of a count or viscount, but effectively under the leadership of the consuls, whose mission was to watch over the destiny of the city. The Aragonese, for example, had a form of election for the coronation of their king that became celebrated: "We who are worth the same as you, and can do more than you, elect you king, with the pact to keep these fueros [laws] between us. If this is not so, no!"

By contrast, in Narbonne the archbishop, viscount, and citizens governed together. In Marseille, each one of these three powers had its own circumscription inside the city. In Nice, Arles, and Avignon, only the burghers governed. These rich and proud citizens had their palazzi, complete with towers, and defended the rights of the city with sword and lance. If they desired, they could become armed knights, and compete with the barons in tournaments. Without losing any of their dignity, these ennobled burghers dedicated themselves to overseas commercial transactions, as in the Greek city-states.

Agriculture, the best sustenance of every community and state, was flourishing. The land produced cereals, particularly millet, in abundance, as well as grain brought from Asia at the times of the crusades. Olive oil and wine flowed in torrents. Commercial treaties united the coastal Occitan cities with Genoa, Pisa, Florence, Naples, and Sicily. In the port of Marseille, Italian, Greek Levantine, Moorish, and Norman ships dropped anchor, traded, and sailed back home.

The intermediaries between Occitania and the commercial cities of the Mediterranean were the exchange agents. In Occitania, Jews could live and work without being disturbed, and they enjoyed the same rights as the rest of the citizenry to hold public office and teach at the universities. Occitan nobility protected and encouraged them; the Trencavel of Carcassonne employed Nathan, Samuel, and Moses Caravita as their ministers for economy and finances. Some of the Jewish professors who taught classes at Occitan universities were famous in both the West and the Orient. Students came from afar to listen to Rabbi Abraham at Vauvert, near Nîmes. In Narbonne, where Rabbi Calonimo taught, he was known as "the son of the great hierarch and Rabbi, Theodore, of the House of David." This dynasty of rabbinic hierarchs was called "the family of the Israelite kings of Narbonne," and they considered themselves to be a branch of the House of David. The lords of Narbonne placed their immense properties under special protection.

Raimon Trencavel fell dead before the great altar of the Church of the Magdalene of Béziers, a victim of the passion for independence that dominated the free cities of Provence. The crown prince of Carcassonne, Roger Taillefer [Talhafèr], who was still under twenty years of age, wanted to avenge his father's death. For this, he needed the help of his relative, King Alfonso of Aragon. Together with his barons and Catalan noblemen, he marched on Béziers, which surrendered after a two-year-long siege. Roger Taillefer pardoned his father's assassins.

One day, an unhappy baron provoked him:

"You have sold your father's blood, my lord!"

These words pierced his heart. One night, while Béziers slept peace-fully, Aragonese troops acting on the young Trencavel's orders took over the city and stabbed all the gentile males of the town. Only the women and Jews were spared.

The following morning, the viscount and his bishop, named Bernard, forced all the daughters and widows of the murdered burghers to marry their Aragonese killers, and demanded an annual tribute of three pounds of pepper from them as well.

Without wishing to attenuate young Trencavel's responsibility in these events—he governed from then on in an indulgent, tolerant, and chivalrous way—we have to say that those really responsible for the bloodbath were Bishop Bernard and the King of Aragon. The nobles fired the flames of bloody vengeance in the Viscount's son only for their personal gain. The bishop did not know how to control the impetuous young man, and Alfonso II wanted to assure himself of a base of sup-port between his County of Rousillon and his possessions in Provence without losing sight of the fact that Béziers represented an advance post facing Toulouse and Carcassonne.

Soon Roger Taillefer understood. To disarm the danger that he him-self had provoked, he established an alliance with the Count of Toulouse and asked for the hand of the count's daughter Adélaide.

The court of Carcassonne was the focus of poetry and chivalrous courtesy, and in the words of Arnaut de Mareulh, "the most chaste court, full of grace, because the scepter was in Adélaide's hands."

The troubadours gave Raimon Roger, the crown prince of Foix and cousin of Roger Taillefer of Carcassonne, the sobriquet "Raimon Drut," which means "Roger the beloved."

The castle of the count of Foix was situated in the savage valley of the river Ariège, which descends from the snow-covered mountains of Andorra bordering the important mountain chain of Montcalm and Saint Bartholomew's Peak, and flows toward the Garonne.

According to legend, a sanctuary dedicated to Abellio, the sun god of the Iberians, was situated on the rock where the Castle of Foix is built.[27]

According to another tradition, Foix was a Basque colony of Phocea, a city in Asia Minor. During the Gallic wars, Foix was the *pal* (meeting place) of the Sotiates, who in 76 B.C. favored Sertorius over Pompey, and who twenty years later were defeated by Caesar's deputy Publius Crassus in the vicinity of vicus Sotiatum (now the town of Vicdessos). From then on, Foix was nothing more than one of the many Roman castella that guarded the Pyrenean passes, assuring safe transit through them.

Under Visigoth domination (414–507), the Catholic bishops, who were unhappy with the leadership of the Gothic kings because of their links to Arianism, succeeded in enlisting the help of the French King Clovis. Volusian, a king who was suspected (not without reason) of having opened the doors of Tours to the Franks, was taken prisoner by the Visigoths and executed in Foix. After the battle of Vouglé, Clovis gathered Volusian's mortal remains and had the French clergy proclaim him a martyr and a saint. Clovis founded a monastery next to Volusian's tomb, and around it, on the ruins of a Roman colony, built a small town which Charlemagne later fortified and converted into an important support base against the Aquitanians to the north and the Moors to the south.

In the rocky Castle of Foix, the bards, guests of Arcantua, the chief of the Sotiates, sang Celtic and Iberian *cantares de gesta*, accompanied by Grecian-style lyres. In the twelfth century, when monetary and amorous worries preoccupied the troubadours, they were always welcomed with great hospitality.

Roger Bernard I, Count of Foix (died 1188) and his wife, Cecilia de Carcassonne, had four children: a son, Raimon Roger (the Raimon Drut of the troubadours), and three daughters. We know the names of only two, Cecilia and Esclarmonde.

Raimon Roger took charge of the inheritance of his father, who had died shortly before the start of the crusade after accompanying Philip of France and Richard the Lionheart to the Holy Land. His domains included the fertile plain that extended from the borders of the County of Toulouse through the gorges of Hers, Lasset, the Ariège with its deafening waterfalls, and the lonely pastures of the Pyrenees, accessible only to those shepherds who knew the mountains and herded their agile flocks there.

Almost all the vassals of the counts of Foix were "Sons of the Moon" (or "Sons of Belissena" as they also called themselves).[28] They claimed to be descended from the moon goddess Belissena, the Celt Iberian Astarté. On their shields were a fish, the moon, and a tower—the emblems of the moon goddess, the sun god, and the power of the knights.

Peire Roger was also a Son of Belissena. His castle was located in Mirepoix (Mira piscem = contemplate the fish). From his Tower (as his castle was called) he could watch the fish swim in the crystal-clear waters of the Hers river, which originates on the majestic Saint Bartholomew's Peak; he could also see the new moon rising above Belissena's forest to the east. Before the Christian era, his city was called Beli cartha (city of the moon). It was believed to have been founded by the Phoenicians, who were searching for gold and silver in the neighboring Pyrenees.

There was hardly a single castle in the Pyrenees that didn't belong to a Son of Belissena. Above all stood the Barons of Verdun, whose dominions under the mountains almost equaled their aboveground holdings in area, and easily surpassed many in beauty. The marvelous lime grottoes of Ornolac and Verdun extended kilometer after kilometer into the bowels of the Ariège mountain range.

This part of the Ariège valley is called the *Sabarthès* (after the Church of Sabart, where the Mother of God had foreseen Charlemagne's victory over the Saracens). The Sabarthès is protected by two cities that belonged to the counts of Foix: Tarascon, which served for years as a Moorish advance post against Charlemagne, and Ax, where Phoenician merchants, Greek colonizers, and Roman intruders healed themselves in its thermal springs.

As vassals of the House of Foix, the Barons of Lordat, Arnave, and Rabat shared the Sabarthès with the lords of Verdun. The castles of Lordat, Calamès, and Miramont rose majestically on rocks like authentic eagles' nests, at an altitude of more than a thousand meters [3,000 feet].

In Olmès (the Valley of Elms) on the northern face of the Saint Bartholomew's range, the Peyrotta and Perelha lived in their fortresses. The most heavily fortified of these were Montségur, Perelha, and Rocafissada. Raimon de Perelha was, together with the counts of Foix, the Lord of Montségur. Montségur signifies "Secure Mountain."

From this bastion, outlawed troubadours, ladies, and knights were to watch in horror as the crusade threw hundreds of thousands of their brothers, who couldn't flee to the still-secure mountains, onto the execution pyre or into subterranean dungeons.

Never existed a better place to defend
Than Munsalvaesche

Wolfram von Eschenbach[29]

Sons of Belissena were not only in the County of Foix; they could be found as vassals and parents of the Counts of Toulouse and the Viscounts of Carcassonne throughout the Languedoc: in Castres, Termès, Fanjeaux, Montréal, Saissac, and Hautpoul.

The castles of the lords of Saissac, Cab-Aret, and Hautpoul were located in the nearly impenetrable forests of the "Black Mountain Range," from whose summit it was possible to see the fifty towers of the city of Carcassonne.

Ermengarde de Saissac ("the beautiful Albigense," as she was called by the troubadours), Brunisenda de Cab-Aret, and Stéphanie the "She-Wolf" were among the most celebrated ladies of Languedoc. Three barons and two troubadours sang and courted these three women, the most beautiful of them all. The nobles who dominated the harp as well as the lance were Raimon Drut, the crown prince of Foix, Peire Roger de Mirepoix, and Améric de Montréal. The troubadours were Peire Vidal—the future "Emperor of Constantinople"—and Raimon de Miravalh.

Peire Vidal, who "asked from all noble ladies their love," couldn't resist the temptation to also try with the "She-Wolf." He fell crazily in love with his "Dulcinea," but nothing was to come of it. The "She-Wolf" paid no attention to the genteel words and love songs of the *trobère*. Neither his magnificent horses, rich armor, imperial throne, nor campaign bed made the slightest impression on the woman. Finally, Peire tried to get Donna Loba's attention in another way. He put on a wolf's head and his warrior's outfit and dedicated himself to passing in front of her castle. This also came to nothing.

Love is ingenious. Because the wolf's head had failed to make the desired impression, the troubadour dressed himself in an authentic wolf's skin and terrorized Donna Loba's shepherds and flocks every night. One of the shepherds' dogs managed to catch him and fell on the hypothetical "Isengrim" with grinding teeth. The shepherds, who were quite perplexed to hear a wolf shouting for help, had to work hard to save him. They took him, bloodied and wounded, to the castle of the She-Wolf. This was exactly what the wise Peire wanted, because in this way he could be taken care of and cured in Cab-Aret. Michel de La Tour, his biographer, did not lie when he said that all the ladies cheated on him. The "She-Wolf" cheated on him with Raimon Drut, the crown prince of Foix.

Améric, "who remedied the necessities of the troubadours with a good horse, livery, and a cape," was the lord of Montréal, a small town halfway between Carcassonne and Foix, and also a Son of the Moon. His sister Geralda was the famous mistress of the castle of Lavaur. No troubadour or beggar ever left her castle without being welcomed as a guest and receiving some coins for the journey. A chronicler related, "Geralda was the most noble and generous lady of all Occitania." Nevertheless, during the crusade against her homeland, she suffered an awful death. For consummate heresy, she was thrown in a well and covered with stones:

> The grass in the castle courtyard in Lavor
> Grew alone, undisturbed, and high
> Soon it overtook, and cast its shadow over
> Scattered, and unburied bones.
> Carrion birds, which pulled them out
> Fly high in silent circles
> The burned and blackened old walls
> Mourned by the dark sky,
> At the well, she still stands, the Linden-tree
> Once a witness of prettier times,
> Moved by the wind, she lets
> Her leaves glide silently by
> To the well, the briars push with eagerness
> To the well, thistles even, the rough ones
> Overhang the marble edge
> As if to look down
> A singer stands at the deep well
> To cry out his last song,

Where all delights are buried,
Giralda rests, covered with stones.

LENAU, *THE ALBIGENSES*

Guyot de Provins was a trobère from the north of France who wandered through Europe, visiting the most important courts of France, Germany, Aquitania, and Occitania.[30] We can place him in Maguncia on Whitsunday 1184, enjoying a festival for knights organized by Frederick Barbarossa. At the beginning of the thirteenth century, already very elderly, he compiled his "Bible," a satire on the different feudal estates of his time. In it, Guyot named his protectors for us:

The Emperor Fredrick Barbarossa, *l'empereres Ferris.*
Louis VII, King of France, *li rois Loeis de France.*
Henry II, King of England, *li riches rois Henris.*
Richard the Lionheart, *li rois Richarz.*
Henry, the "young king" of England, *li jones rois.*
Alfonso II of Aragon, *li rois d'Arragon.*
Raimundo V, Count of Toulouse, *li cuens Remons de Toulouse.*

Guyot followed the procession of troubadours to Toulouse. From this center of the world of courteous poetry, there were two ways to reach the residence of his Maecenas, Alfonso de Aragon: one, by returning to Foix, the home of Raimon Drut, and following the Ariège, later crossing the Sabarthès to reach the border of Aragon through the pass at Puymorens; the other, which was easier, by passing through Carcassonne and Perpignan in the Roussillon, hugging the coastline until Barcelona, and from there to Saragossa. It is possible that he used one road when he left, and the other when he returned. Whether in Carcassonne or Foix, troubadours felt at home. In Foix, he could have met with Raimon Drut and his sister Esclarmonde and celebrated her beauty.

Esclarmonde's aunt Adélaide, the daughter of Raimundo V of Toulouse and Constance of France, reigned in Carcassonne. After the death of her husband Roger Taillefer in 1193, all the possessions of the Trencavel family came under her indulgent scepter.

Now Kyot laschantiure was the name
Of one whose art compelled him
To tell what shall gladden no few.
Kyot is that noted Provençal
Who saw this Tale of Parsifal
Written in that heathenish tongue.
And what he retold in French
I shall not be too dull
To recount in German

WOLFRAM VON ESCHENBACH

Wolfram cites Kyot, a Provençal, as the person who inspired his Parsifal and claims that Chrétien de Troyes (the author of *Perceval le gallois,* written circa 1180) "has done wrong by this story."[31]

"Coinciding with the very words of Wolfram, it is supposed that Guyot refashioned and completed the Perceval of Chrétien de Troyes, which was its sole model." It has been proved as well that Wolfram, as he himself admitted, used a poem by the Provençal Kyot, a deduction that "is confirmed conclusively by the fact that only Wolfram knew the epochal poem in its uniform totality, and consequently, only he was capable of modifying it."

We do not know the exact dates of the birth and death of Wolfram. Because his *Parzival* dates from the first decade of the thirteenth century, we could deduce that his birth took place in the last third of the twelfth century. Regarding his death, Püterich von Reichertshausen (1400–1469), the author of a chivalrous poem entitled *The Letter of Honor,* confesses that he couldn't decipher the date of his death on his gravestone "in the Church of Our Lady, in the little town of Eschenbach."

Wolfram was poor, and went "from court to court" as a knight and traveling singer. He did not know how to read or write.

Reading is unknown to me
(I do not know a single letter)
Neither what is written in books
For this fact, I am ignorant.[32]

Because of this, somebody had to read Guyot de Provins' *Parsifal* to him if in reality he were to succeed in composing his version of the poem. Wolfram learned to speak French during his relations with the Western poets of the Minne. He seems to have been proud of it, because he never lost an opportunity to flaunt his knowledge of French in *Parzival,* although his misunderstandings and mistakes are frequent—above all, when the time came to translate names of places and persons (which can be verified with the original French version of the epochal poems of the Grail and Parsifal). Nor should we be surprised by such mistakes in the verbal transcription if we admit that Wolfram needed an oral translation of a subject so rich in its depictions.

The formulation of his phrases shows such fidelity, and expresses historical events with such clarity, that the presence of an intermediary can be excluded. It is difficult to find an explanation other than that "Kyot" and Wolfram met. The German cantor took the subject of the author.

It is possible that Wolfram and Guyot met on the occasion of the festivities organized by Frederick Barbarossa for knights in Maguncia or on the Wartburg in the court of the Landgrave Hermann of Thuringia. As we know, the Wartburg was the German court most frequented by the poets of the Minne, and Wolfram was there circa 1203.

The intense relations between the Minne singers (cantors of the idyllic love) of Germany, France, and Occitania are surprising. For example, under the pseudonym of Sembelis, Bertran de Born sang to Princess Laina de Plantagenet, sister of Richard the Lionheart. He remained in contact with his domina even after she became Duchess of Saxony, if you recognize as sufficient proof the Provençal poems that he sent her, which have since been found in Germany. Some have even come to the conclusion that Frederick Barbarossa, sovereign of the Kingdom of Arles from 1178, composed poems in Provençal on the banks of the Verdon River. Whatever the case, multiple links certainly united the chivalrous and loving poetry of the North with the South, and they influenced each other.

We will never know if the "true legend" came to Wolfram through the person of Guyot or from others reading from a manuscript of his *Parsifal,* which may allow us to forgive Wolfram's confusion of "Provins" for "Provenza."[33]

Along with the love poems already mentioned, "conjectural poems" appeared. It was the custom that a patron would entrust a troubadour with the composition of poetry that praised his grandeur or expressed in poetic form thanks for his hospitality and protection. For this reason, it is not strange that Guyot de Provins would have celebrated in *Parsifal* (lines that have not survived) his Maecenas, Raimundo of Toulouse, his daughter Adélaide de Carcassonne, her granddaughter Esclarmonde de Foix, and the King of Aragon, the cousin of Roger Taillefer (Adélaide's husband).

And that is the way it happened!

King Alfonso II of Aragon and Catalonia, better known as Alfonso "The Chaste," is Wolfram's "Castis" who was promised to Herzeloyde.[34]

To Wolfram, Herzeloyde was the mother of Parsifal; to Guyot de Provins [Wolfram's source], Herzeloyde is the Viscountess Adélaide de Carcassonne, the *domina* of Alfonso the Chaste.

The son of Adélaide is Trencavel, a name that Wolfram translated as "pierce-through-the-heart," the name of Parsifal. Raimon Roger, the Trencavel, served as Wolfram and Guyot's model for Parsifal.

As we will see, this deduction does not imply any violence.

The "Court of Love" of the Viscountess of Carcassonne was renowned throughout Occitania. From Barcelona to Florence and Paris there was no lady more celebrated than she. Her court was the center of poetry, heroism, and chivalrous courtesy, and at the same time, as the troubadour Arnaut de Mareulh said, "the most chaste and full of grace, because the scepter was in Adélaide's hands."

This trobère was a poor cleric from the area around Périgueux. One day he hung up his habit, and thereafter went from castle to castle singing the songs he had learned behind the abbey walls. He arrived at the court of Carcassonne, saw Adélaide, and stole her heart. But the high position of the crown prince of Toulouse, the aim of the kings of France (to destroy Occitania), frightened the humble harpist.

"The honor to aspire to the love of Adélaide corresponds solely to kings. But doesn't love make all humans equal? Who accepts is worthy. Before God, social classes do not exist. He only recognizes feelings from the heart. O beautiful and pure Lady, loyal transcription of divinity, why don't you act like her (a loyal transcription of divinity)?" Arnaut was right to be worried about his Minne. King Alfonso proposed something far more prosaic than homage and pretensions of sublime love to Adélaide. As he was, together with the Count of Toulouse, the feudal lord of the Viscounty of Carcassonne and Béziers, he proposed marriage to his cousin—Roger Taillefer's widow since 1193—because he wanted to assure for himself, if not the exclusive possession of her domains, at least his feudal supremacy.

Alfonso never believed that the Minne should exclude marriage; in fact, he thought that one had nothing to do with the other. In this way, he killed the Minne's enchantment, which demanded chastity as an absolute condition. He belonged to the world of profane knights, seeking a crown and a marriage bed, and by doing so lost his knighthood according to the leys d'amors that the hawk had brought from the sky.

Arnaut de Mareulh also became unworthy of the kingdom of love. One day, Adélaide kissed him, but he betrayed the grace he received by revealing this in two poems. In fact, this was a grave infraction of the rigorous laws of the Occitan world of the Minne. Moreover, these kisses awoke feelings in him that had nothing at all to do with sublime love.

> As I like that the wind
> Blows in my face in April,
> Before May begins,
> When the trilling of the nightingales
> Threshes the night
> Each bird happily trills
> His songs, as they please him,
> Under the pearled lilies of the dew
> Coupled with his small female. . . .
>
> ARNAUT DE MAREULH

Dismissed by the Viscountess Adélaide, the poor troubadour had to seek refuge in the court of Guillaume VIII of Montpellier (whom Guyot de Provins calls his protector Guillaumes).

"They could separate me from her, but nothing or nobody can break the links that bind me to my loved one. My heart is full of tenderness and certainty. They belong only to her, and God. Happy fields where she lives! When will we see each other again? How is it that somebody from there does not come to me? A shepherd who brought me news of you is for me a noble baron. If I found you in the desert, it would become Heaven for me."

Arnaut de Mareulh celebrated only Adélaide. He died of nostalgia. Love sickness was the mortal affliction of the troubadours; its only remedy, the Minne.

While Adélaide resided in her castle of Poivert, which was surrounded by splendid Pyrenean forests, many princes and troubadours passed through. The most delicate love problems were submitted for her judgment. When Richard the Lionheart, Alfonso of Aragon, or Raimon Drut de Foix had "sins" against love on their consciences, it was Adélaide who had to administer justice. There was no way to appeal her verdict, and all had to submit to it—it was not for nothing that she was considered the most noble, chaste, and gracious lady of all Occitania.

While in Poivert, troubadours like Peire d'Alvernha honored the wine of the Roussillon and "intoned songs to the happy torchlight" or filled the forests and fields with the sound of satires, jokes, and songs. She remained alone in her abode and prayed. She was a pious lady, but the God she prayed to was not our God. Her Christ did not die on the cross. For her, the threatening God of Israel was Lucifer.

Adélaide was a heretic!

This was not the only reason she rejected the amorous proposals of troubadours and princes. Being a heretic and understanding the troubadours were not mutually exclusive. Quite to the contrary, the greater part of the troubadours were heretics; all the Cathars were troubadours, and almost all the ladies of Occitania, once time had left its mark on their faces, became heretics. This was not the only motive that kept the Viscountess of Carcassonne far from the mundane activities of her court at Poivert.

During her life, Adélaide became all too familiar with bitter tragedies. Her husband, Trencavel, contracted a huge debt during the bloody reprisals against the burghers of Béziers for which he now had to answer to God. The Trencavel were enterprising and chivalrous but impulsive people. She was afraid of the possible antics of her only son Raimon Roger. Along with the heretic Bertran de Saissac, who was designated by her husband Roger Taillefer as young Trencavel's tutor, she oversaw the education of her son—a son who was destined never to become an ordinary knight, but a knight of the supreme Minne. He had to be worthy of the "Round Table" in Montségur, that inaccessible Pyrenean castle of carved rock where the Pure Doctrine of the Consoling Paraclete was preserved.

> *Upon my word, you are Parsifal!*
> *Your name means, "Pierce-in-the-heart"*
> *Great love ploughed just such a furrow*
> *Through your mother's heart . . .*
> *Your father left sorrow for her portion*
>
> WOLFRAM VON ESCHENBACH[35]

Parsifal had to show himself worthy of the Knights of the Grail!

Upon a green achmardi
She bore the consummation of heart's desire,
Its root and its blossoming—
A thing called "The Grail"
Paradisal, transcending all Earthly perfection!
WOLFRAM VON ESCHENBACH[1]

PART TWO

THE GRAIL

The empire of love is open,
The fable starts to unfold.
NOVALIS

THE INVISIBLE *Amor-Eros* extended his protecting hand over the world of the Occitan Minne. He was no longer the winged boy depicted in antiquity; now he appeared as an adult male. Troubadour Peire Vidal believed that he met him in flesh and blood as he headed one day from Castlenaudary to Muret and the court of Raimundo V of Toulouse:

> It was in the springtime, when the bushes begin to take on color, flowers bloom on the fields, and the birds trill jubilantly. An elegant and strong knight approached on horseback. Blond hair fell on his bronzed face, and his clear eyes glistened. The smile of his mouth revealed mother-of-pearl teeth. The shoe on one of his feet was adorned with sapphires and emeralds; the other foot was bare.
>
> The knight's cape was covered with violets and roses, and he wore a crown of marigolds on his head. Half of his horse was as black as night, and the other half, white like ivory. The forepart of the horse was jasper, and the stirrups were of agate. On the harness shone two diamonds, as beautiful and precious as any possessed by the Persian king Darius. On the bridle, a stone shone as splendorous as the sun. . . .
>
> Alongside the knight rode a lady a thousand times more

beautiful than he. Her skin was white as snow. Her pink cheeks were like rosebuds. Her hair shone like gold.

Behind the lady rode a servant and a lady-in-waiting. The servant carried an ivory bow and three arrows on a belt: one was gold, another steel, and the third lead. Regarding the lady-in-waiting, I only saw that her hair was very long and fell to the saddle of the horse. The knight and the lady sang a new song that the birds repeated.

"Let us stop at a well in a field surrounded by forests," said the lady. "Because I cannot stand castles."

"My lady," I answered her, "there is a very lovely spot under a laurel tree, and a spring is there among the stones."

"Peire Vidal," said the knight, "you should know that I am *Amor,* and my Lady is called *Grace.* Her lady-in-waiting and my servant are *Modesty* and *Loyalty.*"[2]

Wolfram prefaces *Parsifal* with a long prologue about Loyalty and Infidelity. He doubts that God would ever endanger the salvation of the soul; only the spirit of chivalry, that "prize of the intrepid man," could provide this coveted salvation. Nonetheless, whoever is dominated by disloyalty is punished with Hell.

> *If vacillation dwell with the heart,*
> *The soul will rue it.*
> *Shame and honor clash,*
> *Where the courage of a steadfast man*
> *Is motley like the magpie*
> *But such a man may yet make merry,*
> *For Heaven and Hell have equal part in him.*
> *Infidelity's friend is black all over, and takes on a murky hue,*
> *While the man of loyal temper holds to the white.*
>
> *I shall set these marks as a challenge to women:*
> *With God as my witness I bid good women to observe restraint*
> *The lock guarding all good ways is modesty—*
> *I need not wish them any better fortune.*

If I should describe for you here completely
Man and woman, as I could,
It would seem to you long and boring[3]

Wolfram did not need to explain the roles of man and woman to the *Minnesingers* of his time. We now know that the development of the world of the Minne in Germany closely followed its evolution in Occitania. According to the Mosaic dogma of Genesis, Yahweh first created an androgynous Adam, who was both the father and mother of Eve; this doctrine was never well received in Occitania. According to Occitan myth, Adam and Eve were two fallen angels, condemned to wander from star to star with Lucifer before their Earthly exile. Eve enjoys the same rights as Adam in Heaven as on Earth. She is not the "fe-male" of Adam; rather, she is his domina, because, like their ancestors the Iberians and Celts, the Occitanians saw in womankind something prophetic and divine. The Jewish Eve is placed beneath man: she must first bear her father's name and later her husband's, and can never have her own. The most ancient families of Languedoc, especially in the Pyrenees where the Celt Iberian tradition had achieved its highest degree of purity, always bore the names of their female ancestors. It was said, the Sons of Belissena *de Imperia*, *de Oliveiria*. These ladies' tools were not the spindle and the cradle; they preferred the pen and the scepter.

The troubadours were poets, and all poets suffer from unsatisfied nostalgia. Those who couldn't find satisfaction in the Minne knew the road that led them to the Round Table of nostalgia where the "Consoler"—whom Christ had first announced through Saint John the Evangelist—could be found.

The troubadours were poets in a country where the sun was more radiant than ours, the stars closer to Earth, and it was easy to pray.

These errant poets were no longer crazy rhymers, but "Pure Ones" or Cathars who, as we will see a little further on, transported the leys d'amors to the world of the spirit. In place of their ladies' favor, they sought freedom in God. In place of the Minne, the Consoler.

To pray and compose verses were the same thing. And so it was in Occitania, whose inhabitants very well appreciated the gifts of poetry and prophecy, qualities identified today as intuition and inspiration. The prayers of the Cathars—the errant troubadours—were nothing other than stanzas of the hymn to the luminous divinity that they received day to day in the symphony of tones and colors of their homeland. They were truly poets.

And like all poets, they felt themselves strangers on Earth; they aspired to a better Hereafter, where man, according to their mythology, had been in his time an angel, and where his real home could be found: the "House of Songs" or the Kingdom of the Light of Ahura Mazda, as he was called in remote times by the Babylonians.[4] The Cathars were so convinced of a better Hereafter that they radically renounced this life, considering it only a preparatory period for the true life that they knew existed beyond the stars.

The mountain peaks that rise to the heavens and the gorges that are lost in the eternal night of the Earth have always delighted poets and priests. On the summits, poetry and prayer blossom instinctively. Mankind feels closer to God there. In all great myths, the divinization of man is achieved in the mountains: Hercules became Olympic on Mount Oeta; Christ was transformed on Mount Tabor. The troubadours knew all this perfectly well, because in their time, the bridge that united the Orient with the West over the Mediterranean had not yet fallen: its first arch extended from the gigantic mountains of Asia to the sacred Paradise of the Greeks, and the second one from there to the Pyrenees, where Heliades had placed the Garden of the Hesperides: the luminous land of souls.

Mankind came from the Orient, just as our great myths come from the Orient, the last of which were the "Good Tidings." The sun rises in the East.

When it disappears behind the clouds, the desire to follow it is awoken in more than one—but how? Man must be a fallen god who feels an immense desire to return to the sky. Perhaps a poet's nostalgia is nothing more than the yearning for a lost Paradise, where man is the image of divinity, not its caricature.

When the sun sets in Provence and Languedoc, it arches in golden cirri over the intrepid and noble Pyrenees, which rise into the blue of the sky. When night falls over the Provençal plains, they continue blessed, transformed by the rays of the setting sun for a long time. Saint Bartholomew's Peak, one of the most beautiful summits of the Pyrenees, is still called "Mount of Transfiguration" or "Tabor" by the people of Provence. The Pyrenean Tabor is located between the valley of the elm trees known as the *Olmès* and the Sabarthès—the valley of Sabart—where the mother of God promised Charlemagne victory over the Saracens. A lonely and rocky pathway leads from the idyllic Olmès to the cliffs and caves of the Sabarthès: the Path of the Cathars, the pathway of the Pure Ones.[5]

In the heart of the desert solitude of the Tabor rises a rock whose ruggedness defies description; its summit is sometimes enveloped by golden clouds illuminated by the sun, and its walls fall precipitously to the fortifications of a castle called *Montségur*. One day as I was climbing the Path of the Cathars to the summit of the Tabor, I met an old shepherd who told the following legend:

> When the walls of Montségur were still standing, the Cathars, the Pure Ones, kept the Holy Grail inside them. Montségur was in danger; the armies of Lucifer were before its walls. They wanted to take the Grail to insert it again in the diadem of their Prince, from where it had broken off and fallen to Earth during the fall of the angels. At this most critical moment, a white dove came from the sky and split the Tabor in two. Esclarmonde, the keeper of the Grail, threw the precious relic into the mountain, where it was hidden. So they saved the Grail. When the devils entered the castle, it was too late. Furious, they burned all the Pure Ones, not far from the rocky castle on the *camp des cremats*.

> *A troop left it on Earth and then rose high above the stars,*
> *If their purity drew them back again*
>
> WOLFRAM VON ESCHENBACH[6]

The pathway of the Pure Ones starts out from Olmès, borders Montségur, and passes over the summit of the Tabor. Finally, it reaches the caves of Sabarthès, the last home of the Cathars. Once there, so far from the world, they meditated on the supreme Minne in a trance-like state.

> *Yes, if the true Amor calls,*
> *Love like today*
> *The supreme Minne requires it.*
>
> WOLFRAM VON ESCHENBACH

The Cathars left their hermetic life in the bowels of the mountains only to bring the "last consolation" to the dying, or to recite ancient myths to noble ladies and gallant knights gathered in the great halls of castles. With their long black garments and Persian-style round caps, they looked like Brahmans or acolytes of Zarathustra. After they finished, they would pull out the Gospel According to Saint John from a roll of leather that they carried on their chests; then they would read aloud:

> *In the beginning there was the Word, and the Word was with*
> *God, and the Word was God. God is spirit, and those who adore*
> *him must adore him in the Spirit. It may be that I die, because*
> *if I do not die, the Consoler will not come to you. But when the*
> *Consoler that I shall send to you comes. . . .*

Dieus vos benesiga! Shall God bless you!

The Pure Ones would return to their caves, the "Cathedral," the "*Gleysos*" (churches), the "Hermit's Cave," and the "Cave of Fontanet."[7]

> *The beast made for Fontane La Salväsche,*
> *This was the abode of the austere Trevrizent. . . .*
> *From Trevrizent, Parsifal is about to learn matters concerning the*
>   *Grail*
> *That has been hidden*
>
> *His host led Parsifal into a grotto. . . .*
>   WOLFRAM VON ESCHENBACH

The caves of the Sabarthès are so numerous that they could house an entire city of cave dwellers.[8] Next to these large caves, which penetrate leagues and leagues into the mountains, are innumerable grottoes. In the walls of these grottoes, niches still clearly show where carpentry was installed, and how authentic hermitages existed. But because of fires and the passage of centuries, only the burned limestone walls have survived, corroded by time, together with remains of tarred or burned wood, drawings, and inscriptions:

A tree of the word or of life can be found, as they say, in the
middle of Paradise, and the Hellenes already knew this. The
people of the Hesperides guarded its golden apples.

A boat with a sun on the sail.

A fish, symbol of divine luminosity.

A dove, the emblem of God the Spirit.

Monograms of Christ, in Greek or Latin characters.

The word "Gethsemane": the garden where Christ was handed
over to the authorities.

The initials "GTS," artistically entwined, probably an abbreviation of the word "Gethsemane."

Fragments of a phrase, of which only "Sant Gleysa" can be read.

Two of these grottoes have kept their names: the Grotto of Jesus
Christ and the Grotto of the Dead Man. Before the entrance to the first
one, traces of a small garden and a small terrace remain where the hermit who lived there must have meditated:

> Alas wicked world, why do you do so?
> You give us more pain, and bitter sorrow,
> Than ever joy!
>
> WOLFRAM VON ESCHENBACH[9]

The Cathars did not feel that Earth was their homeland. They compared it to a prison that an architect, lacking experience, had constructed
from low-quality materials. They were conscious of the fact that their
real home could only be somewhere beyond the stars. "Up there" had
been built by the Spirit, *Amor*: neither hatred nor war, but life; neither
sickness nor death, rather—God. In the beginning was the Spirit. In it
was the Word, and they were God.

Just as within us two worlds may fight each other—the spirit, which
is fat, and the flesh, which is thin—there are two principles of action in
the universe: the Yes and the No, the Good and the Bad. The Good is
God; the Bad is Lucifer—the eternally negative spirit.

The Word created a world that extends beyond the arch of golden
clouds, past the stars. Our world is the work of Lucifer. The Word is
creative; Lucifer is only a plagiarist, an untalented modeler.

We humans—the fallen angels—must adapt ourselves to these two principles that have determined who we are. The spiritual man, the soul, is the work of the divine Word. Material man, the body, is Lucifer's creation. Our soul is divine, eternal. Our body is non-divine, perishable. The soul, created by God, is Spirit. Banished to the Earth for having rebelled against the Spirit, it has to remain in the body until it has recognized the vanity of Earthly life and wishes to return to the Spirit. A person should begin to redivinize himself now on Earth in order to return. In this case, souls, as they wander from star to star, must dematerialize themselves until the doors of their real home open for them.

> *The stars perhaps enthrone the exalted soul*
> *As here vice rules, there virtue has control.*
>
> VON HALLER

In his *Universal Natural History and Theory of Heaven* (1755), Immanuel Kant wrote:

Who is so bold to dare an answer to the question whether sin exercises its sway also in the other spheres of the cosmic structure or whether virtue alone has established her control there? Does not a certain middle position between wisdom and irrationality belong to the unfortunate capacity to sin? Who knows whether the inhabitants of those distant celestial bodies are not too refined and too wise to allow themselves to fall into the foolishness inherent in sin; whereas the others who live in the lower planets adhere too firmly to material stuff and are provided with far too little spiritual capacity to have to drag their responsibility for their actions before the judgment seat of justice?

The Cathars considered Earth to be Hell. To have to live in the midst of sin was a more atrocious punishment than having their flesh torn with pincers, pricked and tortured by devils with horns and tails in an icy lake or a burning oven. "Earth is Hell," they said. . . .

For them, death was nothing more than changing dirty clothes, a little like butterflies abandoning the chrysalis to lose themselves in the radiant springtime. The Greeks had called the soul *Psiche,* which literally means "butterfly."

What happens with souls who "have not seriously forced themselves," who have found their home in the material? In his condition as father, God cannot remain deaf to the pleas of his children. Their souls can stay down here, emigrating from body to body as long as they like, until the day when they too yearn for the stars.[10]

The largest cave in the Sabarthès is at Lombrives. In very remote times, during a period whose night had hardly been illuminated by the science of history, it was a temple of Ilhomber, the sun god of the Iberians. The simple shepherds and pastors of Ornolac, a nearby town, call it "the Cathedral."

Ornolac is in the lateral valley where the Path of the Cathars snakes its way up to the summit of the Tabor. A marvelous small Romanesque church dominates the town. On the square in front, a Mother of God, sculpted by peasant hands, holds the baby Jesus in her arms and a tassel of wheat in one hand—a sign that her protecting cloak extends over the fields and vineyards.

The steep pathway leads past *menhirs* [prehistoric stone monoliths]— one has fallen over—and then you arrive at the gigantic vestibule of the Cathedral of Lombrives. This is the entrance to an amazing subterranean kingdom, where history and fairy tale have found refuge together from a world that has become dull and ordinary. The path leads into the depths of the mountain between stalactites of white, jasmine-like chalk and walls of dark brown marble, studded with brilliant rock crystal.

A cavern 107 meters [350 feet] high became an authentic cathedral for the heretics. The Earth—another creation of Lucifer—furnished the Cathars with their most precious home, where they could ponder the beauty created by the great artist beyond the stars. So they would not be forgotten, a heretical hand drew the sun and the silvered disc of the moon—the only revelations of God who is love and light—on the marbled wall of the cave. As the water falls to the ground drop by drop from an arched ceiling lost in eternal night, it never changes its rhythm. Its stalactites still form church benches for all those who wish to contemplate this wonderland for a moment.

When there is a storm in the Ariège valley, the whole mountain resonates with the din of thundering waters that widen a passage through the limestone fissures in the rock. When Lucifer, the god of tempests and death, hits the trembling world, his hammer flashing sparks, the entire mountain shakes to its foundations.

A stone stairway leads from the cathedral of the heretics to another part of the cave at Lombrives. After a hike of several hours, the foot stops seized by terror before an abyss hundreds of meters deep.

There, a gigantic stone can be found, upon which, drop by drop, the water has sculpted a marvelous stalagmite in the form of a hammer, which the peasants of Ornolac call the Tomb of Hercules.

THE GOLDEN FLEECE[1]

———•———

Heracles or Hercules
And the Greek Alexander
Could speak from great knowledge of precious stones . . .
WOLFRAM VON ESCHENBACH

SILIUS ITALICUS, A ROMAN POET and historian of the first century after Christ, has passed on to us a legend in beautiful hexameters according to which the gigantic block of stone in the cave of Lombrives, adorned with a stalagmite hammer, is in fact the sepulchral stone of Hercules.

After stealing Geryon's cows, Hercules was received by Bebryx, king of the Bebrices, in the "savage mansion." There, he seduced the king's daughter Pirène, abandoning her afterwards. She feared the anger of her father, and desiring to have Hercules' love again, escaped from home. As she walked the paths of the world, ferocious beasts fell upon her. Defenseless, Pirène called out for Hercules' help, but when he arrived, it was too late; she was already dead. When he saw her he began to weep. His moans made the mountains tremble, and all the rocks and caves echoed Pirène's name, which he repeated between sobs. Then he buried her. The name of Pirène will never perish because the mountains will always bear her name—the Pyrenees.

The Throne of King Bebryx and the Tomb of Pirène are the names of three magnificent groups of stalagmites in the heart of the cave of Lombrives, on the banks of a lake filled with mysteries. The water falls incessantly on Pirène's tomb, as if the mountain is weeping for the unfortunate princess. From the roof and the walls hang in a petrified state the garments that she preferred.

Latin authors (among them Pliny) thought that the first inhabitants of Spain were Persians who migrated from the Caucasus. Greek historian Dion Casius wrote that the Bebrices were the first inhabitants of the eastern Pyrenees. According to the Byzantine historian Zonaras, the Greek grammarian Stephanus of Byzantium distinguished two different Bebrice peoples: one that lived on the coast of the Black Sea and another that was settled in the Pyrenees not far from the "Bebrice Sea," a primitive name for the Gulf of Leon.

Dasqueius, a commentator on Silius Italicus, asserts that the word "Bebryx" is only an adjective and that the king of the Bebrices was named Amykos, a prince who challenged and killed in a boxing match any foreigner unfortunate enough to arrive in his kingdom, until the day Pollux the Argonaut killed him. Festus Avienus, a Roman historian, supports this.

Let's summarize these sources, and expand them. In the third century B.C., an emigration of peoples from the Caucasus to the West took place: Phoenicians, Persians, Medeans, Getules (actually Berbers of North Africa), Armenians, Chaldeans, and Iberians. This last group found a home on the Iberian peninsula. The Bebrices were part of this people and lived in the area of the Pyrenees that, under Roman domination, belonged to *Gallia narbonense* in the region of Saint Bartholomew's and Montcalm Peaks. Thanks to Strabon, a Greek geographer, we know that there were as many gold mines in Spain as in Asia. The gold mines of the Bebrices attracted the Phoenicians (1200 B.C.) and Phocians (600 B.C.). At the beginning of the third century before Christ, the Phoenicians in the so-called Semitic migration founded a new homeland in Syria. We still do not know if from Tyre, their most important city, they were already in contact with the inhabitants of the Spanish and French coasts, or if they arrived there together with the Iberians over land. The most probable scenario is that they began maritime commercial trading from Asia Minor to the western Mediterranean coasts, and from there they returned by sea to Syria with all the riches of the Pyrenean subsoil.

Through Herodotus, we know that a temple was dedicated to "Melkart" (the king of the city of Tyre), and that he was also worshipped as the Phoenician Hercules, the protecting god of navigation and the colonies at the end of the world in the West. The Old Testament calls the god of Tyre "Baal" (lord).

Originally, every god who was believed to inhabit a specific place where he exercised his power, and therefore was of local importance in contrast with other gods, was called Baal. In this way, there was a Baal-Lebanon, a Baal-Chermon, etc. Little by little, Baal-Melkart of Tyre became the "God-Lord" of Phoenicia and Canaan, the "All-Mighty," the masculine generator, personified in the solar disc. His complement ("wife" as she was called in mythology) was Astarté, the feminine principle, receptive, enlightened, and personified by the moon.

An inscription uncovered in Malta gives Hercules the title of proto-guide.[2] It is well known that the cult of ancestors and mythology almost always has the same starting point. Consequently, we could suppose that a Phoenician prince may have served as a model for Melkart. Could this Hercules-Melkart have led his people from the Caucasus to Tyre or from Tyre to the West? We cannot prove it, and it doesn't really interest anybody. The only thing that matters is the fact that the Iberians had a Hercules-Melkart who was their proto-guide and they received orders from Tyre's colonists.

In very remote times, the cave of Lombrives, where the legendary tomb of Hercules is located, was consecrated to Ilhomber, the Iberian Hercules.[3] This local god of the Iberians, more precisely of the Bebrices, who was also called Bel (Baal) under the influence of Greek colonists, was converted into A-bel-lio (Apollo).

Phoecaea was a Greek colony on the Ionic coastline of Asia Minor. Its inhabitants, known as Phocians, were engaged in maritime commerce with the Iberians, other continental Greeks, and the citizens of Argos. Apparently, circa 600 B.C., they managed to overtake the colonial preponderance of the Phoenicians, and assumed the exploitation of the metal mines of the Pyrenees for themselves. When Phoecaea fell under the pressure of the Persian tyrant Harpagon in 546 B.C., they abandoned their homeland in Asia Minor and fled in ships to their western colonies, above all to Massilia (Marseille), Portus Veneris (Port Vendres in the French Roussillon), Kerberos (Cerbère, on the Spanish border), and present-day Monaco, where they built a temple to Heraclius Monoikos.

The tale of the Argonauts is the oldest epic poem of the Greeks. Not only is it the most ancient of the Greek mythological legends that we have, it is an amalgam of primitive Greek colonization and Hellenic ancestor worship—Homer assumed that everyone knew it as fact—and it also provides us with interesting geographic concepts of the ancient Greeks.

Fifteen sailors equipped with fifty oars set out across the sea from Argos aboard the ship *Argo* in search of the Golden Fleece. The best known among them were Hercules, Orpheus, Castor, Pollux, and Jason. After many twists and adventures (like the combat with Amykos, the king of the Bebrices) they arrived at Colchis where, with the help of Medea the bewitched sorceress, they stole the Golden Fleece which they found hanging from a branch of the sacred oak tree.

This shows that there were ancient Greek authors who knew about the existence of the Bebrices in Asia Minor and the Pyrenees, and who associated them with the legend of the Argonauts. What meaning could the conquest of the Golden Fleece have?

Let's take a leap through the centuries to the Middle Ages, following the destruction of the original Mediterranean civilizations, when the center of intellectual gravity had moved north.

What were those innumerable alchemists searching for when they mixed mysterious ingredients in their retorts and tried with mystical incantations to achieve the "great work"?

The Philosopher's Stone, or what others called the Golden Fleece!

What was Parsifal seeking in Wolfram's poem that was referred to as "the Grail"? A stone![4] The *Lapsis exillis (Lapsis ex coelis)*—the "Desire for Paradise"!

For some, paradisal pleasure consists in the possession of everything beautiful and precious the world has to offer. For others, Paradise can be found closer to the stars.

Some alchemists who sought the Philosopher's Stone wanted to transform low-quality metals into gold. By contrast, the truly expert alchemists transferred their secret formulas to the realm of the spirit. For them, inferior metals were nothing other than human passions that had to be revalued. Instead of gold, they expected to find God. In the legend of the Argonauts in Nonnos, the navigators see a "cup" float on the "Mountain of the World with the tree of lights."

The Argonauts found the Golden Fleece, and they were summoned like demigods to the stars with their prize. Hercules prepared to become a god, between the "Lyre" and the "Crown." Castor and Pollux awaited the "Coachman" to take them to the supreme altitudes of the sky. And the *Argo,* which carried the precious relic beyond the sea, was transported as a charm to the radiating Milky Way of the boreal hemisphere of the heavens, where together with the "Cross," the "Triangle," and the "Altar," it irrefutably proved the luminous nature of the eternal God. The triangle symbolized the holy trinity; the cross, the divine sacrifice of love; and the altar, the table of the Last Supper where, on the night of the first Holy Thursday, stood the chalice of rebirth.

> *In truth, I tell ye: he who is not born again*
> *Cannot see the Kingdom of God.*
>
> JOHN 3:3

Undeniably, there were alchemists who sought gold, the "Great King"; others sought God. There were astrologers who wanted to find in the stars the science of tomorrow, and three of them were led by a star to Bethlehem, where in a cave, the Word of God had become a man. It is also said that a pagan astrologer read the mystery of the Grail in the stars:

> *Flegetanis, the heathen saw*
> *With his own eyes in the constellations things*
> *He was shy to talk about,*
> *Hidden mysteries that trembling revealed it:*
>
> *He said there was a thing called the Gral.*
> *Whose name he had read clearly in the constellations*
>
> WOLFRAM VON ESCHENBACH[5]

The celestial archway rotates from east to west. The moon and the stars move during the night, replacing the sun, the star of Helios: Apollo.

Apollo was the god of pure solar light who freed the Earth in the springtime from the claws of winter; for this he was also known as the *soter* (savior) who purified the dead sinner and led him to redemption at the entrance to the luminous land of souls. This god brought help and benediction. In a boat pulled by swans, he reached the land of the Hyperboreans. The clouds sang like the rainfall. The trickling of the water was the song of nature. For this reason, Apollo was the magister of the muses, and his attributes were the lyre and the laurel, whose branches formed the crowns of poets.

When the rays of the springtime sun warm the Earth, humidity in the form of vapor rises to heaven. These vapors and fogs were always seen as oracles because their rise and fall foretold the weather. For this reason, Apollo was also a god with the gift of prophecy. To be a poet and prophet is the same thing.

Alkaios de Mitilene, a contemporary of Sappho, said of Apollo:

When Apollo came to the world, Zeus gave him a golden miter, a lyre, and a chariot drawn by swans, and sent him to Castalia, the well in Delphi, to preach justice to the Hellenes. Apollo disobeyed, and led his swans to the land of the Hyperboreans. When the inhabitants of Delphi learned what had happened, they composed a paean, placed choruses of children around the tripod, and pleaded with the god to dignify them with a visit.

The Hyperboreans were the chosen people of Apollo. Pious, with pure customs, they lived happily. They lived in the forests of their country, where the sun and fertility reigned, and the temperatures were agreeable. They nourished themselves solely with fruits. They never killed an animal, knew no war or quarrels. When they were tired of life, they sought their freedom in the never-ending waves of the sea. Apollo was their supreme god. The "Radiating One" came to them in a golden chalice "similar to a star whose splendor reached the sky." Apollo loved the Hyperboreans from the first day when the waves of the sea carried to their hospitable coasts that chest where his mother Semele had placed him. From then on, year after year, he came to them, "transported from wave to wave in that marvelous concave litter that Hephaistos had worked in precious gold; a litter that transported him, asleep, on the surface of the waters . . ."[6]

In a mystical casket where objects for the cult of Apollo were discovered two hundred years ago close to Palestine in the mountains of Sabina, an engraved scene depicts the combat of the Argonauts with Amykos, the King of the Bebrices.[7] Yet again we find ourselves confronted with the Argonauts, Apollo, the Golden Fleece, and the Bebrice Amykos and his sacred cup.

GWION'S CUP

---◆◆---

The wise Pythagoras,
Who was an astronomer, and beyond dispute
So sapient that no man since Adam's time
Could equal him in understanding,
He could speak from great knowledge of precious stones.

WOLFRAM VON ESCHENBACH

THE INHABITANTS OF CROTONA, a city founded by the Aqueos on the southeastern coast of Italy where Pythagoras lived and taught, assert that this wise man was Apollo in person, and that he had arrived from the land of the Hyperboreans to bring a new doctrine of salvation to mankind.[1] It is said that he died a martyr. He was the son of an artisan named Mnesarchus and the virgin Pythais. Still others saw him as the son of Apollo.

Pythagoras taught that the soul was immortal but banished in the body, and that as a consequence it was obliged to transmigrate from body to body, even to those of animals, before it could achieve its definitive redivinization. Cicero believed he had learned from a good source that Pythagoras had adopted the doctrine of the immortality of the soul and its transmigration from the Druids, the philosophers of Gaul.

Druidism was more a philosophic doctrine than a religion, and comprised theology, astronomy, natural sciences, medicine, and law. What Caesar called "the discipline" of the Druids was nothing other than a dogmatic synthesis of these branches of knowledge, a synthesis that offered surprising affinities with Pythagorean philosophy and Hindu and Babylonian theogonic philosophies.

The Druids taught that Dispater, the god of death, had created the Earth and all on it.[2] The soul was divine in nature, consequently immortal, but forced to transmigrate body to body until the moment when purified of matter, it could enter into the other world, that of the spirit. Their supreme god was Belenus or Belis, as the Greek historian Herodianos called him. This god Belenus was none other than Apollo-Belio, the God of Light.

Dispater was the Latinized name of Pluto, prince of the underworld, sovereign of the pale souls of the dead, and keeper of all subterranean treasures.

The Druids considered the riches of this world to be of no importance. On their orders, the Gold of Tolosa and the treasure of the temple of Delphi were thrown into a Pyrenean lake.

The Path of the Pure Ones leads from Montségur to the Tabor, and from there to the caves at Ornolac. Between Montségur and the summit of the Tabor, there is a mountain lake of dark waters, boxed in by rocky slopes. The inhabitants of the town of Montségur, whose houses, like honeycombs, line the sides of the mountain that dominates the Lasset gorge, call that lake *Lac des Truites* (lake of trout) or *Estang Mal* (pond of sins).

"Don't throw any stones in," my peasant friends told me, "because it is the cradle of thunder! If you throw a stone, it will provoke a storm and a lightning bolt will destroy you! Evil has its home in the lake. That is the reason why there are no fish in it . . ."

"And why then do you call it the Lake of Trout?" I asked them. They replied:

> Properly, it should be called the *Lac des Druides* [Lake of the Druids], because the Druids were the ones who threw the gold, silver, and precious stones in it. It happened long before our Lord and Savior was born. The people were dying *en masse* because of an inexplicable disease. A person who was perfectly well in the morning could be dead by the afternoon.
>
> Never before had such a disease devastated our mountains. The all-knowing Druids advised everyone in this desperate situation to throw all their gold and silver in the lake as tribute to the powers of the underworld, the powers that were lords over sickness and death. In stone-wheeled carts, they transported their riches to the lake and threw them into the fathoms. Next, the Druids drew a

magic circle around the *estang*. All the fish died and its green waters turned black. From that moment, the people were cured of their terrible affliction. All the gold and silver will belong to person who is capable of breaking the magic circle. But as soon as anyone touches the gold and silver, they will die of the same disease that in another time killed so many before the gold was thrown into the lake.

Ptolemy of Alexandria makes a reference to the Bebrices, who belonged to the Volcae Tectosages.[3] Let's go back into history.

At the dawn of the sixth century before Christ, under the reign of Tarquino Prisco, the part of Gaul between the Garonne, the Mediterranean, the Alps, and the ocean was referred to as "the Celtic" by Aristotle, Herodotus, and Hiparchus. It was inhabited by a people who were a mixture of immigrant Celts and native Iberians. One of these Celt Iberian tribes was the Volcae Tectosages; their territory had its capital at Tolosa (present-day Toulouse) and its principal maritime city was Narbo (Narbonne). Aproximately 163 years after the foundation of Rome, which is to say circa 590 B.C., some of the Volcae Tectosages immigrated to *Hercynia Silva* [the Hercynian Forest], which was nine days' walk wide and sixty days long. It went from the foothills of the Alps to the Sudets and the Carpathians, and from the Black Forest and the Odenwald to Spessart and the Rhône. This branch of the Volcae settled in the plains of the Danube. For centuries, they remained barbarians.

By contrast, their brothers under the sun of the fertile Celtic had become accustomed to a civilized way of life. They were gradually transforming themselves into semi-Greeks. This was partly due to their commerce with Greek colonies that were established along the coastline. The Marsillians taught the Volcae how to cultivate crops, fortify cities, and plant vineyards and olives; in all, they brought them into contact with Greek civilization. This influence was such that Greek became the official language in the Celt Iberian provinces, and remained so until well into the third century A.D. The Volcae adopted Hellenistic fashions and intoned paeans in honor of their Abellio.

Greek ships brought westward the news of the immense treasures in the temple in Delphi. In their condition as semi-barbarians, the Volcae decided to steal Apollo's gold in order to be able to offer it to Abellio.

In the year 278 B.C., on the orders of their military commander

Brennus, some 200,000 warriors on foot and horseback left the Celtic to invade Greece. This provoked panic. The Greeks let the barbarians advance to the Spechio River, but they continued to occupy Thermopiles, the door to their homeland.

The Volcae tried to throw a bridge over the river, but they had to give up. Nonetheless, one night 10,000 soldiers chosen by Brennus swam across the river on their shields. The Greeks, who had received the order to defend the Spechio River, had to retreat to Thermopylies. Thermopiles, crowned with the halo of Greek patriotism, has seen two great invasions: the first, when Leonidas and his 300 Spartans lost their lives repelling the Persians in the year 480 B.C. This, the second one, took place a century later when the barbarians attacked.

Several times, Brennus attempted to cross the pass, but nothing could overcome the Greek phalanx.

The Volcae discovered a path that, passing over Mount Oeta, led from Herclea to the ruins of the city of Trachine; but the heroic resistance of a Greek detachment repulsed the invaders.

This reverse did not dampen Brennus' confidence. He ordered 40,000 infantry and 800 cavalry to destroy Etolia, hoping that the Etolians, who were defending Thermopylae, would hurry back to protect their threatened homeland. Brennus was not mistaken. The ploy worked. Faced with the horrific news of the sacking of their town by the Volcae, the Etolians abandoned their positions.

In this way, Brennus managed to pass through Thermopylae. The Greeks fled toward the port of Lamia, where they boarded the ships of the Athenians. Without hesitating for a moment, Brennus led his army against the Parnassus.

At the moment when the Volcae assaulted Delphi, a tremendous storm broke. As Pausanias and Justino wrote, the Earth began to tremble. Gigantic blocks of rock fell from the tops of the mountains, crushing numerous besiegers. The following night Parnassus began to tremble again; the temperature fell and hailstones and snow buried numerous attackers.

The inhabitants of Delphi recovered their confidence. An oracle announced that Apollo would not leave them in the lurch, and that the storm was confirmation of this. Encouraged, they launched an audacious counterattack. From this point forward, the historical accounts differ. According to some historians, the inhabitants of Delphi inflicted a massive defeat on their attackers, forcing them to withdraw. Before retreating, however, the Volcae killed all their wounded and dying. Brennus, gravely wounded, didn't want to be an exception and killed himself.

According to other accounts, the Celts succeeded in taking Delphi, stole its treasures, and transported them back to Tolosa, where all succumbed to a contagious illness. Their Druids discerned by the flight of birds that only throwing all the stolen gold and silver into a sacred lake could cure the population.

A hundred years later, Toulouse, still the capital of the Volcae Tectosages, had become the commercial center of Western Europe—a fact that excited the jealousy and appetite of Rome more than ever before. When Consul Cepio managed to take the city by surprise, he allowed his troops to pillage it. During this looting a large portion of the Delphi treasure was stolen. However, a multitude of good reasons exist to posit that Cepio did not reach the national sanctuary of the Celt Iberians, which until well into the Middle Ages was located in the range of Saint Bartholomew's Peak. The Volcae Tectosages had the custom of consecrating all the gold extracted from their mines to their god Abellio. During this period, there was a famous temple of Abellio-Apollo in Tolosa. Granted that the city was sacked by Roman troops, it is possible that only the temple gold fell into the hands of the looters. Nonetheless, it is undeniable that Cepio ordered the transport of 150,000 talents to Marseille, an ally of Rome. On the way, the convoy was assaulted, and the gold never reached Marseille. The Roman authorities accused Cepio and his presumed accomplices of stealing the money. They must have had miserable deaths, and Cepio was pursued by ill fortune until the end of his days. His bad fortune became a proverb in Rome: *Habet aurum tolosanum* [he has the gold of Tolosa], which means a person with bad luck, for whom nothing goes as it should.

The Celts did not see the Iberians as savage, uncivilized people. They were related to the Persians and Medeans, both highly evolved, and during their seven thousand years of sedentary life, they had completely civilized their new homeland. The Celts, upon entering it for the first time, found the remnants of an extremely ancient civilization.

According to some experts, the prehistoric pictures that can be seen on the walls of the caves in the Sabarthès—above all, those at Niaux—are close to 20,000 years old. The cave drawings of groups of wandering mammoth and deer hunters are proof of a fidelity to nature that presupposes a very developed intelligence and a very fine capacity for observation. In addition, we shouldn't lose sight of the fact that when we discuss the religion (Druidism) and the philosophy of the Celts, we find ourselves confronted with intimately intertwined religious concepts, perhaps similar to those of the original natives. This is certainly the case for the Celt Iberian theogony, because the god Belis, Latinized as Belenus-Apollo, is the Iberian god Ilhomber-Abellio. The Celtic theogony only appears dualist; the Celt Iberian certainly was. They became polytheistic only under Roman domination. There can be no doubt that they could maintain themselves for centuries in their original form in the inaccessible, wild valleys of the Pyrenees and on the mountaintops. As we already noted, the Celt Iberian Druids saw in Dispater-Pluto the Greek-Latin Zeus Chthonios: the god of death, storms, and fire and the creator of the Earthly world. He reigns in the depths of the Earth with his hammer of thunder in hand, or rides across the sky in his chariot pulled by rams, sowing desolation and death. He looks similar to Wotan and Thor but, despite his Greco-Latin name and his affinity with the aforementioned Nordic divinities, he is nothing other than the Celt Iberian variation of Ahriman (Devastator) of the Iranians, Medeans, and Parthians.

According to Iranian Mazdaist doctrine, there have been two conflicting principles since the beginning of time: one is life-fertility, and the other death-destruction.[4]

The first is symbolized by the sun. The effusion of spiritual light, truth, and generosity was venerated in Ahura Mazda (Ormuzd), the omniscient god. The second, symbolized by the darkness of night, contains error, evil, and lies, and finds its incarnation in Ahriman, the Devastator.

Ahura Mazda created the sky and the Earth. His creation survived, but remained incomplete because of the intervention of Ahriman. Mankind has the moral obligation to fight in favor of the "good" against "evil." In nature, it has to destroy all dangerous plants and animals—above all others the serpent, "the enemy of God"—and promote the growth and development of useful creatures.

When the souls of the dead head for the bridge of Tchinvat, the good cross it and arrive in Garodemana, where Ahura Mazda has his throne in the House of Songs. The sinners pass by him and remain in this world, the Drudjodemana (House of Lies) until the day when the savior Saosyat will show all mankind the way to Ahura Mazda.

The fight between God and his adversary will last 12,000, years but in the end Ahriman will be beaten thanks to the intervention of the savior Saosyat. This will happen on the Final Judgment Day. Ahriman will fall to his knees before Ahura Mazda to intone an eternal hymn of praise to the supreme and true God.

The savior Saosyat was born from a virgin, and will return from the dead. He will separate the good men from the bad, and will judge them. The Pythagoreans also called him Rhadamanthys, the judge of the dead.

Of course, the Final Judgment will not mean eternal condemnation for all sinners. Converted by the generosity and justice of Ahura Mazda, they will recognize and adore him as their only god. Henceforth, there will be only light, love, and celestial songs.

The undeniable beauty of the Mazdaist theogony was in truth disfigured by an accumulation of pedantic and eccentric statutes. This is why Voltaire said of the *Zendavesta* (the "Sacred Writing" of Mazdaism) that he couldn't read "two pages of this brew, attributed to the horrible Zarathustra, without feeling compassion for human nature." At any rate, Voltaire liked to exaggerate.

Not very long ago, a stone head of the Buddha, probably of Iberian origin, was discovered in a burial chamber in the south of France.[5] Dating from the first millennium before Christ, in all probability it belonged to an Iberian or Celt Iberian Abellio, who was invariably depicted with crossed legs in the style of the Buddha.

We should point out in passing that swastikas appear as a religious symbol on all the statues and altars of Abellio that have been found in the Pyrenees. (Swastikas have also long been a Buddhist symbol.) Even today, the stone portals of old Basque farmhouses display swastikas as a way to keep evil spirits from their homes and families.

The fact that the Celt Iberian-Iranian Dispater-Ahriman exists also in Sanskrit under the name *Dyaus pitar,* in Greek under the name of *Zeus pater,* and in Latin as *Jupiter,* indicates the richness and intensity of the relations between the Aryan Mediterranean world and the Oriental world of Hindu civilization, its neighbor. All the priestly castes of the primitive Aryans learned Celt Iberian and Iranian dualism during the formation of the esoteric mysteries.

We must keep this in mind when, in our considerations, we speak of dualist Manichaeism and its Western variant Catharism. Were the Cathars Druids who were converted to Christianity by Manichaeist missionaries?

The Druids engaged themselves with theological, philosophical, juridical, and pedagogical problems. The superior of each local caste was called "good-father." In the Pyrenees, as in Ireland, Druidism managed to survive for a long time against the unstoppable advance of Christianity. It was not so easy to penetrate into isolated regions where the native peoples, under the influence of their own priests, clung to their traditions.

The *vates* were astrologers, soothsayers, and medical doctors. For their time, they had a profound knowledge of astrology. Many marvelous tales were told of their methods for curing illnesses.

The *bards* were poets and cantors. They were also called *privairds* (in Provençal, *trobère*; in English, troubadour or inventor). In religious ceremonies and palace festivities, they accompanied the songs of the gods and heroes with the *chrotta,* a type of harp. They found copious material for their mythological epochal poems in Druidic theories of salvation.

So it is that the Druids were not solely the keepers of dualist mysteries— mysteries that we can only guess at, because they were transmitted orally from teacher to student. Like the oligarchy of princes and nobles, they constituted a closed hierarchy that included both the vates and bards.[6]

The word "druid" has three meanings: the first is "Seeing-thinker" or *tro-hid.* The second meaning is "Wiseman" or magician. The third, which is the best known and probably the most correct, comes from the Greek *drys* or the Gallic *drou,* which means "oak."

From the Septentrion to the Indus, the oak was *the* sacred tree, linked to all the myths and cults that were close to nature. An oak was an object of special veneration in Dodona, in the north of Greece. The will of God was interpreted from the rustling of its leaves and the trickling of the holy well that sprang from its roots.

When the Argonauts left in search of the Golden Fleece, which they would find hanging from an oak, they put a piece of wood from the sacred tree of Dodona on the bow of their ship.

The druidic oak and the medlar tree, whose fruits were gathered by the Druids during ceremonies, are referred to so frequently that we will examine them again.

HOW THE BARD TALIESIN CAME TO THE WORLD

———•———

ONE DAY, AS GWION THE DWARF was guarding the sacred cup that contained the precious "Water of Regeneration," three drops fell on his hand, crackling like fire. When he brought them to his mouth, the veil that shrouded the mysteries and the future of the world was lifted. The guardian goddess of the water then tried to kill him. But thanks to the magical virtues of the water, the dwarf was able to transform himself into a hare, a fish, and finally a bird. To chase him, the goddess assumed the form of a hunting dog, a beaver, and a sparrow. Finally Gwion transformed himself into a kernel of wheat and hid himself in a huge pile of grain. Then the goddess changed herself into a black hen, discovered him with her penetrating eyes, and swallowed him. Once inside her body, he impregnated her, and in nine months she gave birth to the bard, Taliesin.[1]

THE LEGEND OF THE BARD CERVORIX

SEATED ON A SOLITARY ROCK on the banks of the Saone, in a forest dedicated to Belenus, the bard Cervorix taught his disciples. Accompanied by an ivory lyre with golden strings, a gift from the Druids of an island in the Seine, he sang about the marvels of the universe and the rhythmic and eternal course of the stars.[1] Suddenly, the horizon darkened and black clouds approached. Nocturnal birds began flying above the bard's head. A great storm was unleashed, a hurricane whipped the trees, and the wolves howled in the mountains. Then Cervorix raised his voice and thundered:

"Man is material. His corporeal wrapping prevents his soul from leaving and represses his authentic desire to quit the Earth for a happier world. What is life? Nothing! Celtic sons, live in peace, think of eternity, and say to all you see that you have known the bard Cervorix."

After he had spoken, he broke his lyre and threw himself into the waves. Ever since, the rock has borne his name.

The following day, the Druids piled up firewood and placed his corpse on it, covering it with flowers and aromatic herbs. Toward midnight, when the seven stars of the Big Dipper reflected the seven holes of the altar in the water, the Druids set the funeral pyre on fire. Two Druids, a woman, a virgin, and a bard circled the fire. One Druid threw a cup of amber into it, the other an ivory lyre; the woman threw her veil, the virgin a locket of her blond hair, and the bard his cape, white like irises.

His ashes were gathered up and deposited in a crystal urn, on which the Druids engraved this inscription:

"Mortal man! Don't forget from where you come and where you're going. Look at this dust. He was what you are; you will be what he is."

Once a year, Apollo went to the land of the Hyperboreans and, as Hölderlin said, was closer to the "men who loved him."

He crossed the sea pulled by swans in a chalice that Hephaistos had fashioned of precious gold, and fell asleep under the tree of the world. Its branches extend over the universe and in its foliage, the sun, the moon, and the stars rustle like golden fruits. It was thought that the Garden of the Hesperides was in the land of the Hyperboreans, a mansion for the fortunate from which God, always in his sacred chalice, symbol of eternal rebirth, leaves for the Orient to begin the day.

It is said that Pythagoras was Apollo in flesh and blood, and that he had come from the land of the Hyperboreans to preach a new doctrine of salvation to mankind. As we have seen, there were other authors in antiquity who claimed that the Pythagoreans were none other than Greek Druids. Could the Hyperboreans have been Celt Iberians?

We can answer this question affirmatively. To find the Garden of Hesperides, you have to look to the land of the Hyperboreans. The ancients called the Iberian Peninsula Hesperia; Apollo was the supreme God of the Druids and the Hyperboreans. Both peoples lived in forests in a sun-drenched land with pleasant temperatures. The Hyperboreans fed themselves exclusively with fruits and never slaughtered animals. The Druids believed that the souls of men were enclosed in the bodies of beasts, and because of this they refused to eat meat. We also know that they refused to use arms and that, consequently, they never took part in wars or conflicts of any sort. The Hyperboreans sought freedom from worldly life by throwing themselves into the waves. Regarding the bards, we already know how Cervorix died.

THE "PURE ONES" AND THEIR DOCTRINE

> *Astaroth and Belcimon*
> *Beleth and Radamant*
> *And others I could name—*
> *This bright heavenly company*
> *Took on a hellish hue as a result of their malice and envy*
> WOLFRAM VON ESCHENBACH[1]

JESUS OF NAZARETH NEVER INTENDED to found a new religion; he only wished to satisfy the messianic aspirations of the people of Israel. What Jesus himself hoped for, and what he expected would happen in a short time, was the intervention of God in the history of the world and the establishment of a "New Israel" on the ruins of the old.

> *These twelve Jesus sent forth and commanded them saying:* Go not into the way of the Gentiles and into any city of the Samaritans, enter ye not. But go rather to the lost sheep of the House of Israel . . . I am not sent but unto the lost sheep of the House of Israel.
> MATTHEW 5:5, 6; 15:24

Jesus was not the founder of the Christian religion, which hardly has anything in common with the hopes for which he was martyred. The Church was born only after his death and burial. Until the crucifixion, Jesus and his disciples coincided with the Jews' messianic aspirations, and the condemnation and execution of the Messiah by them were nothing other than errors.[2] The Christian religion came into being only after Christ's passage, and based its existence as a universal religion on the conceptualization of him as the Savior of mankind—an idea that he never espoused while he was traveling back and forth across Palestine, preaching. The Christian religion created within itself a means that permitted its believers to participate in salvation. As the gospel was originally conceived, it should have collapsed by itself, and the ignominious end of the man on the cross should have marked the end of his doctrine. But because Jesus announced that a brief lapse would occur between his death and his return, his disciples, enthralled by the idea that the Kingdom of God was coming to Earth, preached his resurrection. To win over more converts, they quickly announced that he was already seated at the right hand of God. As always, intense faith finds attentive ears in a suggestible people. Moreover, Jesus' doctrine was a Jewish heresy whose converts went to the Temple every day and broke bread in the seclusion of their own homes.

Paul, the apostle of the prophet who had claimed to be the rightful King of Israel and was already sovereign of the Kingdom of Heaven, announced the coming of the Kingdom of God. He was the first to speak of Jesus as an impartial judge of Gentiles and Jews, who would be rewarded or punished according to their deeds:

"You are all the children of God through your faith in the Christ Jesus. [Galatians 3:26] . . . There is no longer Jew or Greek. . . . [Galatians 3:28] Is he God of the Jews only? Is he not also of the Gentiles?" [Romans 3:29]

This concept implies the negation of Judaism, and is in clear disagreement with the Gospel. Jewish hopes for an Earthly Messiah were deferred. The Jewish Christ had died. Those who believed in the real Christ—the Christ of the spirit, whose kingdom is not of this world—belonged to another world. Paul makes a clear distinction between this world and the other, between the body and the spirit, between the first man, Adam, and the other man, the Lord of Heaven. Both men have co-existed since the beginning of time. Sin came to this world through the first Adam, and with this sin, death. Jewish law could never change this situation. Only the death of another man, the Savior, could bring salvation and freedom to mankind.

When Luke writes in *The Acts and Deeds of the Apostles,* "On the first day of the week when we were gathered together to break bread," the day of the week that is dedicated to God is no longer Saturday but the following day, the first day of the week.[3] Following the example of the solar religions of the Orient, the "day of the sun" was transformed into the "day of the Lord," and a solar divinity emerged from the Jewish Messiah. On the pagan "day of the sun" they found the tomb empty. After the sun had risen, Jesus Christ returned from the dead as a solar divinity: "And very early on the first day of the week, they went to the tomb when the sun had risen." (Mark 16:2)

In the Apocalypse of Saint John, what does the white horse ridden by one called "faithful and true" resemble? "He had eyes like flame, many crowns and a name none but he himself knows and is called the 'Word of God.' Out of his mouth is a sharp sword with which he rules nations." This vision described by John on Patmos corresponds in great detail to a representation of Mithra [the ancient Persian God of Light]. On his vesture is even written, "King of Kings and the Lord of the Lords."

Christ, the solar God who descended to this world to be crucified for and by humanity, came—according to Paul—for both the Jews and the Gentiles, for both Indo-Europeans and Semites.

> The first religious institutions of the Indo-Europeans were based in the adoration of nature. But it was a deep and moral naturalism, a loving embrace with nature, delicious poetry filled with the sentiment of the infinite, of the beginning. In sum, it was everything that Celtic and Germanic genius, that a Shakespeare, or a Goethe, would express much later. It wasn't religion nor meditated morality, rather melancholy, tenderness, imagination; it was above all else, something serious, like the essential condition of morality and religion. Humanity's faith however could not come from there, because its ancient cults had great difficulties abandoning polytheism and they did not have a clear symbol. . . .The glory of creating the religion of Humanity corresponded to the Semitic race.[4]

Is not the honor "to suffer persecution to further justice" also incumbent on this religion of humanity, created by the Semitic race and expounded as dogma?

We should hang a thick veil on the first four centuries of our era, when the Christians sent more of their coreligionists to martyrdom than did the pagans. Although the first Christian persecutions of heretics could not keep up with the cruelty of pagan oppression of Christians, there was an aggravating circumstance: These cruelties were committed in the name of the man who had said that the House of the Father has many abodes, that you shall not kill and that you should love your neighbor as yourself.

By A.D. 400, the plains of Provence were already Christianized. Convents and basilicas had been built over the ruins of pagan temples, making good use of their stones and columns. Relics of the martyrs of the new doctrine were deposited in these churches. By becoming saints, the martyrs became more acceptable to the pagans, who were accustomed to numerous gods and semi-gods. Only the Druids in the Pyrenees continued their sacrifices to Abellio, their "God of Light," which had nothing to do with others' persecutions or cruelties. This divinity had created neither the world nor the humans who inhabited it. Christianity, as the Judeo-Roman Christologists preached it, could not make any inroads with these spiritualists. Because the Church couldn't convert these ascetic pagans, it repudiated them by becoming progressively more materialistic and opulent before exterminating them.

For the Druids, a Christ emerging from the house of the adulterous and murderous king David appeared as a contradiction. The Christ who died on the cross could never be the divinity of light. A god cannot die, they said, nor would he allow others to kill those who think differently in his name. Persecuted and cursed, the Druids spent their nights on the most inaccessible mountaintops and in the deepest darkness of their caves, "praising the Universal Father, according to their holy and ancient custom."

> *A man of the people:*
> *Would ye instant death attract?*
> *Know ye not the cruel threats*
> *Of the victors we obey?*
> *Round about are placed their nets*
> *In the sinful heathen's way*
> *Ah! upon the lofty wall*

Wife and children slaughter they;
And we all
Hasten to a certain fall.

A Druid:
Thus far 'tis right
That we by night
Our Father's praises sing;
Yet when 'tis day,
To Thee we may
A heart unsullied bring
'Tis true that now,
And often, Thou
Fav'rest the foe in fight
As from the smoke is freed the blaze,
So let our faith burn bright!
And if they crush our golden ways,
Who e'er can crush Thy light?

GOETHE, *THE FIRST WALPURGIS NIGHT*

And the Christians came to the Pyrenees. They were persecuted by their brothers, who declared them heretics in the councils of Saragossa (A.D. 380) and Bordeaux (A.D. 384). Together with six of his most famous converts, their teacher Priscillian was tortured and executed in Trevesin in 385 by the Roman emperor Magnus Maximus, himself a convert to Christianity, and Bishop Itacius.[5] The Priscillianists—as the members of this Gnostic-Manichaeist sect were called—were welcomed by the Druids, who assigned to them a new homeland in the Sarralunga forest between Sabarthès and Olmès, in the mountain range of Saint Bartholomew's Peak. The Priscillianists were the ones who finally managed to convert the Druids to Christianity.

From the Druids and vates [soothsayers] emerged the Cathars. Out of the bards, the troubadours.

To understand the philosophical and religious doctrine of the Occitan Cathars with any sort of clarity, we should consult their literature, which was once very rich; it was destroyed in its entirety by the Inquisition as a "source of contamination of a horrible heresy." Not a single Cathar book has survived for us. Only the Inquisitors' notes are left: notes that we can complete by examining similar doctrines such as the Gnosis, Manichaeism, and Priscillianism.[6,7]

The Occitan Cathars taught that God is spirit. For all eternity, love [Amor] is absolute, perfect in itself, immutable, eternal, and just. Nothing evil or transitory can exist in it or come from it. Consequently, its works can only be perfect, immutable, eternal, just, and good, as pure in the end as the fountain from which they flow.

If we contemplate this world, its imperfection, impermanence, and changeability are self-evident. The matter from which it is made is perishable and is the cause of innumerable evils and sufferings. This matter of life contains within it the principle of death, a death from which no one can escape.

Out of this opposition between imperfect matter and God's perfection, between a world full of misery and a God who is love itself, between creatures who are born only to die and a God who is eternal life, the Cathars came to the conclusion that an incompatibility exists between what is perfect and what isn't. Don't the foundations of modern philosophy establish the principle of cause and effect? If the cause is immutable, so are its effects. Consequently, a being with a contradictory nature could not have created the terrestrial world and its creatures.

If the creation is the work of a good God, why did he not make it perfect like himself? And if he wanted to make it perfect and couldn't, it is obvious that he is neither all-powerful nor perfect. If he could have made it perfect and didn't want to, he would be in conflict with the perfection of love. Consequently, for the Cathars, God did not create the terrestrial world.[8]

> *If a God can be called an invalid*
> *Who constructed a world in feverish ardor*
> *Only soon to destroy it, with feverish shudders*
> *Is the World's destiny none other than freezing or burning?*
>
> *Wasn't it only a son of the Gods*
> *To whom this world fell,*
> *As a plaything of colors,*

That as fast as it entertains, it behaves badly
Without any other power than the stuttering of its desires?

LENAU, THE ALBIGENSES

If so many things that happen in this world have nothing to do with divine providence and the desire of God, then how can we believe that God is happy with so much disorder and confusion? And how to explain that all the creatures whose only purpose is to disturb and torture mankind come from a creator who is pure kindness for man? How can the fires and floods that destroy crops and cause the death of so many people or destroy the shacks of the poor be ascribed to this God? A God who is used by our enemies to justify our destruction, we who only wish for and seek the truth? Such were the thoughts of the Albigensian Cathars.

And how could a perfect God give man a body whose ultimate destiny is death after having been tortured by all types of evils?

The Cathars saw far too much intent in visible creation to somehow deny it an intelligent origin. From the analogous principle of cause and effect, they deduced that bad effects came from bad causes and that our world, which could never have been created by a good God, had to have as its creator a bad principle. This dualist system, which we have already found in Mazdaism, Druidism, and Pythagorean philosophy, bases itself in the fundamental opposition between Good and Evil.

Seizing on the New Testament, the Cathars believed that they could refute the opinions of the doctors of the Church, to whom "Evil" was without any doubt the antithesis of "Good," but really nothing other than the negation or absence of Good, with no basis in a special principle.

When the devil tempted Christ—"All these things I will give you if you fall down and worship me"—how could he offer it if it did not already belong to him?[9] And how could it belong to him if he wasn't its creator? When Christ speaks of the plants that his celestial Father did not plant, it is proof that they were planted by somebody else. When John the Evangelist speaks of "the children of God that are not born from flesh and blood," from whom do the children of flesh and blood come?[10] Are not these children from another creator—the devil—who according to Christ's own words is "their Father"?

Ye are of your father the devil, and the lusts of your father ye will
do. He was a murderer from the beginning, and abode not in the
truth, because there is no truth in him. When he speaketh a lie, he
speaketh of his own: for he is a liar, and the Father of it. . . . He
that is of God heareth God's words: ye therefore hear them not,
because ye are not of God.

JOHN 8:44, 47

For the Cathars, all passages of the New Testament that mention the Devil, or the fight between the flesh and the Spirit, or the old man who should be cast out, or the world submerged in sin and darkness, were sufficient to demonstrate the antithesis between God, whose kingdom is not of this Earth, and the true prince of this world, Lucifer.

The Kingdom of God is the invisible world, absolutely good and perfect, the world of light and eons: the eternal city.

God is the "Creator" of all things, because "to create" signifies producing something that did not exist before. He also created matter, which before was nonexistent. He created it from nothing, but only from principle. It was Lucifer, himself a creature of God, who gave "shape" to matter; this was his principle.

Who is the cause of this world? Can you resolve this question?

The spirits are of God; the bodies are of the Evil one.

The Cathars believed that Lucifer, whom they also called Luzbel, had created everything visible, material, and perishable. Not only do all terrestrial things belong to him, but he also governs them and tries to keep them under his domination.

But the Old Testament tells us that Jehovah is the creator of Heaven and the Earth and virtually everything on it. This is true, the Cathars said: He "created" human beings, man and woman.

In the New Testament, you can read, "There is neither man nor woman, but you are all one thing in Christ Jesus" and that "For God was pleased to have all his fullness dwell in him (Jesus) and through him to reconcile to himself all things, whether things on Earth or things in heaven." By contrast, Jehovah said, "I will put enmity between you and the woman." How does this work out? Jehovah curses and God blesses. All the "children of God" in the Old Testament sinned, and in the New

Testament, "those born of God do not sin." Don't they contradict one another?[11]

The Cathars referred specifically to the passages of the Old Testament that speak of the vengeance and anger of Jehovah. They were convinced that Jehovah—who sent the Great Flood, destroyed Sodom and Gomorrah, and repeated over and over that he wanted to destroy his enemies and transfer the sins of fathers onto the sons of the third or fourth generations—was neither God nor absolute and eternal love.

Jehovah forbade Adam from eating from the tree of science. He either knew that human beings would eat the fruit or he didn't. If he knew it, he did nothing other than to push Adam toward temptation, make him a sinner, and provoke his destruction.

Above all, the Albigensian heretics invoked the seventh chapter of the Epistle to the Romans, where Paul calls Mosaic Law a "law of death and sin." Lot committed incest with his daughters, Abraham lied and committed adultery with his servant, David was a murderer and adulterer, and the rest mentioned in the Old Testament were not any better, affirmed the Cathars. For them, the law that Jehovah announced to the Jews through Moses was of satanic inspiration, and if it contained some good things, for example the seventh commandment, it was in order to gain some hearty souls for the cause of Evil.

A divinity who reveals himself in a burning bush to a man—Moses—cannot be "God" because God is spirit and does not reveal himself to mortals in physical matter. Jehovah is not God. He is the Antichrist; he is Lucifer.

> *When Lucifer made the descent to Hell*
> *With his following, a man suceeded him*
> Wolfram von Eschenbach[12]

The Cathars explained the fall of Lucifer, the origin of the Earth, and the birth of man with the following mythological formula:

Seven heavens. The purest and most brilliant was the Kingdom of God and the celestial Spirits. Each one of these heavens had special superior angels, whose hymns of praise rose incessantly to God's throne in the seventh heaven. Beneath the celestial regions four other elements existed, immobile and without form, but separate one from the other.

Beneath heaven: the air, with clouds; further down, the ocean with its endless rolling waves; further down still, the Earth, and in the interior of the Earth, fire. Air, water, earth, and fire: the four elements, each one presided over by an angel.

Commanding the celestial armies was Lucifer, to whom God had entrusted the administration of the heavens. Flying high, he visited all the regions of the infinite celestial world, from the deepest abyss to the throne of invisible eternity. His privileged position sparked rebellious thoughts in him; he wanted to be like his creator and lord. First, he seduced the four angels of the elements and then a regiment of the celestial army. Then God expelled him from the Kingdom of the Heavens. The light that until then had been soft and pure was taken from him and replaced by another, reddish, similar to incandescent iron. The angels seduced by Lucifer were stripped of their finery and crowns and expelled from the heavens. Lucifer fled with them to the outer limits of the firmament. Tormented by remorse, he said to God, "Have patience with me, I will return everything to you."

And God, having compassion for his preferred son, gave him seven days—which meant seven centuries—to do everything that he thought was proper. Then Lucifer established his residence in the firmament and ordered the rest of the angels who had followed him to shape the Earth. He took his crown, which had been broken since his expulsion from the Kingdom of the Heavens, and with half of it formed the sun, and with the other half, the moon. Then he converted his precious stones into the stars. From the primitive mud he fashioned the first terrestrial creatures, animals and plants.[13]

The supreme angels of the third and second heavens desired to share power with Lucifer and pleaded with God to allow them to descend to Earth, promising to return immediately afterward. God read their thoughts, but he did not deny their wish. He wanted to punish them for their lie, but he advised them not to fall asleep during their voyage, because if they did, they would forget the way to return to Heaven. If they fell asleep, he would not call them before 7,000 years had passed. The two angels began their journey. But Lucifer put them into a deep sleep and locked them in bodies that had been shaped from the original clay. When the angels awoke, they were human beings: Adam and Eve.

To get them to forget Heaven, Lucifer created Earthly paradise. But he decided to cheat them with a new strategy: He wanted them both to sin in order to make them his slaves forever. When he put them in paradise, he forbade them—to give more encouragement to their natural curiosity—to eat from the tree of science. He transformed himself into a snake and seduced Eve, who in turn induced Adam to commit the original sin.

Lucifer knew very well that God had also forbidden the first pair to eat the wretched fruit. Because God would never want to see the multiplication of Lucifer's nature, Lucifer acted as if the prohibition of eating the fruit came from himself, to triumph in this way with greater certainty.

For the Cathars, the apple of the tree of science was the symbol of the original sin: the sexual union of man and woman. Through carnal sin, Adam and Eve were disobedient. The sin of the flesh, however, was and continued to be the most serious grievance, because it was committed with their full approval and represented a conscious rebellion of the soul against God.

Humanity had to reproduce, because Lucifer needed fresh souls. In the new bodies produced by Adam and Eve, he confined all the angels who had abandoned the celestial regions with him.

And then, with the death of Abel, murder entered in the world!

After a while, God had compassion with the fallen angels who had been expelled from Heaven and transformed into humans. So he decided to reveal himself to them, and sent his most perfect creature down to the Earth, his supreme angel, Christ, who would assume an outwardly human appearance. Christ came to the world to indicate how they could return to heaven, to the Kingdom of the eternal light.[14]

> *I am come a light into the world, that whosoever believeth on me should not abide in darkness. While ye have light, believe in the light, that ye may be the children of the light.*
>
> JOHN 12:46, 36

Christ did not become a man, a creature of Lucifer; he only appeared as one. He only gave the impression that he ate, drank, taught, suffered, and died, revealing to humans a sort of shadow of his real body. This is the reason he could walk on water and transform himself on Mount

Tabor, where he revealed to his disciples the real substance of his body. Since the fall of Lucifer, Jesus Christ was the greatest of all angels, and for this reason he is called the "Son of God." When Jesus said that he wasn't of this world, but rather from above it, the Cathars applied this passage of the New Testament not only to the spiritual nature of the Savior, but also to his body. With this ethereal body the Eon Christ entered the body of Maria, like the "Word of God," through her ear. He left her as pure as he had entered her, without taking any of her matter. For this reason, he never called her "mother," and this is why he said to her, "Woman, what do I have to do with you."[15]

The Cathars did not recognize the reality of the miracles of Jesus. How could he cure physical illnesses when he considered the body an obstacle to the redemption of the soul? When he cured the blind, he was curing men who were blinded by sin and allowing them to see reality. The bread that he divided among the five thousand was his Word, the bread of the soul that gave real life. The storm that he calmed was the storm of passions unleashed by Lucifer. In this respect, it is possible to apply the words of Christ: The written word kills, but the spirit breathes life.

Because the body of Christ was not of Earthly nature, his crucifixion was only an apparition; this was the only way possible that he could rise to Heaven. A heavenly ascension with a body of flesh and blood appeared absurd to the Cathars. A human body cannot go to heaven; an Eon cannot die.

> *Ye judge after the flesh, I judge no man.*
>
> JOHN 13:15

For the Occitan heretics, the passion of Christ represents nothing other than the grandiose myth of the "sacrifice of love" that renders divine.

> *The total Christ has not appeared on Earth,*
> *His divine human image must still be completed,*
> *Once when the salvation of the World will be consummated, the*
>   *rendition, when God and man unite in a form, living in the*
>   *Spirit*
> *Also the image of Jesus, reflected in all ways, will become agitated*

and shall dissipate in the intense flow of time, when the entire
testimony of Jesus will disappear, the God-Man will be the
nucleus, the luminous heart of all the worlds.

LENAU, "THE CAVE" FROM THE ALBIGENSES

Occitan Catharism aspired to be at the same time a philosophy, a religion, a metaphysical creed, and a cult. As a philosophy, it was the result of speculation on the relations between God and the World, between good and bad. From this philosophic system, the Cathar troubadours fashioned a real mythology. According to Albigensian dualism, the confrontation between good and bad was not eternal. There would be a Last Day when God's victory over Lucifer would be consummated as the final victory of spirit over matter. Then Luzbel, as the repentant prodigal son, would return to his creator and Lord. All the souls of mankind would convert back into angels, and the situation would be reestablished exactly as it was before the fall of the angels. Good fortune would be as eternal as the Kingdom of God. As all souls would reencounter God, eternal condemnation would not exist, because it would be in contradiction with the absolute love of God.[16]

As we can see, Cathar dualism was linked to metaphysical and religious mysteries of Pythagorianism, Orphism, and Mazdaism. Despite everything, the Occitan heretics never stopped insisting that they were Christians. And they were, because they followed the supreme commandment of Christ:

These things I command you, that you love one another. By this
shall all men know that you are My disciples: if you have love one
for another.

JOHN 15:17; 13:35

The abyss that separated Catharism from the Christianity of Wittenberg and Geneva was considerable; although not expressly dualistic, neither was it monotheistic. As we have already seen, the Cathars rejected the Old Testament, and regarding Jesus Christ, they said that he was not the Jewish Jesus of Nazareth and Bethlehem, but instead the hero of a mythology transformed by a divine halo.

Cathar morality, as pure and rigorous as it was, was not the same as Christian morality. The Christians did not demand the mortification of everything corporeal, the scorning of terrestrial creation, or the dissolution of all Earthly links. With imagination and desire, the Cathars wanted to achieve general perfection on Earth, and out of fear of losing themselves in the materialism of the Catholic Church, spiritualized everything: religion, cult, and life.

Even more surprising is the fact that this doctrine, at the same time the most tolerant and intolerant found in all Christianity, should expand with a vigor unprecedented in history. Without any doubt, the fundamental reason for this was the pious and pure life of the Cathars, in stark contrast with the type of life led by the orthodox clergy. The underlying cause for the expansion of Catharism in the south of France can be traced to the fact that Occitan Catharism was indigenous: the Occitanians felt closer to the myths and allegories of the Pure Ones than the sermons of the orthodox clerics, which were normally uncultivated and undignified.[17]

Neither should we forget that Cathar dualism provided a beneficial contrast to the fear of the devil so extensive in the medieval Catholic Church. The oppressive influence of demons in the intellectual behavior of the Christian Middle Ages is well known. In Catholicism, the Antichrist was the rival of God, with his Hell, his armies, and his Satanic power over spirits. Compared with Catholics' fear of the devil, a desolate obsession that lasted an entire millennium, the Cathar idea to engage Luzbel was somewhat more conciliatory. For them, Lucifer was a rebellious angel, non-spiritual and mendacious, the embodiment of the world as it was and continued to be. According to the heretics, when humanity looks for the path of spirituality, it will have crushed the power of the prince of this world. He will have no other choice than to submit to the Spirit with contrition and penitence.

If we strip the Cathar doctrine of all its mythological accessories, we are left with Kant's famous quadruple base:

First: Coexistence of man in the principle of good and bad.
Second: Conflict between the good principle and the bad for supremacy in the human being.
Third: Victory of the good over bad, the beginning of the Kingdom of God.

Fourth: Differentiation of true and false under the guidance of
the good principle.

As we can see, poetry and philosophy in Occitania formed an undis-
solvable reality.

The Occitan Church of Amor (Minne) was composed of Perfecti
["Perfect Ones"] and the faithful or "imperfect ones."[18] The latter were
not constrained by the severe rules of the Perfecti in their condition as
Pure Ones. They could do whatever suited them: marry, dedicate themselves to business, compose songs of the Minne, go to war—in sum, live
their lives as one did in those days in Occitania. The name "Cathar" was
reserved for those who, after a precisely prescribed period of prepara-
tion and through a sacramental act (the *consolamentum,* or consolation,
which we will describe a little further on), were initiated into the esoteric
mysteries of the Church of Amor.

The Cathars, like the Druids, lived in the forests and caves where
they dedicated themselves almost exclusively to the functions of their
cult. A table covered with a white mantle served as an altar. Placed on it
was a New Testament in [old] Provençal, opened to the first chapter of
the Apocalypse according to Saint John; "In the beginning, there was the
Word and the Word was with God and the Word was God."

The religious ceremonies were equally simple. They began with
comments by a Perfect One on a passage in the New Testament.
Benediction followed. The faithful who attended the religious ceremony would bring their hands together, kneel, and repeat three times
to the Perfect Ones:

"Bless us."

The third time, they would add:

"Pray to God for us sinners, so that he will make us good Christians
and lead us to a good end."

Each time, the Perfect Ones would raise their hands and give their
blessings, answering:

"Dieus vos benesiga. Shall God bless you! Shall God make good
Christians of you and lead you to a good end."[19]

In Germany, where there were also Cathars, the faithful asked for
the benediction in rhymed prose:

"For nothing in the world shall wish to die, without before you to achieve that my end shall be happy."

The Perfect Ones would answer:

"And shall you become a good man."

After the benediction, all those attending recited the Lord's Prayer— the only prayer permitted by the Church of Amor. Instead of saying, however, "Give us our daily bread," they said, "Give it to us, the supra-earthly daily bread." Somehow for the Cathars, it did not appear dignified to ask for Earthly bread. Although their desire for supra-earthly bread corresponds to the Latin Vulgate, which in Matthew 6:2 says, *Panem nostrum supersubstantialem da nobis hodie,* Rome reproached them for falsifying the passage.

When a Perfect One was present, before every meal a solemn *particion* [sharing] of the *pan* [bread] took place. At the table, the faithful recited the Lord's Prayer before asking the Cathar for benediction. Finally, this person (or the eldest person present if there were several) took the bread, blessed it, and distributed it with these words:

"Shall the grace of our Lord be with you all."

With these "feasts" that recalled the early days of Christianity, they wanted to symbolize not the enjoyment of the Christian sacrament but rather the spiritual communion between the Perfect Ones and the faithful of the Church of Amor. During the period of persecution, when the Cathars were obliged to hide and could no longer visit their faithful regularly, they used couriers to take the blessed bread to the cities and towns.

Catharism rejected the Eucharist (transubstantiation) of the Catholic Church. It did not believe that bread could undergo a supernatural mutation during the sacrament, or that it could convert itself into the Body of Christ, which was ethereal and apparent. Even though the Church still had not declared the doctrine of transubstantiation as dogma, it denounced and cursed this heretical Cathar concept. At the time, the same doctors of the Church [who were denouncing the Cathars] didn't understand this idea very clearly. The Cathars recognized the word of the Lord: "Who eats my flesh and drinks my blood will have eternal life," but they added, "The spirit refreshes, meat serves for nothing and his words are spirit and life." The bread of heaven that brings eternal life is not the bread of the Perfect Ones but the Word of God. The body of

Christ is not in the hands of the priest or on the altar. He is the community of those who cultivate the supreme Minne: the Church of Amor.[20]

> *Also the era of Christ, covered by God's veil*
> *Passes and the New Alliance gets old*
> *Then we will conceive of God as the Spirit,*
> *Then the eternal Alliance will be celebrated*
> *"The Spirit is God!" Resonates with power,*
> *A thunderous happiness in the night of springtime.*
>
> Lenau, *The Albigenses*

In chapters fourteen and fifteen of the Gospel According to Saint John, Jesus promises his disciples that he will ask his Father to send them another Consoler (in Greek, parakletos; in Provençal, consort = consoler; in Luther's German, Tröster = consoler): the Spirit of the truth, which the world cannot receive because it neither sees nor knows him.[21]

Together with Nadal (Christmas), Pascos (Easter), and Pentecosta (Pentecost), the principal Cathar holiday was the Manisola, the festival of the Paraclete (the Hindu Mani, the Platonic "Idea," the Latin *mens*).

One of the symbols of the Spirit that is also God—a symbol taken from Buddhism by the Cathars—was the Mani, a precious stone that illuminates the world with its flashing, and makes all Earthly desire disappear. The Mani is the emblem of Buddhist law that disperses the night of error. In Nepal and Tibet, it is considered the symbol of brotherly love, of the Dhyanibodhissattva Avalokitecvara or Padmapani.[22]

Yet God existed in the eternal, the unfathomable principle, he who has a thousand names and yet, it is he who is: God!

In the principle the Word was with God. His Father is God, his Mother, and the Spirit that is in God. The Word is God.

In the principle also existed the Spirit. He is the Amor with which God spoke: the Word that made Life and Light. The Spirit is Amor. The Spirit is God. The Amor is God. The Amor is more resplendent than the sun and more brilliant than the most valuable precious stones.

We have no real knowledge of the mysterious Cathar Manisola. The Inquisition's torturers couldn't pry knowledge of the consoling Amor, the supreme Minne, from the Cathars. The secret remained buried with the last heretics in the caves of Ornolac! The Inquisition's reports speak only of the Consolamentum Spiritus Sancti [the consolation of the Holy Spirit], the most solemn sacramental ceremony of esoteric Catharism. The only "believers" who spoke of attending this ceremony were those who talked in the torture chamber.

The Cathars rejected baptism with water and replaced it with a baptism of the Spirit, the consolamentum. Because in their opinion, water is only matter, it could not sanctify nor achieve redemption. They refused to believe that God would free souls from the yoke of Satan through his own creation. They said: Either a person who is to be baptized shows remorse for his sins or not. If he shows remorse, what good does baptism serve, if it is not justified by the testimony of faith or penitence? If he is not repentant, baptism counts for nothing, because he neither wanted it nor earned it. Furthermore, John the Baptist said that he baptized with water but that Christ would baptize with the Holy Spirit.

The consolamentum was the goal that all the faithful of the Church of Amor aspired to and worked for. The rite would assure them a good end and the salvation of their souls. The Cathars believed that if a believer died without receiving the consolamentum, his soul would transmigrate to another body. If he had committed many or grave sins, even to an animal, only until someone in another life had atoned for his sins and made himself worthy of the consolamentum, could he start moving closer, from star to star, toward the throne of God.[23]

This is the reason why the consolamentum was celebrated with such solemnity: a solemnity that contrasted enormously with the simplicity of the Cathar cult.

Once the neophyte had overcome the long and hard preparatory period, he was taken to the spot where the consolamentum would be imparted. Quite often, it was in a cave in the Pyrenees or the Montagne Noir.[24] The way was illuminated with numerous torches along the walls. In the middle of the chamber rose the "altar," and upon it was placed the New Testament. Before the start of the ceremony, the Perfect Ones and the faithful washed their hands so that no impurity would profane the sanctity of the place. All the participants would form a circle in absolute silence. The neophyte would stand in the middle of the circle, a short distance from the altar. Then the Perfectus, who was officiating at the sacramental function, would remind the *credent* (believer) that he was about to be consoled by Cathar doctrines, which meant that he was going to assume special responsibilities and face dangers in case of persecution.

If the neophyte was married, his wife was asked if she was prepared to break their marriage bonds to donate her husband to God and the Gospel. If a woman was going to receive the consolamentum, the questions were directed to the husband.

The priest asked the believer, "Brother, do you wish to embrace our faith?"

"Yes, Father."

Then the neophyte would kneel, touching the ground with his hands and saying, "Bless me."

This was repeated three times; each time, the neophyte would move a little closer to the priest, adding after the third time, "Father, ask God to lead me, a sinner, to a good end."

"Shall God bless you, make a good Christian of you, and lead you to a good end."

The solemn oath of the new member followed.

"I promise," he continued, while still kneeling, "to dedicate myself to God and his Gospel, never to lie, never to take an oath, never to have any contact with a woman, never to kill an animal, never to eat meat, and to feed myself only with fruits. Furthermore, I promise never to travel, never to live or eat without one of my brothers, and in the case that I should fall into the hands of our enemies or be separated from my brothers, to abstain for three days from all nourishment. In addition, I promise never to betray my Faith, whatever death awaits me."

He then asked for a benediction three times as all those present fell to their knees. Then the priest would come up to him and let him kiss the Bible, which was then placed on his head. Then all the Perfecti entered. Some put their right hand on his head, others on his back, and all those present said, "Let us pray to the Father, the Son, and the Holy Spirit."

The officiating priest asked God to dignify the neophyte by letting the Holy Spirit and Consoler descend upon the new brother. The assembly recited the Lord's Prayer and the priest read the first seventeen verses of the Gospel according to Saint John. Then they dressed the consoled brother with a plaited sash, which was symbolically called the "habit."[25]

Finally, the Perfecti gave the new Pure One the kiss of peace. This was done by giving it to his closest neighbor who in turn gave it to the next one and he to the next, until the end. If the consolamentum was conferred to a believer, the priest touched his back with the Bible and held out his arm. In this way, the Cathar passed the symbolic kiss of peace to the person who was nearest.

When the ceremony was ended, the neophyte retired to solitude, to fast on bread and water for forty days and nights, although before the ceremony, no less rigorous fasts had also been performed. The fasting just prior to and after receiving the consolamentum was called the *endura*.[26]

When the consolation was conferred on dying believers, two Cathars accompanied by a few faithful would enter the death chamber. The eldest asked the sick person if he wanted to consecrate himself to God and the Gospel. Then the usual ceremony proceeded, the difference being that they placed a white towel on the chest of the dying while one Cathar stood at his head and another at his feet.

Often, after receiving the consolamentum and during the endura, Cathars would voluntarily kill themselves. Like the Druids, their doctrine permitted suicide, but demanded that it should not be done out of fear, suffering, or boredom but instead in a state of perfect disengagement from matter.

This class of endura was permitted only at the moment of mystical vision of divine beauty and generosity. A suicide who ended life out of fear, suffering, or mere boredom would, according to the Cathar doctrine, continue to suffer from fear, suffering, and boredom. Because the Cathars prophesied that real life began after death, suicide was allowed only when someone wanted to "live."

From the fast to suicide, there is only one small step. The fast demands courage but the supreme definitive act of death requires heroism. The transit from one state to the other is not at all as cruel as it may appear.

Let us contemplate the mask of the "Inconnue de la Seine."[27] Where does the fear of death, the terror of purgatory or Hell, trial before God's tribunal, or divine anger make itself apparent? She wasn't a very good Christian, because Christian dogma prohibits suicide. Neither does she look as if she were consumed by pain, because such women do not have the same look. She was a young person who was more attracted by the Hereafter than her present reality, and who had the heroism to kill her body to continue being only a soul. Her body died in the dirty waters of the Seine, but her saintly smile lives on.

Deep down, the death of Faust was also a suicide. If he had not broken his pact with Mephistopheles by saying "Stay, you are so fair!" nothing would have stopped him from continuing to live on Earth. This fact implies a profound lesson: Suicide is only permitted in the moment of maximum happiness—the greater it is, the less Earthly it is. Only when a person has relinquished sadness and lies (those sovereigns of this world) for the peace of his soul can he affirm, "I have not lived in vain."

What did "not to live in vain" signify according to the old heretical doctrine? First: to love your fellow man like yourself, which meant not to let your neighbor suffer when you have it in your power to bring him consolation and help. Second: not to cause harm to your fellow man, and above all not to kill him. Third: to spiritualize yourself, which means to divinize life in such a way that at the moment of death, the body abandons this world without regrets. Otherwise, the soul will not find any rest at all. If you have not lived in vain as a person, if you have only done good and perfected yourself, this is when, according to the Cathars, you can take the definitive step as a Perfectus.

Two always practiced the endura together. After sharing years of continuous effort and intensive spiritualization in the most sublime friendship, only together could the Brothers decide to co-participate in the next life, the true life of the intuitive beauties of the Hereafter, and the knowledge of the divine laws that move worlds.

The Cathars had a further reason for suicide in pairs. It was painful to have to leave your brother. At the moment of death, the soul should not undergo any pain, because if it does, the pain would continue in the Hereafter. If you love you fellow man as yourself, you cannot submit him to the pain of separation. Pain inflicted on others must be atoned for in the Hereafter, through the slow process of divinization, from star to star (as Dante says, from step to step on the mountain of purification).[28] Even approaching Divinity, separation is perceived as painful.

Five classes of suicide were accepted by the Cathars: poison, starving to death, cutting veins, throwing oneself from a precipice, or, after a hot bath in the winter, lying down on cold blocks in order to catch pneumonia, which invariably brought a fatal end. There is no doctor capable of curing a sick person who wants to die.

Because death at the stake was always a possibility for a Cathar, he considered this world a living Hell. After receiving the consolamentum, he could "let himself die," as it was said then, to escape this Hell of burnings that were alight, for to this world, he was already dead.

If God is better and more intelligent that human beings, shouldn't he have reserved for the heretics all they aspired to and yearned for in the Hereafter? For this, they were capable of withstanding the cruelest self-denials and displaying the most extraordinary force of will to perform—as we will see—unheard-of heroism. What they wanted was the divinization of the spirit. What they pined for was the Kingdom of the Heavens: in other words, life after death.

Those who received the consolamentum were henceforth known as Perfect Ones [Perfecti]; the name Cathar corresponded only to them. They were also called "bonshommes" or good men, "Weavers," or "Consolers." Their life in solitude was rigorous and monotonous; it was only interrupted when they went preaching in the countryside or the cities, attended to their faithful, or imparted the consolamentum to those who asked for it and were worthy of it. They rejected all material goods and did not belong to themselves; instead their lives belonged to the Church of Amor. They administered the goods that their Church received, and put them into the service of the love of their fellow man. The life of the Cathars was one of privation and the rejection of Earthly goods. Not only did they break all ties with family and friends, but they were obliged to undergo a fast of forty days three times a year and feed themselves solely with bread and water three times a week.

"We live," they said on one occasion, "a hard and errant life. We flee from city to city, we are like sheep among wolves, we suffer persecution like the apostles and martyrs, but despite all this, all we want is to lead a pious, severe, and abstinent life, and to pray and work. But all this is no longer a worry because we are no longer of this world."

> . . . he that hateth his life in this world shall keep it unto life eternal.
>
> JOHN 12:25

They were forbidden to kill even an ant. The Cathar doctrine of transmigration of souls prohibited it.[29] This is why they were never allowed to participate in war. When the era of the persecutions exploded upon Occitania, they wandered the battlefields in the shadows of night, caring for the wounded and administering the consolamentum to the dying. They were good medical doctors and had a reputation as infallible astrologers. Eventually, the Inquisitors believed that Cathars could direct the winds, flatten the waves, and calm tempests.

They dressed in long black tunics in a show of the mourning they felt in their souls for finding themselves in the Hell of this world, covered their heads with a sort of round Persian cap, similar to the large beret of the modern Basques, and wore on their breasts a roll of cord that held the Apocalypse of Saint John. As opposed to Catholic monks, whose hair was cut and who wore beards, they shaved and let their hair fall to their shoulders.

THE CAVES OF TREVRIZENT
CLOSE TO THE FOUNTAIN
CALLED LA SALVAESCHE

———◆———

IN PRECEDING PAGES, we described why the Cathars built their hermitages and temples in the caves of Sabarthès, and explained how the plot of the fable of Hercules, Pirène, and Bebryx developed around the four stalagmites in the heretical cathedral at Lombrives. A little further on, we will learn that according to Spanish ballads, a skeleton key is hidden in the "enchanted cave of Hercules" which resolves the mystery of the Grail. But before this, we are going to penetrate into another no less mysterious cave in the Sabarthès so that we may finally reach Montségur—Wolfram von Eschenbach shows us the way.

Before leaving for the Grail Castle, Muntsalvaesche, Parsifal makes a visit to a pious hermit named Trevrizent in the cave of the *Fontane la Salvaesche.*

Trevrizent was a heretic because he never ate "bloody foods, meat or fish." In the twelfth and thirteenth centuries, any Christian who abstained from eating meat was instantly suspected of Cathar heresy.[1] Quite frequently, the pontifical legates who were entrusted with exterminating the heresy and the heretics gave anyone suspected of Catharism the choice between eating meat or being thrown into the fire.

> . . . *He had no mind for such food*
> *As fish or meat or anything with blood.*
> *Such was the holy life he led.*

God had inspired this gentleman
To prepare to join the heavenly host
He endured much hardship from fasting.
Self-denial was his arm against the Devil.

WOLFRAM VON ESCHENBACH[1]

Doesn't Trevrizent's desire to overcome the devil's power nested in meat by fasting, and his belief that life is a period to prepare for the soul's return to heaven from whence it came, make him a Cathar?

When a person "suffers the fast," it is only normal that he would be emaciated and pale, developing the outward aspect of an ascetic. From the fourth century until the end of the twelfth, the Catholic Church considered paleness a symbol of heresy. Even orthodox Catholics who appeared pale because of their fasting and macerations were often accused of heresy, and many good Catholics were killed because of the mistaken belief that Christians with a gaunt countenance were heretics.

Trevrizent the hermit lived in a cell next to the La Salvaesche fountain. He led young Parsifal to a second cave in which an uncovered "altar" was located. One cave in front of the cathedral of Lombrives is called the Hermit's Cave, and not very far away, a second one is called the Cave of Fontanet. In its deepest chamber stands a snow-white stalagmite: the Altar.

Just thirty years ago, four young men went into that cave and disappeared forever. Their bones must have found an eternal resting place in one of the still-undiscovered Phoenician or Phocian funeral chambers. Or did the four find the pathway that leads to the summits of the Tabor and Montségur? Was it one of these young men who wrote the question on a wall in the cave's entrance in big letters: *Why did I not . . . ?*

In the caves of Sabarthès, a question comes to mind, but there is no known answer. When, as if by magic, my lamp conjured the Altar out of the darkness of the Cave of Fontanet, I would often ask myself: What sort of reliquary was placed on the altar in Trevrizent's cell before which Parsifal was initiated in the secrets of the Grail?

An altar-stone stood there bare of its cloth;
On it a reliquary could be seen

WOLFRAM VON ESCHENBACH

Was this reliquary casket part of "Solomon's Treasure," which was taken by the Visigoth king Alaric from Rome to Carcassonne in A.D. 410? According to Procopius, it was filled with objects that had once belonged to Solomon, the King of the Hebrews. Removed from Jerusalem by the Romans, the largest part of this treasure was moved to Ravenna by Teodoric, and later from there to Byzantium by none other than Belisario, the celebrated general of the Greek emperor Justinian. Nevertheless, a portion remained in Carcassonne. According to multiple Arab accounts, the "Table of the Hebrews" was part of this treasure. Did the great King of the Jews, whose tomb according to legend is situated between the Altai and the Hindu Kush, know of the Grail?[3]

> There was a heathen named Flegetanis
> Who was highly renowned for his acquirements.
> This same physicus was descended from Solomon,
> Begotten of Israelitish kin all the way down from ancient times.
> He wrote of the marvels of the Grail
>
> WOLFRAM VON ESCHENBACH

In the seven-day battle for Jerez de la Frontera (A.D. 711), the Arabs vanquished the Visigoths, and Solomon's treasure fell into the hands of the infidel in Toledo. However, the "Table of Solomon" was not there.

> The famous master Kyot found the prime version of this tale in
>   heathenish script
> Lying all neglected in a corner of Toledo.
>
> WOLFRAM VON ESCHENBACH

Trevrizent kept the reliquary in his cave as well as the "Grail legend." The two were inseparable. Were the reliquary's treasure and the "original source of the legend" brought to his cave to protect them from the infidels?

According to Spanish ballads, the Table of Solomon, also known as the "casket" or reliquary, was kept in the "enchanted grotto of Hercules." It was said that the Gothic king Rodrigo penetrated the cave, and found the casket in a dark corner with three chalices in it.

Before taking young Parsifal to the casket in the cave in order to initiate him in the mystery of the Grail, Trevrizent dressed him in a coat.

> His host led Parsifal into a grotto
> Well protected from the wind . . .
> There was a coat lying there
> The hermit lent it him to put on
> And then took him to another grotto
>
> WOLFRAM VON ESCHENBACH

The coat or tunic, the fish, the bridge, and the boat are all elements that appear in poetic contemplations of sacrosanct relics, not solely in Wolfram von Eschenbach's epic. In all myths and epics about the Grail it is easy to find similar images. Let's examine how the greatest German poet of the *Minne* relates Parsifal's visit to the castle of Muntsalvaesche, where the Grail was kept.

> In the evening, he came to a lake.
> Some sportsmen, whose lake it was had anchored there.
> One of those he saw in the boat was wearing clothes of such quality
> That had he been lord of the whole Earth, they could not have
>   been finer.
>
> Parsifal set off and moved into a brisk trot
> Along the right path, as far as the moat.
> There he found the drawbridge raised.
>
> "The fisherman asked me," said Parsifal,
> "To follow the path up to the castle."
> Seeing that it was the angler who said so
> "You are welcome Sir!"
>
> "My lady the Princess Repanse de Schoye was wearing it,"
> Said the discreet Master of the Wardrobe.
> "It is lent to you from off her person."
>
> WOLFRAM VON ESCHENBACH[4]

Invariably, a vast expanse of water and an enchanted mountain appear in all these legends and myths. In the *Vision of Gregory the Great*, a magnificent countryside leads to a bridge, which is open only to the good; it is a reminder of Garodemana [paradise] and the bridge of Tchinvat in Babylonian mythology. Everyone who wants to reach the magical mountain has to cross the waters in a canoe, which above all in ancient mythology is a chalice, a ride on a fish, or the crossing of a bridge. Once there, they find a magnificent field:

The field of the Asphodelos, of the Greeks.

The valley of Avalon of the Celts where, according to Robert de Borron's poem, Joseph of Arimathea, the first keeper of the Grail, is buried.

On the branches of oaks in a sacred forest hangs the Golden Fleece.

The fountain of youth is found in the Garden of the Hesperides.

The enchanted forest of Oberon surrounds and protects the Castle of Monmur.

The forest of Briciljan separates the Grail temple Muntsalväsche from the rest of the world.

The Argonauts leave in their ship, the *Argo*, for the land of the Golden Fleece. Apollo is transported across the seas in a chalice to the Hyperborean, and eventually to Hesperides, the garden of the golden apples. According to the Greeks, the souls of the dead are taken to the land of light in a boat. This is why so many drawings of boats are found on the walls of Greek tombs. The same custom is repeated in Christian catacombs. Many times a fish, or specifically a dolphin, replaces the boat. In this way, Homer speaks of the fisherman Orpheus who captured the sacred fish.[5]

The first Christians used the fish as a symbol of their Savior, Jesus Christ, who accompanied human beings to heaven. The Cathars used the symbol of a canoe as a means of transport to celestial life: the vessel of the dead whose candle is the sun, symbol of the enlightened Savior. For them, as for the first Christians, the fish was the emblem of "Jesus Christ, Son of God, Savior" [*Iesous Christos Theou hyios sôter*, from whose initials comes ICHTHYS = fish].

In epic poems of the Grail, the Grail King Amfortas is described as the "King of the fishermen." Chrétien de Troyes calls him the "*Rois Pescière*." This name probably has its origin in Christ's words, "I will make men into fishermen."

In the ancient poem *Huon de Bordeaux*, to which we will return, the "tunic" of Mallabron, (a "powerful monk" and, according to another version, a fisherman), is transformed into a dolphin, who takes both Huon and Esclarmonde to the marvelous world of Oberon.

We should remember that after receiving the consolamentum in the Occitan Church of Love, a Cathar would dress in a new tunic and cape—symbolic new garments in place of old clothing, which represented Lucifer's intrigues and the imprisonment of the soul.

Trevrizent's cell was *salvasche* (rugged) and at the same time *salvat* (saved, secure). The Cathars, as spiritual brothers of the ascetic, would have also considered themselves safe in the rugged caves of Sabarthès. When the Inquisitors became lords over the cathedral of Lombrives and the hermit's cave, the Cathars still managed to resist the besiegers in their *spulgas* until well into the fourteenth century. (A spulga is a fortified cave, from Latin, *spelunca* = cave.)

The spulgas of Sabarthès—two exist—were authentic subterranean fortresses. Unfortunately, only a few of their galleries and rooms have been explored. Over hundreds of years, their walls have been converted into steep embankments by the constant leaking of chalky water. They continue to guard the secrets that still sleep behind them.

Until now, science has largely forgotten about the spulgas of Sabarthès.[6] And yet, once past the small springs of Ornolac-Ussat-les-Bains on the Toulouse-Barcelona highway near the pass of Puymorens, you cannot miss, halfway up to the right on an embankment carved out with pickaxes, the impressive entrance to a number caves surrounded by walls that are crowned with parapets. That is where the best-preserved spulga can be found: the fortified cave of Bouan. In it, you find all the fundamental elements of a medieval castle: keep, water tank, stairways, casemates, and watchtowers. The spulga of Bouan is only different from other castles in that it is composed exclusively of subterranean galleries.

On the opposite bank of the Ariège river, between the hermitage and the Fontanet, is the spulga of Ornolac (located not far from the houses of the half-demolished baths of Ussat, which are teeming with snakes).

After a difficult, rutted approach, you arrive at an impenetrable thicket of fig trees and brambles, behind which stands the demolished door of a castle. The pathway runs alongside rocky walls blackened by fire to the ruins of this spulga where a rock juts out above, like a snow overhang. It is no longer possible to determine the exact location of the entrance to the deep entrails of the mountain in times past, because it was buried when the heretical castle went up in flames. The grandeur of its proportions can still be seen in the holes of the supporting beams driven into the rocky walls that had to support four stories.

The spulgas of Bouan and Ornolac are silent sentinels of some extraordinarily violent times. First they served as refuge for the Celt Iberians who were exterminated by the Roman legions here after the fall of their capital, Vicus Sotiatum. Later, the Romans converted them into impregnable fortresses. When the victorious Moors pressed north 700 years later, they stayed here until the armies of Charlemagne defeated them on the field of Lombard, between Tarascon and Ornolac, in A.D. 719. Three hundred years later, the Cathars found their last home in them.

Lupo de Foix converted to the heresy in the spulga of Ornolac, as noted in a document of the Inquisition in Carcassonne, *Lupus haereticavit in spulga Ornolaco*. Lupo was the son of Raimon Drut, the Count of Foix. Like all the sons of the Languedocian nobility, he was initiated into the heretical belief by the patriarch of the Church of Love, Guilhabert de Castres. Guilhabert came from the House of Castres in the region of Albi. A Son of Belissena, he was the neighbor and vassal of Trencavel de Carcassonne. Although documents of the era say nothing in this regard, it is probable that Guilhabert also received Raimon-Roger, the young Trencavel, as a believer in the spulga of Ornolac. When the Inquisitors began to assemble their now sadly famous registries, Trencavel was already long dead—poisoned.

Another *haereticatio* of the patriarch Guilhabert caused an enormous sensation in the Christian world. In the year 1204, he administered the consolamentum to Esclarmonde de Foix.

Esclarmonde was the sister of Count Raimon Drut and aunt of the young Raimon-Roger de Carcassonne. From the tower of her father's castle in Foix, she could contemplate the snowy summits of the Tabor, the gorges of Sabarthès, and the pastures of Olmès. While she was still just a girl, her heretical parents consecrated her to the Holy Spirit.

Esclarmonde's name is the symbol of her life: Its true meaning can be roughly translated as "the light of the Earth" and also as "pure light"— a name that was born and died with Catharism. She was the light of the Occitan world, the pure splendor that illuminated the Church of Amor in the darkness of the Middle Ages.

After a prolonged stay in the court of the Viscountess Adélaide, where she presided over the Minne of Poivert, Esclarmonde married the Viscount Jordan de Lille y Gimoez. Jordan descended from an old family of Iberian nobility; on his mother's side, he was related to the house of Comminges, which together with Foix and Carcassonne dominated the Pyrenees.

We know very little of Esclarmonde's life after her *haereticatio*. Maybe one day someone will discover a clue in a Pyrenean cave that will reveal the true story of this woman who, from the summit of a jagged rock, challenged the greatest powers of Medieval Europe: the Vatican and the Louvre.

The orthodox world of the thirteenth century named her "the Popess of the Heretics." Cathar Occitiania called her Esclarmunda.

> *Esclarmunda, your name means*
> *that you truly give light to the world*
> *and that you are pure having done nothing disloyal*
> *and are thus fully deserving of such a noble name.*
>
> GUILHEM DE MONTANHAGOL[7]

The figure of Esclarmonde belongs at the same time to history, poetry, and legend. Poetry has made her into the queen of the faeries of the castle of Monmur, a legend that was told to me by an old pastor when I was going up to the Tabor from Montségur along the trail of the Cathars. Esclarmonde would become known as "Titania" and "Repanse de Schoye"—the keeper of the Grail.

The historical Esclarmonde de Foix was the lady of the Tabor and of Montségur.

Montségur was Muntsalvaesche and Monmur!

Monmur, the Enchanted Castle of Oberon

———— ◆ ————

IN THE ANCIENT FRENCH POEM of Oberon, "Huon de Bordeaux," which has strong similarities not only to Wolfram's epic but also to the German legends of Ornit and Wolfdietrich, Esclarmonde is the wife of King Huon de Bordeaux. Supported by Oberon, the King of the Faeries, in his struggle with his rebellious brother, Huon promises that after three years he will visit Oberon at his castle in Monmur. When the three years have passed, Huon and Esclarmonde set off in a galley, praying to God to lead them safe and sound to Monmur. After months of odyssey through the *pays des commans* and the *terre de foy*, they arrive at the *bocaige Auberon*, the enchanted forest of Oberon.

There, they find the "castle of the strange monks" where a magnificent banquet awaits them in a sumptuous hall—but to their surprise nobody is there to serve them.

The following morning, when Huon and Esclarmonde go to the church for mass, they discover that there is neither an altar nor a crucifix in the church. Then, as if by magic, a hundred monks suddenly pop out of the floor. Esclarmonde becomes apprehensive. Then Huon remembers that Oberon had recommended that he bring a long shawl with him. With it, he traps a large, horribly ugly monk, and together Huon and Esclarmonde manage to convince him to explain to them exactly what is going on in the castle. He tells them to continue their journey, because all the strange monks are really ghosts. When God banished Luzbel, he banished the monks to this place, where they await redemption on the final Judgment Day.

"Hope is the habit of this fraternity . . ."

The monk then takes Huon and Esclarmonde to Monmur on a magic cape.

According to another version of the ballad, the fisherman Mallabron, who transforms himself into a dolphin, takes them across a great expanse of water to Oberon's castle.

Although Oberon is awaiting death in Monmur, he has refused to die before Huon is elected King of the Elves. Oberon heartily welcomes Huon and Esclarmonde, and a party is organized where wine is served to all the guests from a marvelous cup.

After the banquet, Oberon asks that his crown and javelin, the symbols of his sovereignty over the empire of the faeries, be brought to him. Huon and Esclarmonde are then solemnly crowned sovereigns.

The following morning, Huon, in a show of power, convokes all the faeries and barons of the kingdom. In front of the entire faery world brought together in a magical assembly, Oberon declares:

> *I cannot bear remaining any longer on Earth;*
> *I want to go to heaven as soon as possible . . .*

SONG OF HUON

Oberon says farewell to the faery world and dies. His embalmed body is placed in his coffin, which is suspended in the air while a chorus of elves dance beneath it. Oberon's mortal remains are finally buried in a huge cave.

Of all the similarities between the "Song of Esclarmonde" of the Huon Cycle and the Grail poems (above all, Guyot and Wolfram's versions), we will highlight only the most important and apparent links: The crown and the javelin correspond to the Grail and the blood lance. The magic cup plays the role of the Grail that distributes food. The *Bocaige Auberon* looks like the forest of Briciljan. Still more shocking is the similarity between the strange monks who await their freedom and the angels of Parsifal:

> *When Lucifer and the Trinity began to war with each other,*
> *Those who did not take sides, worthy, noble angels had to descend*
> *   to Earth . . .*

I do not know if God forgave them or damned them in the end.
WOLFRAM VON ESCHENBACH

Especially surprising are the analogies between Anfortas the fisherman on the shores of Lake Brumbane and the fisherman Mallabron beside a vast body of water, behind which is located Oberon's Kingdom of the Faeries. Both Anfortas and Oberon suffer. Both consider that the arrival of their successor will be a moment of salvation.

According to the "Song of Esclarmonde," the enchanted castle of Monmur is to be found in the vicinity of the *pays des commans* and the *terre de foy.* Wasn't the marriage of the historic Esclarmonde with Jordan de Lille the direct association of the *Pays de Comminges* and the *Terre de Foix,* the cradle of Cathar faith (*foy* in old French)?

MUNTSALVAESCHE AND MONTSÉGUR

—◆—

Except for a solitary castle, rich in all Earthly splendors.
If any seeks it out of set purpose, alas he will not find it.
Nevertheless one sees many who attempt it.
I presume it is unknown to you, sir,
Its name is Muntsalvaesche
WOLFRAM VON ESCHENBACH[1]

The Templar knights kept their precious relic, the Grail, in Muntsalvaesche. The symbol of these Knights of the Temple was the lance, a sign to prepare for combat.

Such good demonstration and strong guard
is mounted by the knights of this region
That neither with fraud nor ruse
Could this zone of mountain be penetrated?
WOLFRAM VON ESCHENBACH

The Dutch chronicler Veldenaer wrote in the fifteenth century that the Swan Knight came from the Grail (*dat greal*), the former name of Earthly paradise. But according to him, this was not the Holy Paradise, but rather a place of sin. In the same era, Halberstädt's Saxon chronicle said of Lohengrin, "The chroniclers consider that this young man, the Swan Knight, came from the mountain where Venus is present in the Grail."

Was the Grail Mountain a Venus mountain? Didn't this contradict the Grail circle's precept of chastity?

> *In its service knights and squires must guard against licentiousness:*
> *A noble brotherood lives there, who by force of arms have warded*
> *   off men from every land. Only one man ever came there without*
> *   first having been assigned.*
> *He had not reached years of discretion.*
>
> WOLFRAM VON ESCHENBACH

To better understand this contradiction, we should have another look at the poem of Peire Vidal, in which the troubadour pretends to have found the God-Amor in person. At the side of Amor rides a lady. Venus? No, Grace! The *leys d'amors* prohibited simple love, carnal love.

The troubadours found solace in the grace of their ladies, and the Cathars aspired to a consoling Mani—*the* help. A feminine principle with purpose. But the chroniclers we just quoted were right when they saw in the Grail Mountain a mountain of Venus, sinning and heretical.

In remote times, Montségur was a sanctuary dedicated to the Goddess Belissena, the Astarté-Artemis-Diana of the Celt Iberians. Astarté was the *Paredra de Baal* in Phoenician theogony; Artemis, the sister of Apollo in Greek mythology; and Belissena, the wife of Abellio, in the Celt Iberian cosmos of divinities.

In the sanctuary of the divine twins Castor and Pollux in Delphi and Didyma, as in all the important spots where Apollo was worshipped, temples were consecrated to Artemis. Her priests and priestesses had to take an oath of chastity. A small troop of nymphs accompanied the inaccessible goddess in her hunts in the woods. Her symbol was the half moon.

For their part, the Druids had their own sanctuaries dedicated to Belissena in places that were consecrated to Abellio. Not far from present-day Mirepoix—whose lords, the Sons of Belissena, wore the tower, the fish, and a half moon on their coat of arms—is the sacred forest of Belena. Present-day Belesta, just a few hours from the path to Montségur, was consecrated to Belissena. A sanctuary dedicated to Belissena has been found close to another dedicated to Abellio in Lavelanet, at the foot of the promontory of Montségur, where Ramon de Perelha, a Son of Belissena, commanded the fortress.

Many times in Greek mythology, Artemis is identified with Daphne (laurel), the first legendary Sibilla of Delphi. The Sibillas wrote their oracles on laurel leaves, laurel being the sacred tree of poets and prophets. Peire Vidal knew very well why he invited his Lady Grace to rest beneath a laurel tree.

The dove was a bird dedicated to Artemis. In Dodona, the priestesses of Artemis called themselves "doves." The most sacred oak tree of Greece could be found there, and its timber served as the keel for the *Argo* before the Argonauts visited the prophet and soothsayer Medea, who helped them in their quest for the Golden Fleece.

The dove was the emblem used by the Cathars—as in the gospels—to designate God-Spirit. A Cathar sculpted a dove in the rocky wall of one of the caves of the Sabarthès. In the ruins of Montségur, small clay pigeons have been found. A dove was depicted on the shield of the Grail knights. A dove left a host on the Grail on Good Friday, the day of the supreme Minne. A legend that I heard from the lips of a shepherd in the Pyrenees told how a dove split Mount Tabor in two and how Esclarmonde transformed herself into the emblem of God-Spirit. The concordance of images that are so apparent here are not susceptible to various interpretations.

The creation of Lucifer brings death with it; death that can only be fought by the refusal to propagate the human species. When there are no longer men, there will no longer be death.

This is the reason the Cathars rejected carnal love and replaced it with the celestial Minne; in other words, they only recognized the original divine Amor-love. Dante called Beatrice, the Queen of his Loves, "The Beloved of the First Love." Original love has nothing to do with Earthly love that procreates human beings.

> When a man's life ends in such a way that God is not robbed of
>   his soul
> Because of the body's sinning and who nevertheless succeeds in
>   keeping his fellows' good respect, this is a useful toil.
>   WOLFRAM VON ESCHENBACH

The laws of chastity reigned in Muntsalvaesche, Monmur, and Montségur. In the "Song of Esclarmonde," Oberon say, "Huon, keep yourself from being intimate with a virgin. Remain loyal to the beautiful Esclarmonde who awaits you and who rejects all pretenders." In Wolfram's *Parzival*, the knights are of an immaculate purity and Anfortas, King of the Grail, can neither live nor die:

> *But any lord of the Grail who seeks love other than that allowed*
> *him by the Writing will inevitably have to pay for it with pain and*
> *suffering fraught with sighs*
>
> Wolfram von Eschenbach[2]

Because "There is nothing more pure in the world than a naïve girl," those who guarded the Grail in Muntsalvaesche were virgins. Their Queen was Repanse de Schoye.

It was not easy to arrive at Muntsalvaesche, Monmur, and Montségur. The forest of Oberon and the woods of Brizljan and Serralunga that surround and protect Montségur, where the Priscillianists found refuge from Roman henchmen, were thick and dark.

> *In a remote country, far from your steps,*
> *A castle exists that is called Montsalvat . . .*
>
> Richard Wagner

REPANSE DE SCHOYE

She whom the Grail suffered to cry itself had the name of
Repanse de Schoye.
Such was the nature of the Grail that she who
had the care of it was required to be of perfect chastity
and to have renounced all things false.
—WOLFRAM VON ESCHENBACH[1]

I am going to repeat the legend the old Pyrenean shepherd told me:

When the walls of Montségur were still standing, the Cathars kept
the Grail inside them. Montségur was in danger. The armies of Lucifer stood before its walls. They wanted to take the Grail to insert
it again in the crown of their prince, from where it fell to Earth
during the fall of the angels. In the most critical moment, a white
dove came down from the sky, and split the Tabor in two with its
beak. Esclarmonde, the keeper of the Grail, threw the precious relic
into the mountain where it was hidden; in this way she saved the
Grail. When the devils entered the castle, it was too late. Furious,
they burned all the Pure Ones, not far from the rocky castle, on the
Camp des Crémats, the field of fire. . . .

The tale continued:

All the Pure Ones perished in the flames, except Esclarmonde. Once
she was sure that the Grail was in a safe place, she climbed to the

summit of the Tabor, transformed herself into a white dove and flew to the mountains of Asia. Esclarmonde did not die. She continues to live in Earthly Paradise.

> *. . . Ethnise, where the Tigris flows out of Paradise.*
> WOLFRAM VON ESCHENBACH

My shepherd of the Tabor was relating timeless wisdom. Don't elves play in the moonlight around the crystal clear springs in their native Pyrenees? Don't the oak trees on the Tabor speak to the shepherds, who are so far from God's world, by rustling their leaves? The guaranteed-authentic story that the ninety-year-old peasant of Ornolac told me shows that the grandchildren of the Druids and bards, of the Cathars and troubadours, are today's mystics and poets. He asserted that he saw a snake on the Tabor that bit its tail and shook itself as it formed a circle at the abyss of the Sabarthès toward the snow-covered summit of Montcalm's peak.

Today, Pyrenean peasants still idealize the world that surrounds them and consider it enchanted. The Cathars and the troubadours are long dead, but can the human desire for Paradise and God ever be extinguished? Three times the Tabor was cursed and three times it burned in flames. Six hundred years later, a day worker from the town of Ornolac pretends to have seen the symbol of eternity: a snake that bites its tail.

Esclarmonde did not die, a shepherd told me on the Pathway of the Cathars. She continues to live. . . .

According to Wolfram, the Grail Queen Repanse de Schoye was an aunt of Parsifal. Esclarmonde married the Viscount Jordan de Lille y Gimoez, who was in a way the stepbrother of Trencavel, given that the Houses of Carcassonne and Comminges were united in the tenth century under the scepter of Asnar, a Cantabrian prince. For this reason, the coats of arms of Carcassonne and Comminges were identical.

At the death of Jordan (circa 1204), Esclarmonde renounced her inheritance, divided it between her six sons who were of age, and returned to her mountainous homeland. After receiving the consolamentum at the hands of the Son of Belissena Guilhabert de Castres, she established her residence in the Castellar de Pamier, a place that her brother Raimon-Roger (the Raimon Drut of the troubadours) gave her for her widowhood. From there she could rule her dominions of the Tabor. She was the feudal lady of the castle of Montségur, and Ramon de Perelha, another Son of Belissena, was her vassal.

> The fortress of Mont Ségur was constructed
> With the only purpose to defend other fortresses. . . .
>
> GUILLERMO DE TUDELA

The Romans called Montségur *Castrum montis securi,* their most secure and inaccessible Pyrenean bastion.

Montségur was also the most important fortress of Occitania; impenetrable and highly placed, it dominated the plains of Provence. It was a place for which the Pure Ones had a special affection: the first step toward the stars. Only the snowy summits of the Tabor and the starry sky surpassed that mountain, nearly a thousand meters [3,300 feet] in height.

From Lavelanet, a small town about two hours from Montségur toward the plains, the pathway of the Pure Ones winds through the gorge of Lectouire toward the top of the mountains. It is a place of noisy waterfalls, abrupt stone walls, conifers split by the winds, and farmhouses on the sides of the mountain, with names that recall the Saracen occupation: the door of the Tabor.

When I climbed the rock of Montségur for the first time, clouds swirled around the rocky mountain paths, and a storm howled through the pine and elm trees. When I finally arrived at the cliff *(abbès)* from which a vertiginous pathway leads to the ruins of the heretical fortress, the clouds suddenly parted and before me rose, golden in the sun, a gigantic rocky pyramid, gray and barren. I had never seen anything so savage and inaccessible before. A sea of clouds flew in the periphery like a flag of incense.

Together with Lavelanet *(inuxta castrum montis securi),* Montségur defended the access to the Tabor and the caves of Ornolac, which were protected on the Tabor's other flank by the Castle of Foix, the fortified city of Tarascon, and the fortifications of the Sons of Belissena: Miramont, Calmés, and Arnave. The Sons guarded the access to the Tabor in Mirepoix, Montréal, Carcassonne, Rocafissada, Belasta, Quéribus, and other cities and castles of similar names.

In Montségur, only the noblest knights of Occitania protected the

Church of Amor. The mountains, where myths and fables were woven together over thousands of years; the caves, where the memory of ancestors and ancestral civilizations lived on in their magical labyrinths; the woods and springs that inspired songs and prayers—all were sacred for the Occitanians! The Tabor was their Great National sanctuary.

Even today, you can find at each step unmistakable vestiges of that grand civilization. The caves of Sabarthès contain fossilized skeletons, mammoth bones, and Stone Age utensils revealing the presence of prehistoric man, along with countless shards of Greek pottery, Phoenician glass works, and Celt Iberian bronze ornaments. On the rocky white walls, prehistoric pictures shine and mysterious runes await deciphering. At the tops of the mountains, underbrush and brambles hide the impressive ruins of temples and cities.

In the twelfth and thirteenth centuries, the Druids and the bards were no longer the custodians of the Parnassus of Occitania; this task had fallen to the Cathars and the troubadours. In the fourth century, the Priscillianists rebaptized the range with the name Tabor and dedicated it to Saint Bartholomew, the Apostle of India and Persia. The sacred mountain of Abellio was converted into the Tabor of the exalted Trinity. The peaks of Saint Bartholomew, Soularac, and the rock of Montségur symbolized the divine trinity: Agnostos [the unknown], the Demiurge, and the Paraclete.

The Cathars roamed around the lakes of the Druids telling their converts stories of the golden coins that their spiritualist ancestors, like themselves uninterested in money, had thrown into the depths of the waters. In the shade of a *menhir* or seated on a cromlech, they spoke of the Grail:

> *A stone whose essence is most pure:*
> *This stone is also called the "Grail."*
>
> WOLFRAM VON ESCHENBACH

Maybe the Pure Ones told their attentive disciples a legend that is well known today in Provence and Languedoc; it recounts how Lazarus, Martha, Maria Magdalena, and Saint Dionysus Areopagite (a disciple of the Apostle Paul) took the Grail to Marseille, where Maria Magdalena kept it with her in a cave near Tarascon until her death.

The supreme Minne changed men into poets and poets into sons of

God, sons of the muses whose sovereign was Apollo, Artemis' brother. Are not Heaven and the gods inventions that come from the desire for paradise, a desire of every human being?

Troubadours, knights, and ladies who ascended Montségur to await the "kiss of God," as the Talmud calls the scythe of death, lived in an immense monastery whose doors were protected by strong castles, whose walls were the rocky walls of the Tabor, whose roof was the blue of the sky, whose cloisters were caves, and whose "Colegiata" was the cathedral at Lombrives.

The Church of Amor was religiously the faithful counterpart of the empire of the Occitan Minne, whose *leys d'amors,* as was said, were brought to the Earth from the sky by a hawk. The Grail in turn fell to the Earthly world when Lucifer was expelled from God's throne. The *leys d'amors* and the Grail were two symbols of the religious and temporal Minne that Heaven presented as gifts to the Earth.

The laws of the Minne established as its fundamental thesis that it should exclude bodily love and matrimony. The Minne is the union of souls and hearts; love is passion that dissipates with sensual pleasure.

Catharism demanded chastity as *sine qua non* for the "perfect" life. The supreme Minne was the marriage of the human soul with God-Spirit. Carnal love carries with it the death of the contemplation of God and fusion with him.

Troubadour Guilhem de Montanhagol's poem (which we cited earlier when we tried to explain the Occitan idea of the Minne) could be applied to the Church of Amor in the following terms: Men have to have a pure heart and think only about the supreme Minne. This is in no way is heresy, but rather the sublime virtue that makes humans into the children of God.

The troubadours were the legislators of the *leys d'amors.* The law of the Minne, of the Church of Amor, was the Gospel of the disciple whom the Lord loved:

> *This is my commandment: that ye love one another as I have*
> *   loved you.*
> *When I go to heaven I will pray the Father, and he shall give you*
> *   another comforter, that he may abide with you forever. . . .*
>
> JOHN 15:12; 14:16

Two men ride at the head of the army:
Abbot Arnaud, who the Pope sent as his legate, and
Count Simon, whom the knights named
As their commander to lead the crusade
Horrible pair! Cold and clever, the one,
Fast as windswept flames the other,
So Simon and Arnaud ride together
Associates, in thought and action.
Wherever their horses ride,
Followed by brash shock troops,
Not only the grass of Languedoc is lost,
But also the future sowing of joy
LENAU, THE ALBIGENSES

PART THREE

THE CRUSADE

THE DOCTORS OF THE CATHOLIC CHURCH and their Inquisitors considered Catharism a neo-Manichaeism because of its dualist theories. In reality, like the heresy of Manes (A.D. 216–276/77), it was a Manichaeism adapted to a Western mentality. The Mani, the symbol of Buddhist faith, found its faithful Cathar transcription in the Holy Spirit.[1]

Following the example of the Hindus, a stone that fell from the stars, a *lapsis ex coelis* (Wolfram speaks of a *lapsis exillis*, an erroneous expression that makes no real sense) that illuminates and consoles the world, symbolized the pure doctrine, which signified nothing other than Catharism.

Esclarmonde, the "Light of the World," kept the oriflamme of the Cathar faith in Montségur. At the most critical moment of the siege, four audacious knights took that emblem, "the treasure of the heretics" (as the Inquisitors called the Cathar relic), to the caves of Ornolac in a mountain journey filled with adventures. If we find a reference to the Grail in the "treasure of the heretics," we will have found several points to support our hypothesis. As superficial as our reading of the poems in question may have been, it is clear that the Grail of Chrétien de Troyes, Guyot, and Wolfram has nothing to do with the Last Supper or a "Christian" relic. Priestly interventions appear nowhere in its story.

The Grail was a heretical symbol. Those who venerated the Christian cross cursed it and a crusade pursued it. The Cross undertook a holy war against the Grail.

The Cathars saw in the veneration of the cross an insult to the divine

115

nature of Christ.[2] The repudiation of this symbol was such that—as an example—we can cite the cry of one of the Sons of Belissena: "I would never want to be redeemed by such a sign!"

> *What could have happened that drove the happy troubadour Fulk*
> *To join the priestly order*
> *To become the Church's blood and staghound*
> *Sniffing without pause after the traces of the heretics?*
>
> LENAU, *THE ALBIGENSES*

The son of a rich Genoese merchant from Marseille, Fulk was a bad troubadour; but when it came to fanaticism and greed, even the most bloodthirsty enemies of the heresy could not be compared to him.[3]

Over a long period, Fulk celebrated the wife of the Viscount Barral de Marseille in his songs; she accepted his homage but not his affection. Eventually she dismissed him because of his impetuous demands for *plaisir d'amour*. Throughout his life he ran after money and fame. When he found himself abandoned by all his patrons because of his immoral conduct, he took the priest's habit, because this was the fastest way to advance in medieval life. He was not mistaken. Shortly after entering the Cistercian order, he was named prior of the monastery at Floreja. Five years later he was bishop of Toulouse. When a pontifical legate who arrived in Provence to eradicate the heresy learned that the ex-troubadour had been chosen bishop of Toulouse, he exclaimed, "All is saved, because God has entrusted the Church to such a man!"

Soon his parish income was insufficient to satisfy the demands of this troubadour in a cassock, and he sank into debt. The townsfolk held the despicable priest in such contempt that he could not go out in the street without someone jeering or insulting him. It is told that one day in a sermon, when Fulk compared the heretics with wolves and the Catholics with sheep, one of those whose eyes had been gouged out, and whose nose and lips had been cut by Simon de Montfort, the butcher of Occitania, got up, pointed to himself, and said, "Has a sheep ever bitten a wolf like this?"

Fulk answered that Montfort had been a good dog.

Esclarmonde's brother, the Count of Foix, accused this bishop before Pope Innocent III of causing the deaths of more than 500,000 persons.[4]

Through a fatal turn of events, Occitania and its Tabor were inundated with hatred and damnation. Obeying a deadly law, the powerful of the world rewarded the supreme Minne of the Cathars with the most violent hatred!

> *They were those who knew also the Father;*
> *Where are they then? They were burnt alive.*
>
> GOETHE, *THE ETERNAL JEW*

During the second half of the twelfth century, the Pure Doctrine marched triumphantly across the Occitan provinces of the south of France. Knights, townsfolk, and even some of the clergy saw in the "good men" the enunciators of the true Evangelism, and very little more was needed to sweep Rome's power over Christianity from Provence, Languedoc, and Gascony.

No country could boast of its spiritual freedom and religious tolerance with greater reason than Occitania. All opinions could be freely expressed, all religious confessions were treated equally, and it is quite possible to assert that no real antagonism existed between classes. We have already learned the necessary requirements to be armed as a *chavalièr*.

In no other part of Europe did chivalry flourish as in Occitania. Occitan knights were as at home in the Holy Land or Tripoli—which was really nothing other than an Occitan province—as in the Roussillon or Toulouse. For certain, it was their spirit of adventure, not religious fervor, that led them to the Orient. Almost all who returned brought, instead of religious edification, an unforgettable recollection of the splendor, mysticism, and pleasant life of the Orient. Added to this was the fact that the Church demanded a spiritual and temporal submission that was incompatible with Occitan honor and pride in being free men. Almost all the barons and knights of the country were Cathar believers. With great respect, they welcomed the Perfect Ones to their castles, served them at their tables, and entrusted the education of their children to them.[5]

At last, after a long and brutal fight against feudalism, the burghers of Occitania's cities had achieved their autonomy and freedom. Enriched, and proud of their extensive commerce with Oriental ports, they defended their municipal privileges with ever-growing success. The burghers imitated the customs of the nobility and competed with them in bravura and palatial spirit; like them, they dabbled in poetry, and if they wished to, they could easily become "knights." Jealous of their independence, they rejected the influence of the clergy and temporal authorities, although they shared the latter's antipathy for the Church and its clerics.

On one occasion, the Bishop of Albi was called to the deathbed of a dying relative. He asked him in which monastery he wished to be buried. "Don't worry. I want to die together with the '*bonshommes*' and to be buried by them." The Bishop declared that he would not allow it. "The more you try to hinder me," declared the dying man, "I will drag myself on all fours to them." And so it was: The *bonshommes* took care of, consoled, and buried the relative of the Bishop of Albi.

Without any doubt, the rampant corruption in the Church was primarily responsible for the anti-Rome movement in Occitania. Many bishops visited their diocese only to collect arbitrary taxes, and for this purpose they retained entire armies of tax collector-robbers. The disorder that reigned among the clergy was indescribable. They fought and excommunicated one another. To avoid recognition, priests hid their tonsures and wore lay clothing. If they managed to escape the glares and taunts of the people in the street, they could not silence the revilement of the troubadours:

> Soon the day will come
> When the world will be completely reversed.
> The priest will go to the tournament
> And the women will preach.
>
> PÈIRE CARDINAL[6]

When a heretic preached, people came in throngs and listened enthusiastically. If by chance a Catholic priest spoke, the crowd would ask him ironically how he could dare to preach the Word of God.

The Church recognized that the heresy's progress was stimulated by the clergy's depravity and failure at their duties. Pope Innocent III declared "that the responsibility for the depravity of the people's customs belongs fundamentally to the clergy, and that from there flowed all

Christianity's problems. . . ." To combat the sects efficiently, the clergy had to enjoy the esteem and confidence of the populace, but for some time, it had ceased to deserve them.

On one occasion, [Saint] Bernard de Clairvaux said of the Cathars, "Certainly there are no other sermons more Christian than yours and your customs are pure." Should it surprise us then that Catharism—which has been identified throughout the centuries with Occitan civilization—extended itself in such an expansive way and that in the end was considered as the *Sancta Glieiza* of Occitania?

Entire monasteries passed over to Catharism and even ailing bishops were treated and consoled by the *bonshommes*.

Peter Waldo, a rich merchant in Lyon, had the New Testament translated into his mother tongue circa 1170 so he could read it.[7] Soon he realized that the angelic life as Christ and his apostles had taught it was nowhere to be seen. Consequently, he started to preach the Gospel as he conceived it. Soon he had numerous followers whom he sent as missionaries on all the pathways of the world. It was rare indeed if a noble adhered to the Waldensian sect. Its converts were almost exclusively from the lower classes; its preachers preferred to announce the new doctrine (*la nobla leyczon,* as a troubadour called it) in the streets and town squares. Discussions between Waldenses and Cathars were frequently organized, but a perfect harmony reigned between the two "heresies." Rome, which often confused the Waldenses of southern France with the Cathars, classified both under the name "Albigenses." They were two different and independent heresies, and the only thing they had in common was that the Vatican had sworn to exterminate them.

Inquisitor Bernard Gui in his *Inquisitor's Manual,* gives us a description of Waldensian doctrine:[8]

Contempt for Ecclesiastical power has been and still is the main heresy of the Waldenses. . . an error that earned them excommunication and their conversion to Satan. . . .

They argue against all oaths, whether in law or elsewhere . . . in the name of God, and they think that they can back up their claims by alluding to texts of the Holy Gospel.

Again, the followers of this sect hold in contempt the sacrament of penitence and the power of the keys of the Church. They affirm to have received from God the right to listen to confessions, to forgive sins and impose penance. Publicly they manifest that they have not received this power of the keys from the Church, because they were expelled from her, and outside of her, there is neither true penance nor possibility of salvation.

Again, they err regarding the sacrament of the Eucharist, because they maintain that the bread and the wine cannot convert into the Body and the Blood of Christ if the consecration is performed by a sinning priest.

Again, the Waldenses affirm that purgatory does not exist after this life, and that the alms and masses of the believers serve for nothing for those who have died.

Again, they hold in contempt prelates, priests, monks and nuns of the Catholic Church. They say that they are authentically blind and that they lead other blind who in no way preach the pure Gospel and who do not know the real apostolic poverty.

Again, they presume to be the successors of the apostles and to practice true apostolic and evangelic poverty.

Again, the Waldenses eat and drink like everybody else. He who wants and can fast does so Mondays and Wednesdays. And all eat meat, because they say that Christ did not forbid eating meat.

Again, they recommend to their followers continence, but permit to appease the ardor of passion, although through shameful carnal relations. They affirm with the Sacred Scripture: "It is better to marry than to suffer the ardor of passion."

Again, their "Perfecti" do not work and hold money in contempt, not that they don't recognize it and fall into its claws. Again, they call each other "brother" and call the "poor of Christ" or the "poor of Lyon."

Again, the only prayer that they teach and recite is the "Lord's Prayer." They do not know either the "God save you, Maria" nor the "I believe in God the All powerful Father" because they say that both prayers were not introduced by Christ rather the Catholic Church.

If you wish to know if one is a Waldense, it is sufficient to ask him to recite the Credo as the Catholic Church teaches it. He will answer: "I don't know it because nobody taught it to me like that."

While Occitania's clergy remained inactive, either from indolence or a justified fear of the powerful protectors of the sects, the progress of these "heretics of Toulouse and Albi" engendered genuine consternation among the prelates of northern France. At their urging, Pope Alexander III convoked the Council of Tours in 1163. The Pope, sixteen cardinals, 184 bishops, and more than four hundred abbots issued the following decree:

> An abominable heresy has taken hold in the country and from there has poisoned Gascony and the rest of the southern provinces. Consequently, we forbid, under the penalty of excommunication, all bishops and clerics to receive the heretics or to sell or buy a single thing from them.[9]

Two years later, it was the Catholic Occitan clergy's turn to stop the expansion of the heresy, but they were in far too weak a position to contemplate outright persecution. The only solution they saw was to invite the Cathar leaders to a public debate. To this end, the Bishop of Albi invited the most distinguished heretics to the town of Lombers: Constance, the sister of King Louis VII of France and wife of Raimundo V, Count of Toulouse, and Raimon-Trencavel, Viscount of Albi, Béziers, and Carcassonne—all the vassals of the Count of Toulouse agreed to attend. The Cathars who were summoned to the conference energetically refused to be interrogated by the prelates and demanded a debate; the clergy had no other choice than to agree to it. A little bit of everything was discussed until the Cathars declared that they could not find in the New Testament a single passage that would permit priests to live a more sumptuous life than princes, and adorn themselves with luxurious garments, jewels, and trappings.

When the Abbot of Albi launched an anathema against the *bons–hommes,* they replied, "You are the heretic, and we can demonstrate it with the Gospel and Epistles!"[10]

Because a safe-conduct pass had been guaranteed, the Cathars could return to their woods and caves in safety. The clergy, for their part, could gauge just how weak their position was in these provinces, and just how much they were detested.

Toulouse was the bulwark of the heresy. The Cistercian monks tried to convert the laymen, but instead of conversions, all they collected were derision and insults. The "commission for conversions" believed that they could only clean this "stable of Augeas" with brute force, and as their first example they summoned Pèire Maouran [Morand] to appear before them. The most illustrious citizen of the town, Morand was over seventy years of age. The people of Toulouse called this Cathar "priest" or "priest John."

The Cardinal-legate, Pedro de San Crisogono, began by telling him, "Peire Morand, you are suspected of Arianism."

"No." (Peyre Morand was not lying because he was not an Arian.)

"Can you swear it?"

"My word is enough, I am a knight and a Christian."

Peire Morand was firm for a long while. But when they threatened to confiscate his assets, ruin his palazzo and his castles, his strength subsided, and he swore.[11]

They led him naked through the streets of Toulouse to the Church of Saint Estève. The Cardinal had him flogged before the altar. Then he promised him absolution for his sins if, in a period of forty days henceforth, he would abandon the country as a pilgrim to the Holy Land, where he should serve the "poor of Jerusalem" for three years. Until his departure, he should be whipped every day in the streets of Toulouse.

They confiscated all he had, but they promised to return his property to him when he returned from Palestine.

The severity of the missionaries produced the desired effect. Multitudes of *Tolzans* [the inhabitants of Toulouse] rushed to reconcile themselves with the Church. Proof of the sincerity of these conversions is demonstrated by the fact that after he returned from the Holy Land, Peire Morand was elected three consecutive times *capitul* [alderman] by his fellow citizens.

The punishment of Pèire Morand was only the prelude for further persecutions. Cardinal Peyre de San Crisogono excommunicated all the Cathars in the city of Toulouse, who then fled to Carcassonne to be close to Roger Taillefer and Adélaide [Adelasia]. The Viscount of Carcassonne was very tolerant in religious matters. Catholics, Cathars, and Jews lived together in perfect harmony in his domains and benefited from identical rights. A Jew named Caravita was his treasurer and Bertran de Saissac, a heretic, his minister.

When the missionaries demanded that Roger Taillefer extradite the fugitives, Adélaide retired to Castres with the outcasts. The lords of Castres were vassals of the Viscounts of Carcassonne, and they belonged to the family of the "children of the moon." Irmgard, Isarn, and Orbria were the ladies of Castres, and their brother Guilhabert was the patriarch of Occitania; his subterranean church was located in a cave in Ornolac.

The Cistercians tried in vain to convince Adélaide and her barons to hand over the Cathars. They had no other option than to leave Castres empty-handed.

Meanwhile, Pope Alexander III convoked the Third Council of the Lateran in 1179.[12] The Pontiff dictated fresh, harsh measures against the Cathars of Gascony, Albi, and Toulouse: The Count of Toulouse, the Viscount of Béziers, the Count of Foix, and the greater part of the barons of Occitania were all excommunicated.

Pope Alexander, whose missionaries in Toulouse and the Occitan prelates told him in terrifying terms about the growing power and audacity of the sect, believed that the moment had come to send a new special legate to the heretical provinces to guarantee the strict application of the resolutions of the Third Council of the Lateran. For the second time, he entrusted this mission to the Cistercians, under the orders of their abbot, Henri de Clairvaux. To lend more weight to his mission, Henri, whom the Lateran council had named Cardinal-Bishop of Albano, proclaimed a "Crusade against the Albigenses." It was the first time that such a coercive method was employed by the Church against other Christians.

De Clairvaux and his soldier-pilgrims headed for Lavaur, one of the best-supplied castles of the Viscount of Carcassonne.[13] At the time, Roger-Taillefer was campaigning at the side of the Count of Toulouse, and was unable to send any reinforcements to the besieged city. Adélaide assumed command of the defense. But Lavaur could not resist the pounding of the Catholic army, and the Viscountess was soon obliged to open the doors of the city to the crusaders.

The fall of Lavaur forced Roger-Taillefer to sue for peace. Although he renounced the heresy, we shouldn't attach great importance to this: He only wanted to avoid further disasters for his country, which was left in ruins by the crusade. He was not mistaken that diplomacy favored his cause and that of the heretics. Thanks to this act of submission, his country was spared the missionaries from Rome—for a while.

The coat of arms of Lotario de' Conti—an eagle fulminating bolts of lightning—became the symbol of his domination: "Urbi et Orbi" [to the City (Rome) and the world]. Under the name of Innocent III he became God's vicar: for the Cathars, not the God whose angelic choruses announce the good news on the evening of Christmas, but the God of tempests who, from Sinai or Mount Olympus, has his lightning ready for those who scorn his majesty.[14] Without beating around the bush, on the day of his Papal coronation (February 22, 1198) de' Conti defined the powers that he believed to have received from heaven. In his ritualized speech, he said, "God has placed me above the peoples and kingdoms to root out and exterminate, but also to build, and plant. To me, these words were sent: I will give you the keys of the heavens, and what you bind to Earth will be bound in heaven. I find myself between God and men, smaller than God but larger than man. . . ."

With growing anger, he contemplated the expansion of the Cathar heresy, and realized that his Church was in danger—a Church outside of which there is no salvation. Innocent believed that Catharism was so dangerous, he had to tear it out by the roots and throw it into the fire.

Two months after his enthronement, the Pope wrote to all prelates, princes, and nobles, and the French people in general, ordering them to dispossess and burn all heretics who did not return to the true faith. Furthermore, six months later, he gave full powers to his legate, Rainier Sacconi, to radically reform the Church and reestablish ecclesiastical discipline in Occitania for the purpose of eliminating this "source of evil." The Occitan clergy did not look favorably upon Rainier's reforms. With all the means at their disposal, they tried to thwart his mission, almost to the point of allying themselves with the heretics against the Holy See.

Rainier fell ill in the summer of 1202 and was replaced by Pèire and Raoul, two monks from the Cistercian abbey of Fontfroide, not far from Narbonne. They began their mission in Toulouse. Raimundo VI had just succeeded his illustrious father, the patron of the troubadours, as Count. Only two years after coming to power, Pope Celestine III [circa 1106–1198; r. 1191–1198] excommunicated Raimundo "because of his ransacking of churches and convents." (Innocent III rescinded the excommunication in 1198.)

Raimundo VI had always maintained intimate contacts with the Cathar sect. A number of perfecti accompanied him on his travels and military expeditions; he always carried—and this is what the Church always threw in his face—a copy of the New Testament with him, to be able to receive the consolamentum in case of illness or fatal wound. He regularly attended heretical meetings for which the best halls of his castle were used. "He knelt, as all believers, when the *perfecti* recited their prayers, asked for their benediction and the kiss of peace. He exhorted his vassals and troubadours to follow his example, and he was never afraid to publicly display his aversion for Rome and his sympathies for Catharism."[15]

The pontifical legates could do nothing. Innocent III declared, "A new Great Flood is needed to purify the country from sin, and to prepare a new generation." To this end, he decided to put all the strength of the Church into the obliteration of Catharism.

Completely demoralized, the two monks of Fontfroide petitioned the Pope to dismiss them from their duties. Innocent III then named as new head of the Church's commission Arnaud de Cîteaux, "abbot of the abbots," supreme head of the great order of Cister, a somber and implacable man filled with zeal for the cause of the Catholics.[16]

By the end of May 1204, Innocent III had formed a new authority that comprised Arnaud and his Cîteaux monks and Pierre de Castelnau and monks of the Fontfroide abbey, and gave them extraordinary powers. But the outward appearance of the legates and their attendants was not very appropriate for the success of their mission. They traveled across the land on gorgeous horses and accompanied by an army of servants. Considering that the Occitan heretics reproached the Catholic clergy most strongly for their luxury and riches, it is easy to imagine the impression they gave: "Look," the people shouted, "these people want to speak with us about Our Father Jesus Christ, who was poor and walked barefoot!" When the Cistercian monks attempted to convert them, the listeners turned and left, shrugging their shoulders and smiling ironically. The legates quit their endeavors, understanding that their efforts had been in vain. Completely demoralized, they were more decided than ever to request their dismissal from the Pope.

As luck would have it, they met Diego de Acevedo, Bishop of Osma, and his subprior Domingo de Guzmán in Montpellier. Both were returning from Rome where Pope Innocent had denied them the permission they needed to leave the Bishopric of Osma so they could dedicate themselves to the conversion of the heretics. When de Acevedo learned that the Cistercians were thinking of breaking off their mission, he recommended that they renounce their sumptuous retinue and mix among the people, barefoot and poor like the Apostles; they might thus have more success. The idea was so new that at the first instant, the legates vacillated. But when he declared that he was ready to set a good example and help them in their mission, they followed his advice. Pierre de Castelnau, Arnaud de Cîteaux, Diego de Acevedo, Domingo de Guzmán, and the monks of Fontfroide and Cîteaux left Montpellier and began their pilgrimage across heretical Occitania barefoot and dressed in hair tunics, preaching the true Gospel of the Catholic Church.

Roman legates, Cathars, and Waldenses, at the same time and place, claimed to be the true successors of Christ. Poor like him, they proclaimed the Gospel, outside of which there is no salvation.

> *It is true, I tell you*
> *Fortunate are those who suffer*
> *Persecution for the sake of the Gospel,*
> *Because the kingdom of the heavens belongs to them. . . .*
>
> MATTHEW 5:10

Two by two, three by three, the Roman legates crisscrossed the southern provinces, preaching. Their results left a lot to be desired. They were forced to accept the challenges of the Cathars, who believed that they could resolve who was closest to the Evangelical doctrines through public debates. Many debates and conferences took place, but the most important was the one that took place in Pamiers, in 1207.[17]

Pamiers is a small town on the banks of the Ariège, located in the northern part of the County of Foix. Since 1204, it had been the residence of Esclarmonde, who was Princess of Foix and Viscountess Jordan y Gimoez. As we have already mentioned, Esclarmonde had married the Viscount Jordan, from the illustrious house of Comminges and Selio. After her husband's death, she renounced the favorable clauses in his will and left Gascony to take up residence in the Castellar de Pamiers, a place that her brother Raimon-Roger had given her for her widow-hood. Under Esclarmonde, Pamier became the mystical "metropolis" of Occitania, the Cathar equivalent of Toulouse chivalry. From the caves of Sabarthès and the Montagne Noir, the heretical philosophers streamed there to discuss with her the philosophy of Plato and the wisdom of Saint John the Evangelist.

It was there that Esclarmonde, with the permission of her brother, invited the pontifical legates and the most erudite Cathars. Our knowl-edge of the particulars of the conference is insufficient. Nevertheless, a detail exists that reveals for us the difficulties of the Roman legates. When Esclarmonde reproached Rome for the bloody crusade of Albano, a monk shouted in anger, "Madame, you should be with your spindle! Everything is lost on you in such a meeting!"

The Bishop of Osma and Domingo de Guzmán spoke on behalf of Rome. We don't know if Domingo participated in the discussion. Perhaps the moment for "miracles" had not yet arrived for the future "Saint Dominic."

The Pamiers conference made evident once again the extraordinarily grave situation the Cathars were in. A year earlier, Gauceli, patriarch of heretical Aquitaine, had brought together a congregation of hundreds of perfecti and innumerable "believers" in the Tower of Pierre-Roger de Mirepoix. They harbored the suspicion that the Church, faced with the impossibility of eradicating the heresy through conferences and mis-sionary work, would soon resort to violence. As a consequence, they decided to request from Esclarmonde and her vassal Raimon de Perelha the castle Montségur as a supreme refuge during emergencies. With an escort of heretical bishops, deacons, and knights, the patriarch went first to see Raimon de Perelha, and then to Castellar de Pamiers to speak with Esclarmonde, because the entire mountainous zone of the Tabor belonged to her widow-estates. Raimon, one of the Sons of the Moon—the most fanatical adherents of Catharism—was immediately willing to put the castle of Montségur in shape and refortify it with advanced works. By giving her acquiescence, Esclarmonde did nothing other than see her own desires satisfied that the knowledge that the safety of the castle of the Paraclete and the Tabor would be guaranteed. That is how Montségur—the "Temple of Abellio," the *castellum montis securi,* the citadel protecting the sacrosanct mountain of the Tabor, the "Parnassus" of Occitania—was fortified and made ready.[18] Over half a century, this Noah's ark would be able to resist the waves of blood and crimes that would suddenly flood Occitania, destroying its culture and civilization.

Domingo de Guzmán established his residence in Fanjeaux, where he could observe Montségur. It was in Fanjeaux where Domingo, "through the intervention of the rosary, finally succeeded in moving the Virgin Mary to exterminate the heresy." It was also from Fanjeaux that the Inquisition would extend itself around the world, tormenting it for centuries like a horrible nightmare.

In the meantime, Pierre de Castelnau launched his fulminating excommunication of the Count of Toulouse, putting his lands under Papal interdiction. On May 29, 1207, the Pope confirmed the sentence of his legate. Innocent III announced the punishment that God had in store for the Count of Toulouse in this life and the next. He added that in the name of God, he himself would exhort Christian princes to expel him from Toulouse and authorize them to divide his county between them, so as to be free of the heresy once and for all. The communiqué said the following:

To the noble Count of Toulouse:

What pride has taken over your heart, leper! Without any interruption, you have waged war on your neighbors, scorned the laws of God, and allied yourself with the enemies of the true faith. Tremble, atheist, because you are going to be punished. How could you be capable of protecting the heretics, cruel and barbarous tyrant? How can you pretend that the faith of the heretics is better than that of the Catholics?

Still, you have committed other crimes against God: you do not want peace; you make war on Sunday and ransack convents. To shame Christianity, you have given public offices to Jews.

Our legates have excommunicated you. We have backed their decision. But because our mission is to forgive sinners, we order you to seek penitence to merit our indulgent absolution. Because we cannot leave your offenses to the Church and to God unpunished, we inform you that we are ordering the confiscation of all your worldly goods, and to raise all princes against you, because you are an enemy of Jesus Christ. But the anger of the Lord will not stop there. The Lord will destroy you!

Events were clearly leading to a catastrophe. In a vain attempt to move the legates toward indulgence, Raimundo declared that he was ready to accept all the conditions of the Church. They no longer listened to his plea; they publicly called him "coward and liar."

Against this background, an unknown knight assassinated Pierre de Castelnau.[19] The emissary of the Vicar of God in Rome had fallen—murdered: Rome would know how to avenge his death.

Immediately thereafter, Pope Innocent III excommunicated Raimundo, the assassins, and their accomplices. Sunday after Sunday, throughout the Western world, the Church proclaimed "with bell, book, and candle" their excommunication and the interdiction of any place they might tread upon. Raimundo's vassals were freed of their oath of loyalty. Regarding Raimundo, he could only begin to contemplate a request for forgiveness after demonstrating his repentance by expelling the heretics from his territory.

The Pope called on all Christianity to take up arms. He ordered all bishops to preach a crusade against this irreconcilable enemy of the Church and his heretical subjects, "who are worse than the Saracens." He asked the King of England to make peace with France, and to ally himself with Philip II against Toulouse.

The Archabbot Arnaud de Cîteaux hastily convoked a general chapter of the Cistercian order, which unanimously decided to preach the new crusade. Arnaud and his brothers of the order traversed France preaching the cross against the heretical provinces of the Midi. Bishops and priests added their voices to the Cistercian fanatics. The churches resounded with sermons that exhorted the Catholic populace to take up arms in favor of God's cause.

To make the recruitment of soldiers for this Holy War easier, the Pope promised indulgences that were similar to those given to the participants in the crusades in the Holy Land. Also, the participants in the struggle against the Albigenses were assured eternal salvation: "Any person, as great a sinner as any, can escape the torments of Hell if he fights against the heretics!"

The Vatican called up all loyal Christians to defeat the heresy: "Forward, brave soldiers of Jesus Christ! Fight the agents of the Antichrist. Until now, you have fought for mundane glory; from these moments on, fight for celestial glory. I call upon you to serve God, not for an Earthly reward; I call upon you so that you can win the kingdom of the heavens. For your prowess as warriors I promise you this reward with a tranquil conscience and with the most absolute conviction!"

The imminence of the storm shook the Count of Toulouse. He earnestly implored the Archabbot of Cîteaux to give him absolution. Arnaud refused him on the pretext that he did not have the power to lift his excommunication and referred him to the Pope.

Raimundo's nephew, the young Raimon-Roger from the House of Trencavel, recommended that Raimundo begin preparations for strong resistance. But the Count was completely demoralized. He sent emissaries to the Vatican with the news that he wanted to submit himself to the sovereign decision of the Church. Innocent demanded that Raimundo hand over his strongest castles as a demonstration of his good will. Once done, the Pope would be willing to listen to him and lift his excommunication—if he could prove his innocence. Raimundo accepted these conditions. He didn't suspect that the Pope would trick him with a fictitious indulgence until the moment for his complete destruction had arrived.

Raimundo handed over seven of his most important fortresses to the Papal legate, Milo, who in turn entrusted them to abbots and bishops, and Raimundo swore unconditional submission to the Pope and his legates.

Stripped to the waist, in the atrium of the Church of Saint Gilles he swore again to put himself henceforth in the Church's service, eradicate the heresy, dismiss all Jews from their positions, and personally participate in the crusade. Then the legate whipped the Count's back with a cane and led the penitent to the altar where, in the name of the Pope, his excommunication was lifted. From this moment on, the Count of Toulouse took up the cross against his own vassals.

In July 1209, Innocent III sent him a letter, congratulating him for his submission and penitence, and let him guess the nature of his salvation in this world and the next. What Raimundo did not know, however, was that the same Papal courier brought another letter for the legate Milo with the order to continue chastising the Count.

Two months later, "Because, in the interim he has not managed to exterminate the heretics," the Count of Toulouse was again excommunicated and all his worldly goods put under interdiction.

A crusade such as had never been seen before in all history began to assemble in Lyon. The Church's assurance that all the crusaders would return to their homes in forty days, carrying booty and gaining eternal life, had the desired effect.

In Lille, a thief joined the crusade to escape arrest, but was detained at the last minute. Faced with this infringement of the crusaderss immunity, the archbishop of Rheims excommunicated Countess Mathilde de Flandres and placed her dominions under interdiction; she freed the pilgrim, and he left with the crusade against the Albigenses.

From all over the Western world, new recruits continued to flow toward Lyon: from the Île de France, Burgundy, Lorraine, the Rhineland, Austria, Friesland, Hungary, and Slavonia. Christianity in its entirety wanted to march against Provence and Languedoc to suppress once and for all this scandalous situation that had resisted all the Church's efforts to remove it for nearly three generations.

On June 24, 1209, the crusaders left Lyon and followed the Rhône river downstream: 20,000 knights and more than 200,000 citizens and peasants, not counting the clergy and the merchants, headed for Occitania.

But what a mishmash, this army of Jesus Christ: At its head rode the somber and implacable Archabbot of Cîteaux, the "chief of the Christian armies against the Albigensian heretics." With his monk's cowled habit swept back by the wind, this apocalyptic knight galloped toward a country that did not worship his God. Behind him, the army of archbishops, bishops, abbots, priests, and friars sang the *dies irae*. Together with the princes of the Church marched secular princes with their magnificent armor of steel, silver, and gold. Then came the bandit-knights with their ramshackle armaments: Robert "No, lieutenant," Guy "Doesn't-drink-the-water," and all the other what's-his-names. Then came the citizens and peasants, and behind them the dregs of all Europe: the *ribautz* (ruffians), the *truands* (crooks), and in the temples of Venus on four wheels, the prostitutes of the lords of all the nations. I will not go into details. . . .

In a speech delivered on September 1, 1883, Pope Leo XIII declared that the Albigenses had attempted to overthrow the Church by force of arms.[20] She had been saved, continued the Holy Father, not by military force but through the prayer of the holy rosary of the Blessed Virgin Mary, a rosary that was the invention of Domingo de Guzmán.

This has nothing to do with the truth. Through the chronicles of Guillermo de Tudela and Pierre de Vaux-Cernay, both enthusiastic members of the crusade, let's accompany the soldiers of Christ in Occitania, and penetrate the wildest Pyrenean vales and the darkest caves where only death reigned. . . .

Despite its obvious religious motives, and the fact that the Vatican sponsored it, the crusade against the Albigenses was fundamentally a war between northern and southern France. The nobles of the north were burning to complete the unification of the country, a task initiated seven hundred years before by Clovis I, France's first king. And the people of the south, both Catholics and heretics, unanimously opposed such an invasion, despite the multiple venalities of which their own nobility and cities were capable. There was no religious hatred between the Catholics and the heretics in the Midi. Heretics and Catholics (naturally, I am not referring to the clergy) lived side by side in peace. Very rarely did orthodox Occitanians give any help to the crusaders (here again, we are dealing with laymen). It would have been logical for Occitania's Catholics to receive the crusaders as liberators from the domination or tyranny of some hated enemy belief, but this was not the case. For the Occitanians, secular tolerance had become a custom, and the love of the land was stronger than religious contradictions.

The young Raimon-Roger of the House of Trencavel, Viscount of Béziers and Carcassonne, rode to meet the crusaders. He tried to avoid disaster for his two towns, but he had to return without achieving his goal. In Béziers, his subjects surrounded him:

"Is there any hope?"

"Fight to the death! God be with you!"

And he continued galloping toward Carcassonne.

Béziers awaited the arrival of the crusaders.[21] A dragon belching fire and destruction was coming closer in a deafening march. . . .

An aged priest asked to enter the city. It was Reginald de Montpeyroux, the bishop who had joined the crusade. The bells called the faithful to the cathedral, which was constructed in the Romanesque style by master Gervasi.

"The crusaders are about to arrive," said the old priest; "give us the heretics; if not, you will all perish."

"Betray our brothers? We would rather be cast to the bottom of the sea!"

The bishop mounted his mule and left the town. The unexpected answer provoked such a seizure of anger in the Grand Prior of Cîteaux that he swore to erase with blood and fire both Catholics and heretics, and not to leave a single stone on top of another.

On the afternoon of July 25, the crusaders were in sight. Impatient for their plunder, the *ribautz* and *truands* rode toward the town on their own initiative. For the rest of the pilgrims, there was nothing else to do but follow them. The doors gave way. As the crusaders burst into the town, the inhabitants of Béziers, both orthodox and heretic, fled in terror for the relative safety of the two churches. One of the barons asked the Grand Prior of Cîteaux how they could distinguish the heretics from the Catholics; if we are permitted to believe Caesarius von Heisterbach, Arnaud responded: *Caedite Eos! Novit enim Dominus qui sunt eius!* [Slay them all! God will know his own!]

In the houses of God, where priests adorned with ornaments celebrated the mass for the dead, all the inhabitants of the town were murdered: men, women, and children ("Twenty thousand," wrote Arnaud de Cîteaux to the Holy Father). Nobody was left alive. Even the priests were burned alive before the altar. And the crucifix, along with the safety from the invaders that it represented, was smashed on the stone slab floor.

> *Nothing could save them; neither the cross, nor the altar or crucifix; and these crazed ruffians and beggars cut the throats of priests, women, and children.*
> *Not one, I believe escaped. Shall God receive their souls in Glory!*
>   GUILLERMO DE TUDELA

The town was sacked. While the crusaders were fully occupied with their work as executioners in the churches, robbers devoted themselves to pillaging the town. Because nobody wanted to renounce the spoils that were promised, the flats of swords and heavy sticks were required to separate these wandering thieves from their booty.

Then the town was set ablaze. The thick smoke blackened out the sun on this horrible day in July, a sun that, on the Tabor, was just about to set.

"God is with us!" exclaimed the crusaders. "Look, what a miracle! No vulture or crow is interested in this Gomorrah!"

The bells melted in their belfries, the dead burned in the flames, and the cathedral blew up like a volcano. Blood flowed, the dead burned, the town blazed, walls fell, monks sang, crusaders slaughtered, and gypsies pillaged. So died Béziers—and so began the Crusade against the Grail.

Without vultures and crows, Béziers was left to the wolves and jackals. News of her horrific end sowed panic in every town of the Languedoc. No one had expected this.

Everybody knew that the "crusade" was a war, but that the Louvre and the Vatican would rival each other in barbarity to obliterate Occitania was a shock. When they came to this realization, it was too late: the crusade with its 300,000 pilgrims was already in the heart of the country, and the Count of Toulouse, who participated directly in combat, had lost his authority. This was the worst of all!

Constructed by the Gothic kings and later the House of Trencavel, the magnificent walls of Carcassonne were bursting with refugees. Grape growers from the Lauragais and shepherds from the "Montagne Noir" and the spurs of the Pyrenean mountain range sought refuge with their flocks and their meager possessions from the hurricane that was advancing with the steps of a giant.

On the afternoon of Tuesday, August 1, the lookout on the highest watchtower of the castle announced that the crusaders were in sight. By early Thursday morning, the crusader camp on the opposite bank of the river appeared filled with life.

The *Veni Creator Spiritus,* the hymn of the crusade, resounded the whole morning. It was the signal for the attack. The pilgrims crossed the river and began the assault on the Graveillaude quarter. After two hours of combat, the Viscount's troops had to pull back before the superiority of the enemy and were forced to abandon the district. Graveillaude was razed to the ground.

Friday, the crusaders hoped to take the Saint Vincent district. Passing the smoking ruins of Graveillaude, they attacked the walls of Saint

Vincent. But these fortifications were more solid and better defended. The assault failed.

When he heard of the disaster of Béziers, Raimon-Roger's brother-in-law, King Pedro II of Aragon, "the Catholic" (1174–1213), crossed the Pyrenees, hoping that with the help of his intervention, Carcassonne would not suffer a similar fate. Escorted by a hundred Catalan and Aragonese knights, he entered the crusaders' camp. After a brief rest in the tent of the Count of Toulouse, he headed to the beleaguered city without weapons and in the company of only three knights. Carcassonne was filled with joy: "The King has come to our aid! Are we not his friends and vassals?"

"Viscount," the King of Aragon told his brother-in-law, "in the name of Jesus, Our Lord, did I not advise you on numerous occasions to expel the heretics and their crazy doctrine from the city? I am very worried to see you and your city in such danger. I see no other solution than to come to an agreement with the barons of France. The army of the crusade is so powerful that I am forced to doubt that your cause could have a happy end. I recognize that your city is strong, but it shelters too many women and children. Would you permit me to negotiate on your behalf with the barons?"

In agreement with his vassals, the Viscount answered, "Sire, do as you think best. We give you our full confidence."

The monarch returned to the camp. The French princes and barons agreed, but nobody could promise anything without the approval of the Papal legate. The King of Aragon then went to see the Abbot of Cîteaux and explained the situation to him. Arnaud listened in silence and then said:

"In honor of the great esteem that we profess for the King of Aragon, we authorize his brother-in-law, the Viscount of Carcassonne, to leave the city with twelve companions selected by him. The city and everything in it belongs to the crusaders."

Disconsolate, the King went back to his brother-in-law.

"Sire," exclaimed Raimon-Roger, "do you believe that I am capable of betraying my lowliest subjects? I would kill myself first. I must ask you to return to your home. I know how to defend my city and myself."

Downcast, the King kissed his brother-in-law and began his return to his country, crossing the County of Foix and passing close to Montségur

and the caves of Sabarthès, whose walls had just been repaired and reinforced.

The crusaders renewed their assault, but this time they were caught
under a hail of arrows, stones, boiling water, and pitch, and had no
other recourse than retreat.

"The Lord is with us," exclaimed the Abbot of Cîteaux. "Look at
the new miracle! God, the Lord of the elements, has put them on our
side. We have water, because the Aude is ours; but up there in the nest
of the heretics, the wells are running dry because the Lord has forbidden
the clouds to give the sinners a drink."

In the besieged city, atrocious scenes were taking place. The accumulation of people and animals, the stench of open animal carcasses, clouds
of mosquitoes, and the horrendous lack of fresh water provoked an epi-
demic. Women and children ran wailing and crying through the streets.

One day, a knight presented himself at the eastern door of the city.
He said that he wanted to parley with the Viscount; he had come from
the King of France, and he asked Raimon-Roger to go to the crusaders'
camp to discuss terms under truce. They would guarantee the Viscount
safe conduct.

"Swear it," said Raimon-Roger.

"I swear by God the Almighty."

After a brief discussion with his barons and consuls, Raimon-Roger
decided to go to the crusader camp. In the company of a hundred men
on horseback, he rode to the tent of the Abbot of Cîteaux. The French
barons observed the most famous and valiant knight of Occitania with
curiosity and admiration. The Viscount presented himself before the
abbot of the caster: "Your Eminence desires—?"

"Arrest him and all his knights!" exclaimed the Archabbot Arnaud.

In this way, through betrayal, the Viscount of Carcassonne and his
one hundred companions were neutralized. Intentionally, the crusaders
let a few escape so they could announce the arrest of the Viscount to the
city. When Carcassonne learned of the loss of their leader, they knew that
their fate was sealed—and that the same horrible fate of Béziers awaited
them. The consuls and barons met in council, and the night fell.

The following morning, the crusaders awaited the surrender of
Carcassonne. But the drawbridges were not lowered and the doors
remained closed. Oddly, there were no lookouts on the watchtowers or

on the lake. The city was as silent as a graveyard. The crusaders suspected some trick. Cautiously, they approached the walls. They listened—no noise. Then they smashed open the eastern door.

The city was completely empty. Even the main fortress had been evacuated.

With this news, the legate, barons, priests, and monks came running. The first thing they did was to throw the Viscount into one of the deepest dungeons of his own castle. The second was to install themselves in the castle as if in their own home, and the third was to let the soldiers pillage the city.

They found themselves confronted with an enigma. Not a soul in the city! The steps of the intruders resonated gloomily in the empty streets.

From the balcony of the Count's castle, the "commander-in-chief of the Christian army," Grand Prior Arnaud de Cîteaux, made the following harangue:

"Barons and soldiers, listen to me! As you see, nothing can resist us. The God of thunder performs miracles. In his name, I prohibit you all to pillage; on the contrary, I will excommunicate you and I will curse you. We are going to give the entire booty to an honorable baron who will keep this country that we have conquered in the grace of God."

The army applauded the decision.

Stupefied, the crusade's chiefs asked themselves how thousands of Carcassonne citizens could vanish, as if swallowed by the Earth. The Earth had indeed swallowed them. The night before, the besieged population had fled through a subterranean passage to the Montagne Noir, the woods of the Corbières, and the gorges of the Tabor. In the cellars, the crusaders finally found about five hundred people for whom the flight posed too many difficulties: mostly women, children, and elderly. About one hundred denounced the heresy. The crusaders took their clothes from them, and let them run as they had come into this world, "clothed only in their sins." The other four hundred remained loyal to their faith, and were hanged or burned alive.

In the Cathedral of Saint Nazaire, the crusaders gave thanks to Heaven for the help that was given them. Their *Te Deum* was accompanied by the moans of their victims, and the incense mixed with the smoke of the execution pyres. Arnaud de Cîteaux celebrated a "Mass of the Holy Spirit" and sermonized on the birth of Christ.

Messa lor a cantada de Sante Esperit
E si lor preziquet cum Jhesu Crist nasquit . . .

GUILLERMO DE TUDELA

This occurred on August 15, in the year of Our Lord 1209, day of the assumption of Mary of the Heavens, patroness of the crusade.[22]

Carcassonne had fallen. Centuries earlier, Charlemagne had besieged it for seven long years in vain. It was finally handed over to the genial emperor by its own decision; this was how a city of knights paid chivalrous tribute to the first "knight without fear or stain." And now Carcassonne had fallen through betrayal. The most charming and chivalrous city of Occitania—the city of fifty towers, where Gothic kings and sultans held court, where Adélaide received kings and troubadours, where the Trencavel cast their watchful gaze toward the land of Salvaesche—had fallen through treason.

Victorious, the pilgrims of the crusade against the Albigenses placed the cross, the symbol of their triumph, on the highest tower of Carcassonne.

The Grail was in danger!

After the thanksgiving mass was celebrated in the Church of Saint Nazaire, the Abbot of Cîteaux convoked all the prelates and barons. For him, the moment had come to give this conquered land a new lord. Arnaud first offered the Viscounty of Béziers and Carcassonne to the Duke of Burgundy and the Counts of Nevers and Saint-Paul, but they immediately refused his proposal. They had come to punish the heretics, not to appropriate lands that didn't belong to them.

A committee was charged with the task of naming a new temporal lord. Arnaud de Cîteaux, two bishops, and four knights selected, under the guidance of the "Holy Spirit," Simon de Montfort, Earl of Leicester.

In 1201, Simon de Montfort enlisted in the crusade of Baudouin de Flandres when French knights, lacking the necessary funds for a crusade in Palestine, sold their services to the Venetians, who wanted to reconquer the town of Zara in Dalmatia, which had belonged to Hungary since 1118. Simon, as the only French baron, declared that he had gone to fight against the infidels, and not to wage war for Venice against Hungary, a statement that led him to abandon the crusade.

When the holy war was proclaimed against the Albigenses, a

Cistercian abbot visited Simon in his castle at Rochefort, hoping to convince him to join the crusade. At first, he did not accept. Casually, he picked up his psalm book and haphazardly opened it. He asked the abbot to translate what he had before him.

These were the words where Simon had put his finger: Psalm 91 of the Old Testament.

> For he shall give his angels charge over thee, to keep thee in all thy ways.
> They shall bear thee up in [their] hands, lest thou dash thy foot against a stone.
> Thou shall tread upon the lion and adder: the young lion and the dragon shall thou trample under feet. Because he hath set his love upon me, therefore will I deliver him: I will set him on high, because he hath known my name.

Simon de Montfort took up the cross against the Albigenses "for the glory of God, honor of the church, and the extermination of the heresy." This crude fighter, who was unable to read or write, became the implacable executioner of Occitania. This unjust and cruel fanatic, who devastated one of the most peaceful and beautiful regions of the Western world over a ten-year period, is still considered a "Champion of Jesus Christ" and the "Savior of Rome" by the Catholic Church.

On November 19, 1209 Raimon-Roger, the noble scion of Trencavel, suddenly died.[23]

"He was poisoned!" lamented the Occitanians.

"Cursed shall be those who think so!" exclaimed the pilgrims of the Albigensian crusade. But even Pope Innocent III had the courage to write in a letter that the young Viscount of Carcassonne and Béziers had been *miserabiliter infectus,* miserably poisoned.

With the arrival of Simon de Montfort on the scene, Trencavel— "Parsifal"—had no other option than to end his days in the deepest dungeons of his own castle. The noblest knight of Occitania was forced to drink from the poisoned chalice just as Socrates, that most distinguished thinker of ancient Greece, had.

Let yourself be buried already, cavalry,
And shall no word proclaim you already!
You are ridiculed and without honor,
There is no dead who has less strength,
Express yourself and clericalize
The king suppresses your inheritance,
And all your empire is treachery and sales
And you will be suppressed!

PÈIRE CARDINAL

The first to abandon the crusade were the Count of Nevers and his vassals. Eventually, the Duke of Burgundy and all the other French barons followed their example, one after another. They had spent the forty days of "service" necessary to assure the salvation of their souls. In vain, the princes of the Church tried to convince the knights that God's cause still required their presence. The *ribautz* and *truands* also left; their plunder was enough and they wanted to return home.

Montfort, needless to say, stayed, and with him all the archbishops, bishops, abbots, priests, and friars, but only thirty knights and about four thousand pilgrims, for the most part Burgundians and Germans. He was forced to double the pay for their services. Montfort's situation was extraordinarily delicate. At the zenith of their success, the legates held a council in Avignon where they made all the knights, nobles, and municipal employees in the conquered territories swear that they would do anything in their power to eradicate the heresy.

But this didn't really mean very much because these oaths were mere formalities, and the homage rendered to Simon by his new vassals was in no way sincere because it was obtained by brute force.

Slowly, the country began to recover from its terror. A series of small guerrilla wars compromised Montfort's situation even further. Sometimes, his power did not extend farther than his lance point. Once in Carcassonne, he had terrible difficulties stopping his own troops from fleeing. On another occasion, he found it impossible to find a single knight who was ready to assume command of the garrison of Carcassonne when he wanted to besiege Termès.

Despite all these difficulties, he managed to bring several fortresses under his control and make some inroads into the county of Foix. By 1210, when fresh pilgrims joined the crusade, his situation improved noticeably.

Toward the end of 1209, Raimundo VI visited the Pope and complained about the un-Christian attitude of Simon de Montfort.[24] He hoped that he could count on the Pope's greater indulgence, because the King of France and his most powerful vassals had not hesitated to tell the pontiff of their indignation over Simon's cruelty and the shameful, disloyal behavior of the legates. Raimundo tried to demonstrate to Innocent III how unjustly his legates had persecuted him and his subjects. He assured the Pope that he had fulfilled all the conditions his legate Milo had imposed upon him in Saint Gilles, and asked to be exonerated, once and for all, of the accusation that he had murdered Pierre de Castelnau. The Holy Father received the Count very cordially; the pontiff presented him with magnificent gifts and showed him famous relics—and he even permitted the Count to touch them. He called him "my dear son" and entrusted his legates with the expressed mission to convoke, at the very latest in three months, a council to give the Count of Toulouse the possibility of exonerating himself.

Did Innocent listen carefully to Raimundo's protestations? None of this really mattered to the Pope, because he had no intention whatsoever of deviating from the course of action that he had set down for the Holy See and his legates: the complete destruction of Raimundo. The Count, his heart filled with suspicions, hastened to leave the Eternal City out of "fear of falling ill there."

Instead of preparing the council ordered by the Pope, the pontifical legates dedicated themselves to haranguing the population of Toulouse to rise up against their lord. A religious brotherhood, founded for the "conversion of the heretics," fought almost daily in the streets of Toulouse with those citizens still loyal to the Count.

According to Pierre de Vaux-Cernay, the monk who was the official historian and biographer of Simon de Montfort, "God opened a path for them, which indicated the means they needed to abort the legal exoneration of the Count." This "means" inspired by God for the legates consisted of demanding from Raimundo—again—that he expel *every* heretic from his lands. The good monk's admiring description of the pious lie, so mischievously prepared and so skillfully delivered, reveals for us the secrets of Roman diplomacy as it operated against the Albigenses: "O pious lie of the legate! O cheating piousness!"

Simon de Montfort also contributed to the humiliation of Raimundo VI. He traversed the length and breadth of the County of Toulouse with his pilgrims, bringing death and fire. When he laid siege to Minerve, the Abbot of Cîteaux supported him with fresh troops. Guilhem, lord of Minerve, wanted to hand over the city to the crusaders if they promised to leave his subjects alive.[25] Arnaud desperately wanted to kill all the heretics, but he believed that an order to kill all the besieged indiscriminately was incompatible with his dignity as a priest. Consequently, he decided to spare all Catholics and all heretics who would renounce their faith. Montfort's knights protested: "We have come to exterminate the heretics, not forgive them. Out of fear of death, you will see how they convert."

But Abbot Arnaud calmed them "I know them well enough. Not one will convert." He knew the heretics well. With the exception of three women, the rest refused to buy their lives with the renunciation of their faith and saved their executioners the trouble of pushing them into the blazing pyres—they threw themselves in.

Termès should be razed.

Termès was an impregnable fortress: an admirably fortified city with a periphery encircled by strong walls, and surrounded by a flowing river whose bed was washed granite.

Raimon, the elderly lord of the castle, a Son of Belissena, was ready to defend it. The "army of God" did not lose any time. But the situation became serious only after the arrival of the Bretons, French, and Germans.

A consummate specialist directed the attack: Guillaume, Archbishop of Paris, an expert in siege weaponry. He preached, reproached, gave instructions to carpenters and blacksmiths, and inflamed the soldiers. In a word, he knew his profession. He supervised the placement of the most sophisticated battering rams and catapults around the city.

Months went by. The besieged made fun of the vain efforts of the besiegers: "Our city is strong, you are wasting your time, and we have more food than you!"

The beleaguered townsfolk knew that hunger was wreaking havoc in the crusader camp. Leaves and grass substituted for the bread they needed. But God takes care of his pilgrims in arms. He prohibited the clouds from raining on the heretics. The wells of the besieged city began to run dry. They quenched their thirst with wine, but even this became scarce. Hunger is terrible, but thirst is even worse.

"Tomorrow, we will surrender," Raimon, the lord of the city, told the crusaders.

But Raimon let the whole morning pass. From the keep of his castle, he looked toward the Corbières, and saw a pale, small cloud floating over the Bugaratsch. He knew what it meant.

The cloud got progressively bigger and darker, until the sky was covered. Then a cloudburst brought down a deluge of water. Those half dead from thirst drank buckets of the divine liquid—this would bring their destruction. Dysentery broke out across the city and began to cut down its inhabitants. In a state of panic, the defenders of Termès fought to escape the death that surrounded them. A crusader realized that they were trying to flee during the darkness of night, and alerted the camp.

And once again, the fires blazed.

Montfort returned triumphantly to Carcassonne. Raimon de Termès was thrown into a dungeon. Many years later, he was pardoned. But when his son went down to get his father out of that tomb, he found only the bones of his skeleton behind its walls.

In the meantime, at the request of the Pope, the legates were obliged to convoke a council in Saint Gilles in September 1210. Cold and impassive, they informed the Count of Toulouse that he had not complied with his oath because he had not expelled *every* heretic, and that consequently it was not possible for them to exonerate a perjurer of the accusation of murder. Without listening to his defense, they excommunicated him again.

Confronted with such a miserable fraud, a man with a more energetic character would have probably become furious. Instead, Raimundo burst into tears. His judges interpreted this as another proof of his "congenital evil."

At the petition of the Pope, the legates were obliged to hold another conference, which took place in Arles in January 1211.[26] While they made Raimundo wait "terrified" before the closed doors, the legates cooked up new conditions, knowing full well that the Count would refuse them:

> The Count of Toulouse shall dismiss all his troops. He shall hand over all persons who they designate as heretics to the clergy. Henceforth, there will be only two types of meat authorized in the County of Toulouse. Henceforth, all inhabitants, nobles, and plebeians shall no longer be fashionably dressed; instead they will have to wear dark habits of thick cloth. All the fortifications of the cities and castles shall be dismantled. The nobles, who were until now residents of cities, can only live in flat lands with the peasants. Every head of a family will have to contribute four silver escudos annually to the legates. Simon de Montfort will have the right of passage through Raimundo's estates, and if something is taken, the Count of Toulouse will have no right of recourse. The Count shall serve in Palestine with the Templars or the Knights of Saint John, and cannot return until authorized by the legates. His possessions shall belong to the abbot of Cîteaux and Simon de Montfort all the time that they wish.

This ignominious humiliation awoke the courage that had long been dormant in Raimundo. He finally understood that it was impossible to negotiate with such adversaries, who were lacking fundamental honesty. He had the conditions, which the legates had imposed on him with their hatred and arrogance, published throughout his realm. The effect they produced was stronger than a call to arms.

"We prefer to abandon our country with our Count than to submit to priests and Frenchmen!" exclaimed Raimundo's vassals. The merchants of Toulouse, the Counts of Foix and Comminges, and all the Sons of Belissena promised to help Raimundo. Even the Catholic prelates, who disapproved of this ungodly crusade, publicly supported the disgraced Count.

With a redoubled fervor, the legates preached the crusade in the entire Western world. They managed to recruit fresh troops in Germany and Lombardy. Simon needed reinforcements; he wanted to take Lavaur. The crusaders, in the name of the Son of God who had died on the cross, promised to take bloody revenge on Lavaur. The sovereign of this city, a Belisseno, had once remarked on looking at the cross, "Shall this sign never be for me a means of salvation!"

Lavaur was one of the most heavily fortified cities in Occitania.[27] But there was nobody to direct its defense. The lord of the castle had fallen in Carcassonne, and his wife Donna Geralda was a weak woman.

The city was filled with troubadours who had fled, outlaw knights, and Cathars who had only just escaped the stake.

When Donna Geralda's brother Améric learned that Simon de Montfort had threatened his paternal city, he galloped to the defense of his sister, his people, and his country. Although the crusaders had already begun their assault, he managed to enter Lavaur.

Meanwhile, Montfort was taking great care of his troops. He awaited the arrival of his German troops who had passed Carcassonne and were fast approaching.

These Germans would never arrive. The Count of Foix inflicted an overwhelming and devastating victory on them. Two-thirds of these pilgrims were lying on the ground, dead or wounded. The rest were chased into the forests by the Count of Foix's troops. One of these pilgrims took refuge in a chapel. The Crown Prince of Foix followed him.

"Who are you?" the young count asked him.

"I am a pilgrim, and priest."

"Show it!"

The German took off his hood and showed his bald head. The young prince of Foix split his skull with his broadsword.

Montfort had two mobile assault towers constructed, and on the top of one of them he affixed a crucifix as a good luck charm. A stone launched by a catapult in the town tore Montfort's arm off. "And those dogs," wrote the chronicler, "started to laugh and shout, as if they had obtained a great victory. But the Crucified will miraculously avenge himself, because the day of the Finding of the Holy Cross, he will punish them for this action."

The mobile towers could not approach Lavaur's walls because a deep ditch encircled the city. The crusaders threw all the stakes, tree trunks, and branches they could find into it, so the towers could advance. But the defenders used iron harpoons to fish for the assailants, throwing them off the towers and sending them hurtling to the ground. As the situation in the town became more critical, the defenders dug tunnels under the walls and brought tree trunks into the city. The towers fell apart. During the night, the most daring tried to set fire to the assault machinery, but the German counts and their soldiers were able to thwart their plans.

Montfort and the legates were becoming demoralized. Everything they threw into the ditches disappeared during the night. Finally, a crafty crusader came up with the idea to fill the subterranean gallery with firewood and wet leaves and set fire to it in order to fill it with smoke. They put the proposal into practice, and the towers advanced yet again. But a hail of stones rained down upon the attackers, and the defenders poured pots of boiling tar, boiling oil, and molten lead on them from the parapets of the walls.

Then a fresh miracle occurred: the legates and the bishops of Carcassonne, Toulouse, and Paris sang the hymn of the crusade, the *Veni Creator Spiritus*. Following this, a wall collapsed after being struck by a ballista. Petrified by the pilgrims' singing, without any further resistance, the defenders of Lavaur let the enemy enter the city and clap them in irons.

As predicted by the chronicler, Lavaur fell on the day of the Finding of the Holy Cross, May 3, 1211. During two months the city faced 15,000 crusaders. Simon de Montfort, French and German nobles, abbots, monks, burgers, day laborers, serfs, and gypsies: The army of Christ made its entry into the conquered city. Regardless of their confession, age, or sex, all inhabitants were executed.

When a crusader knight learned that a large number of women and children were hidden in a cellar, he asked Simon de Montfort to spare the weakest. Simon agreed. This knight, whose name was not important enough to be related by the two chroniclers of the siege— neither the monk-historian Vaux Cernay nor the troubadour-historian Guillermo de Tudela—is the only "honorable man" in the crusade against the Grail.

Améric de Montréal, the sovereign's brother, and eighty knights, nobles, and troubadours were led to the place of execution. The gallows were prepared. Améric was the first to be hanged. The gigantic scaffold, which was meant to support the weight of eighty men, broke with just one. The carpenters hadn't built it properly. Montfort didn't want to wait, so he ordered his henchmen to cut their throats.

A woman in chains was standing with the chiefs of the crusade: Donna Geralda, the sovereign of Lavaur.

They threw Donna Geralda in a well
They covered her with stones
Having in it lament and sin,
Because there was nobody, take good notice of it,
Who would leave their house without receiving hospitality?

GUILLERMO DE TUDELA

Donna Geralda was thrown in a well, and covered with stones until her moans were no longer heard. She died twice, because she carried a child in her.

They lit a pyre, a fire for rejoicing: they had managed to capture four hundred Cathars. Those who were unable to recite the *Ave Maria* were taken to the pyre "in an ecstatic state of jubilation."

The happiness the martyrs felt to finally leave this Hell was greater than that felt by their executioners. Giving each other the kiss of peace, they threw themselves into the flames to the cry of "God is Love!" The mothers closed the eyes of their children until the fire closed them forever, and they discovered eternal paradise.

Like an accusing finger pointing to an unpolluted sky, Montségur rose to the west on a towering and commanding rock above the clouds of blood, pyres, and cities in flames: an accusing finger that at the same time pointed to the place where there were only light, love, and justice.

"Lord, forgive them, because they know not what they do. But I tell thee: they will inflict death upon you and think that they are doing something to please God. If you remain loyal to the death, I will give you the crown of eternal life, *Dieus vos benesiga* . . ." So Guilhabert de Castres consoled the terrorized Cathars in the "holy fortress" that dominated the gorges of the Tabor.

After the fall of Lavaur, the crusaders committed fresh atrocities. When they skirted the forest where six thousand German pilgrims had been roundly defeated, Fulk, the bishop of Toulouse (previously a troubadour whom Dante had transported to Paradise), believed he saw a halo and communicated this new miracle to Pope Innocent III.[28] But the Pope had long realized that his "vicars," blinded by fanaticism and ambition, had gone too far. Pope Innocent III understood. He wanted to be God, but he was forced to recognize that he was nothing other than a man, a magician no doubt, but one who could no longer dismiss the spirits that he had conjured.

> Before the image of Christ and in the silence of the night
> Innocent knelt and prayed aloud:
> Did he feel, perhaps the horror of the silence
> That he cast over the world?
> He raised his look to the image of God,
> Whose love and tenderness terrorized him.
> While he thinks about what he did
> In the bloodthirsty way he led the world.
>
> He looks intensely into the face of the image,
> A moth blocked the light
> And everything around him turned dark
> And silent, because he poses no more questions to the image
>
> Soon he sees other lights that rise
> And other crosses that cannot hide
> The flames of the Provence show
> The crosses on the chests of the executioners
>
> The ruins collapse, the swords resonate,
> And the savage crackle of the fire,
> He listens how his name is cursed
> When this horrible vision assaults him
> He presses his conscience in his fist
> And impassive, mumbles: Amen, Amen.

LENAU, *THE ALBIGENSES*

If metempsychosis exists, the soul of Diocletian must have reincarnated in Pope Innocent III. The God for whom the pilgrims of the crusade fought against the Albigenses was not Yahweh, Baal, or Thor, nor even Lucifer. It was Moloch, the god of the valley of the son of Hinnom.

Until the Albigensian crusade, Provence and Languedoc resembled a "tranquil island, happy and flourishing in the heart of a sea of storms." The bloody atrocities of the holy war against the heretics constituted one of the largest and most horrible tragedies that the world has ever witnessed.

A lovely, rich country; a people tolerant, free, and not submerged in darkness or fear at the end of the medieval world; the only civilization, and perhaps the most Christian one, that was a worthy successor to the "simplicity and grandeur" of the ancients—exterminated by a theocrat and jealous, sanctimonious neighbors.

Christ planted love; the world harvested hatred. Christ wanted to repeal ancient laws and erect a new order: but the world made a New Alliance crueler than the old one.

Along with the flower and cream of the country, the flames of the crusade against the Albigenses burned off the tender plants of its poetry, which began to wither away. With the Albigensian crusade, the feeling of absolute tranquility and the spiritual life of pleasure and love disappeared. Occitania lost its spell of peace and well-being, an enchantment that gave way to bigotry and the thirst for blood. The war against the Albigenses gave the coup de grâce to Occitan poetry, which never flourished again.

> We walk sad and led astray
> The splendid tents are lost dreams
> The soft chairs and sumptuous settings
> The bells of silver and the golden bridles.
>
> The arrows are pointed now to the heart
> Not the songs with enjoyment and sweet pain.
> Happy times that we lose!
> Sad days that buried the song!
>
> His two harps lay against the tree
> Until, alone, they rot and corrode:
> The cords tremble with the blowing of the wind
> Their multicolored framework flutters.
>
> LENAU, THE ALBIGENSES

The crusade against the Albigenses continued rumbling for a long time. I only wanted to relate the facts up to this point. And I did so, despite my limitations, in the most faithful way that I could. Raimon-Roger de Carcassonne, Améric de Montréal, and Donna Geralda de Lavaur are only three of the hundreds of thousands of martyrs of the Languedoc.

But Raimundo de Toulouse, Pedro de Aragon, and Simon de Montfort remained alive![29]

The walls of Montségur were still standing, and Esclarmonde continued guarding the Holy Grail!

Pedro de Aragon, who enjoyed the sympathy of the Vatican, came down openly in favor of Toulouse. As an Occitan monarch, he could not remain impassive at the Vatican's crimes against Raimundo. Moreover, faced with the ever-growing power of Simon de Montfort, his own interests were now in danger. Simon assigned the conquered estates exclusively to the French, and organized the subjugated provinces in a French way. What may have finally determined Pedro's anti-Rome attitude was the terrible end of Raimon-Roger. As we know, Béziers was a vassal of King Pedro of Aragon, who was at the same time connected to the young viscount by family bonds and deep friendship.

Pedro was revered as the Occitan knight without fear or blight. He showed his religious fervor in 1204 when, in the company of a brilliant retinue, he sailed to Rome to swear fidelity to Innocent. He was crowned with unleavened bread, and received from the Pope the scepter, cape, and other items of royal insignia, which with great veneration he deposited on the altar of Saint Peter. He gave him the gift of his kingdom, which inspired the Pope to present Pedro with a sword and the title of "flag bearer" of the Church.

By virtue of Pedro's good relations with the Vatican, his ambassadors lodged a formal complaint with Innocent about the methods of the legates, methods that the king considered arbitrary, unjust, and contrary to the authentic interests of the Catholic religion. Following this, he traveled to Toulouse with the intention of intervening in favor of his brother-in-law Raimundo, who had been ruined. His ambassadors induced Innocent to order Montfort to return all the assets that he had confiscated from non-heretics, and to warn Arnaud not to impede the crusade that the Roman curia was preparing against the Saracens by prolonging hostilities in the County of Toulouse—a crusade that eventually concluded victoriously with the battle at Las Navas de Tolosa in 1212, which broke the power of the Moors in Spain. There, he stood out above all the other kings and nobles and so could add "El Católico" to his name.

The manner in which the Pope proceeded, together with the energetic mediation of Pedro, produced a profound impression among the legates, and galvanized the entire hierarchy of Languedoc into action to overcome the crisis.

In January 1213, the King of Aragon gave the pontifical legates a petition that implored them to extend grace more than justice to those nobles who had lost their estates. He presented an act of abdication signed by Raimundo and confirmed by the city of Toulouse, as well as corresponding "abdications" of the Counts of Foix and Comminges, which handed the dominions and rights over to Pedro. They recognized the jurisdiction of the legates to act as they wished, even if their actions were contrary to the orders of the Pope. Only when the Occitan nobles gave the Church satisfaction could their rights be reestablished. Until then, no submission was complete and no guarantees could be sufficient. But the prelates were far too submerged in their fanaticism, ambition, and hatred. The destruction of the House of Toulouse was far too costly for them to be stopped now; they were committed to prosecuting their plan to the bitter end.

The guarantees Pedro offered in his petition did not receive the minimum consideration by the legates. Arnaud de Cîteaux wrote an extremely stern letter to the King of Aragon that threatened him with excommunication if he did not break off his relations with those excommunicated for heresy or accused of it.

Meanwhile, both parties proceeded without waiting for a decision from Rome. In France, the crusade was being preached yet again. The Dauphin Louis, son of Philip, took up the cross together with French barons. In the other camp, King Pedro had strengthened his relations with Raimundo and the excommunicated nobles even further.

In September 1213, a decisive battle took place between the crusaders and the Occitanian coalition at Muret, not far from Toulouse. The crusaders won. Miracles were on their side; incense and supplications were more important than the patriotism and mysticism of the Occitanians. If we are to believe the official chronicler, Monfort's victory at Muret was due to a miracle: To assure themselves that Pedro was on their side, the Albigensian nobles gave him all their wives and daughters the night before the battle. He was so exhausted the next morning that he couldn't keep himself standing during the celebration of the Mass, much less participate in combat. Pedro of Aragon was killed in the battle at the hands of two famous French knights, Allain de Roucy and Florent de Ville.

Simon de Montfort died in 1216. The Abbot Arnaud de Cîteaux, who in the meantime had been named archbishop of Narbonne, and who was now his bitter enemy, had anathematized him. Apparently, this act signified the end of Montfort's power. After Muret, Toulouse rebelled against him. On the Day of Saint John in 1216, when he tried to reconquer the town, a stone thrown at him by a presumably feminine hand killed him. When the news that the "glorious paladin of Christ," the "New Maccabaeus," the "bastion of faith" had fallen as a martyr in the defense of religion, the mourning of all believers in the Western world was enormous.

Six years later, Raimundo VI, Count of Toulouse, Duke of Narbonne, and Marques of Provence, who had been converted into the most unfortunate and cursed monarch of the Western world, died.

When the abbot of Saint Cernin tried to administer the last rites to Raimundo, he could no longer speak. A Knight Hospitaler who was in the chamber threw his cape with a cross on the Count. He wanted his order to take charge of the burial in recognition of the inheritance that the Count had willed them. But the abbot of Saint Cernin threw off the cape, shouting that the count had died in his parish.

An inquest ordered by Pope Innocent IV in 1247 revealed that by virtue of the declarations of 120 witnesses, Raimundo had been "the most pious and merciful of all men, and a faithful servant of the Church." But nothing could change the awful reality that the mortal remains of the Count remained unburied in the convent of the Hospitalers, and eventually it became a source of food for mice. By the end of the seventeenth century, it was possible to observe only his skull as a "curiosity."

Paris and Rome continued preaching crusades against the Albigenses until 1229, the year when Raimundo VII of Toulouse and Saint Louis of France sat down for serious peace negotiations in Meaux; the treaties were solemnly ratified in Paris on April 12, 1229.

In a penitential habit, Raimundo had to kneel before the Papal legate outside Notre Dame and ask him for permission to enter the cathedral. In the atrium, they took his clothing and shoes from him and led him in a simple shirt before the altar where the excommunication was lifted and he had to swear to uphold the treaties. Later, they led him to the

Louvre, where as a condition of the treaties, he had to stay as a prisoner until the day of the wedding of his daughter Joana with the brother of King Louis, a child who was hardly over nine years old.

The conditions for peace were the following: Raimundo had to swear an oath of loyalty to the King and the Church, promise to root out the nest of heretics at Montségur, and offer a reward of two silver escudos to anyone who brought in a heretic dead or alive. Furthermore, he had to give to the churches and convents of Occitania ten thousand marks as an indemnity, and donate four thousand marks for the establishment of Catholic faculty in Toulouse. He was ordered to treat as friends those who had fought against him during the crusades. The walls of Toulouse and of thirty other cities and fortresses were to be demolished, and five castles were to be handed over to the King of France as a guaranty. It was implicitly admitted that the Count of Toulouse had lost his rights to all his estates. Saint Louis graciously left him with the territories of the former bishopric of Toulouse, but only under the condition that after his death they would pass to Raimundo's daughter and her husband, Louis' brother, and so belong forever to the royal French household. From the outset, the King reserved for himself the territories of the Duchy of Narbonne and the counties of Léley, Gévaudan, Viviers, and Lodève, while the marquisate of Provence to the east of the Rhône was left to the Church as a feudal estate. In this way, Raimundo lost two thirds of his dominions.[30]

In the other great cities of Occitania, which had previously been vassals of the Count of Toulouse (but in reality, virtually independent city-states), royal seneschals were instituted.

Raimundo had to take energetic steps to oblige all the vassals to recognize French domination, especially the Count of Foix, who was obliged to sign a humiliating peace treaty the following year. In this way, the sovereignty of the French crown was assured throughout the south of France. The Louvre had triumphed!

However, Rome still believed that the time to put away its weapons had not yet arrived.

Ay Toulouse and Provence!
And the land of Agen!

Béziers and Carcassonne!
How we saw you! How I see you
Ai! Tolosa e Provensa!
E la terra d'Agensa!
Bezers e Carcassey!
Quo os vi! Quo vos vey!

BERNARD SICARD DE MARJEVOLS[31]

There is a deep and silent cave in the forest,
Where the rays of the sun or the breeze of the wind never reach
It is where an old and exhausted beast drags itself
When it wants to die, hidden in the darkness,
Perhaps, we should learn more from the anguished death rattle
Of an animal than from the stars.

LENAU, THE ALBIGENSES

Part four

THE APOTHEOSIS OF THE GRAIL

———•———

ROME HAD MONOPOLIZED ORTHODOXY and the miraculous. As all chroniclers unanimously affirmed, the crusade against the Albigenses had concluded victoriously (of course!), thanks to the miracles the "God of Thunder" had conjured up for his combatants.

One night in 1170, Juana de Aza had a strange dream: The Spanish noblewoman fancied that she was carrying a dog in her body, and when she gave birth to it, it held a burning torch in its mouth which set the world ablaze. When Juana gave birth to a healthy boy and the priest baptized him with the name of Domingo, his godmother had a singular vision: She saw on the forehead of the just-baptized child a star that circled and illuminated all the Earth with its splendor.

We first met Saint Dominic in the year 1206; he was encouraging the demoralized legates of the Pope in Montpellier, and trying to prevent them from abandoning the task they had started: the conversion of the heretics. Then we found him in the council of Pamiers, together with the vexed monk who shouted to the arch-heretic Esclarmonde that instead of mixing in theological discussions, she should remain with her spindle. Finally, he was present at the establishment, not far from Montségur, of the convent of Notre Dame de Prouille, and participated in the search for converts among the Albigenses. We didn't mention that on one occasion in Lagrasse, near Carcassonne, he celebrated a mass on an improvised platform, while at its four corners, stakes had been prepared to burn the accursed heretics.

We are not going to describe which miracles helped him recruit friars for the convent at Prouille or obtain pontifical authorization for the Dominican Order and test how the prayer of the rosary of the Mother of God was absolutely essential for the eradication of the heresy. We are happy to say that almost daily, Saint Dominic brought the Evangelism of Salvation to the jailed heretics; people venerated him as a living saint, taking pieces of his habit as relics, and as the Dominican historian Tomas de Malvenda (1565–1628) noted, the founder of the Dominican Order also has the honor to be remembered as the founding father of the Inquisition.

The Inquisition was officially set up on April 20, 1233, a date that saw the publication of two bulls by Pope Gregory IX, which assigned the persecution of the heretics to the Dominican friars. Analysis of both Papal documents shows that the Pontifical Sovereign did not foresee the consequences of such an innovation.

In the first bull, the Pope insisted on the necessity of destroying the heresy regardless of the means, and of supporting the establishment of the Dominican Order. Then he turned to the bishops:

"We see you immersed in a vast accumulation of worries without being able to breathe under the pressure of these exhausting preoccupations. For it, we will help you carry your burden, and have decided to send preacher-friars against the heretics in France, and the neighboring provinces. For which we ask you, admonish you, exhort you and order you to give them a good welcome, and treat them well, and that you should favor, counsel and help them so that they can fulfill their mission."

Gregory's second bull was directed to the priors and friars of the preaching Order. It alluded to those lost children who continued to support the heretics, and said: "Consequently, I empower you with the faculty, where you preach, to defrock those clerics who, ignoring your warnings, refuse to renounce the defense of the heresy; I empower you with the faculty to proceed immediately against them, even if essential to recur [have recourse] to the secular arm [a euphemism for death by burning at the stake]."

When the Dominican Order received from the Holy See the mission to combat the heretics in the south of France, it found itself saddled with a task that was almost impossible to accomplish. Without any obstacles, from generation to generation, the heresy had established itself so firmly that it affected all social strata; this meant that the Dominicans had to systematically re-educate all of Occitania in the true faith.

Therefore, the Inquisitor was not supposed to impress people with fatuousness—his mission was to paralyze them with terror. The sumptuous garments, eye-catching processions, and escort of servants corresponded to the prelates. The Inquisitor wore the habit of his Order, and when he traveled, a few knights accompanied him to protect him and execute his orders. A few days before visiting a town or village, he would send word of his arrival to the ecclesiastical authorities, asking them to convoke the townsfolk at a predetermined hour in the marketplace. Those who obeyed this order were promised an indulgence. Those who did not were excommunicated.

The Inquisitor would direct his homily to the congregated population. Speaking of the true faith, whose expansion they had to support with all their strength, he exhorted the town's inhabitants to present themselves to him within a space of twelve days. They were to reveal all that they had learned or heard about anybody who could be suspected of heresy, and for what reasons. Those who did not present such a declaration were *ipso facto* excommunicated. Those who obeyed were compensated with an indulgence of three years.

We can imagine the shock that fell over a parish when, suddenly, an Inquisitor arrived and launched his proclamation. Nobody could really know what gossip circulated about him- or herself. "Finally parents were instigated to betray their own sons, sons their parents, husbands their wives, and wives their husbands," as Gregory IX said on one occasion.

Attending the inquest, apart from the Inquisitor and the bailiff, was a secretary who wrote down the proceedings as dictated by the Inquisitor "so that there would be a record in the best possible way." Let us have a look at one of these inquests just as the Toulouse Inquisitor Bernard Gui passed it on as a model, complete with comments pertinent to the case:

When a heretic appears for the first time, with airs of security as if convinced of his innocence. The first that I ask him is for what does he believe he has been called to declare.

The Accused: Sir, I wish that you would tell me the motive.

Me: You are accused of being a heretic, and to believe and teach things which our Holy Church does not permit.

The Accused (before such a question, they always raise their eyes to the sky and adopt a pious demeanor): God and my lord, you are the only one who knows that I am innocent, and that I have never professed another faith than that of true Christianity.

Me: You call your faith Christian because you hold ours for false and heretical. For this, I ask you if ever you have held another belief for more true than that which the Church of Rome considers true.

The Accused: I believe in the true faith, as the Roman Church teaches it.

Me: It is possible that some of your coreligionists live in Rome. It is this what you call the Roman Church. When I preach, it may occur that I speak of questions that are common to your faith and mine, like for example, that God exists, and so you believe something that I am preaching. And yet you could be a heretic, because you believe other things, which should not be believed.

The Accused: I believe in all what a Christian should believe.

Me: I know your tricks. What your sect believes is what, according to you, a Christian should believe. We are wasting our time with a sterile discussion. Tell me simply and fully: Do you believe in one God, Father, Son and the Holy Spirit?

The Accused: Yes!

Me: Do you believe in Jesus Christ, who was born of the Virgin Mary, who suffered, rose from the dead, and ascended to Heaven?

The Accused: Yes!

Me: Do you believe in a mass celebrated by a priest, where the bread and wine convert, through the power of God in the body, and blood of Christ?

The Accused: Why should I not believe it?

Me: I did not ask why you should believe it, but if you believe it.

The Accused: I believe all what you and other good doctors order me to believe.

Me: These good doctors are the teachers of your sect. If my belief is the same as yours, you also believe me.

The Accused: From the moment when you teach me what is good for me, I believe as you do.

Me: You hold a thing for good if I teach it like it is taught by your doctors. Tell me then, do you believe that the body of Our Lord is found on the altar?

The Accused (quickly): Yes!

Me: You know that all bodies are the work of our Lord. For this, I asked you if the body that is on the altar is the body of the Lord who was born of the Virgin Mary, who died on the cross, resurrected from the dead and rose to Heaven.

The Accused: And you Sir don't believe it?

Me: I believe with complete certainty.

The Accused: Me too.

Me: You believe what I believe. But I haven't asked you that. What I asked you is if you believe it?

The Accused: If you twist my words, I really don't know how I should answer. I am a simple man who never studied. I plead with you Sir, not to make a trap for me with my own words.

Me: If you are a simple man, answer me simply without evading the question.

The Accused: With pleasure.

Me: Would you like to swear that you never learned anything that contradicts the faith that we hold for the true one?

The Accused (becoming pale): If I have to swear, I will do it.

Me: I wasn't asking that if you had to swear but rather if you liked to swear.

The Accused: If you order me to swear, I will swear.

Me: I don't want to force you to swear. You consider the swearing of an oath as a sin, and you will blame me if I force you to do it. But if you wish to swear, I will accept your oath.

The Accused: But why should I swear if you do not order me to do it?

Me: Why? To free you from the suspicion that you are a heretic.

The Accused: Sir, I do not know how to swear an oath if you do not teach me.

Me: If I were the person to have to swear, I would raise my fingers and say: Never have I ever had anything to do with the heresy nor believed anything that was contrary to the true faith. As it is the truth, shall God help me!

To avoid swearing an oath properly, and yet to make us believe that somehow he had sworn the oath, the accused stuttered. Some heretics even twist their words in such a way as to give the impression that they are swearing or converting the oath into a prayer, like for example: "Shall God help me, because I am not a heretic!" When asked if he had sworn an oath, the accused answered: "Didn't you hear me swear?" If pressed, irremissibly, he appealed to the judge for compassion: "Sir, if I have done something bad, I will do penitence for it with pleasure. But help me free myself from the accusation that, being innocent, weighs on me!"

An energetic Inquisitor should never let himself be influenced by such methods. On the contrary, it is absolutely necessary that he act with decision to force such people to admit and publicly renounce their error with a view—if it is later proven that the oath was false—to hand them over to the secular arm. When someone is ready to swear that he is not a heretic, I usually say: "If you are swearing to escape the stake, neither ten, one hundred, or one thousand oaths are sufficient, because you are dispensed from the oaths that you have been forced to swear. As I have in my hands proof of your heretical escapades, your oaths will not keep you from being burned at the stake. The only thing you will do is to overload your conscience, without saving your life. If, by contrast, you confess your error, I could concede certain measures of grace."

I have seen people who, pressured in this manner, ended by confessing.

The oath of a certain Joan Tesseire of Toulouse who was accused of heresy has come to our attention:

"I am not a heretic, because I have my wife, and I sleep with her, I have children, and I eat meat, I lie, swear, and I am a Christian believer; because it is all true, shall God help me!"[1]

If the heretical "believers" allowed themselves to be converted, and renounced the heresy while promising to tell all the truth and denouncing their accomplices, the punishment that awaited them was relatively light: flagellation, pilgrimages, or a fine.

Flagellation consisted in the penitent, stripped to the waist, presenting himself with a stick to the parish priest, who then beat him in the presence of the faithful after celebrating Mass every Sunday during the Epistle and Evangelism.

On the first Sunday of every month after Mass, the heretic was required to visit every house where he had associated with another heretic, where the priest would beat him again. During processions, at each station he was thanked with more strokes.

There were large and small *pilgrimages*. The large pilgrimages had, for obligatory destinations, Rome, Santiago de Compostela, Saint Thomas of Canterbury, and the Three Kings of Cologne. Such pilgrimages, because they had to be done on foot, took several years. On one occasion, an elderly man of more than ninety years had to undertake a pilgrimage to Santiago de Compostela for merely having exchanged a few words with a heretic. The so-called small pilgrimages were to Montpellier, Saint Gilles, and Tarascon on the Rhône, Bordeaux, Chartres, and finally Paris. Upon his return, every pilgrim was obliged to present a certificate to the Inquisitor that proved that he had accomplished the pilgrimage as ordered.

In cases where the confession and renunciation were not obtained in a spontaneous manner, the accused was punished with one of the *poenae confusibiles*. The most common among these punishments, and at the same time the most humiliating, was to *wear the cross*. The heretic was forced to wear on his chest and back, yellow crosses that measured five centimeters wide and ten high [two inches wide and ten high]. During a procession, if the convert had committed perjury, they added crosses from the forearm to the upper arm. In this way, the cross carrier was exposed to the mockery of the townsfolk, and had difficulties surviving. A certain Arnaud Isarn complained on one occasion that he could hardly make ends meet, although he had worn the crosses for less than a year. And yet, being condemned to wear the cross was almost always for life. The cross that in the times of the crusades to the Holy Land had been worn with pride on the shield or on clothing was converted into a symbol of infamy.[2]

Once detained and jailed, the "believers" were exhorted by the Inquisitors to convert, and were interrogated in the presence of at least two witnesses. If they were not willing to confess and denounce their heretical brothers, they were handed over to the torturers.

Pope Clement V declared in 1306 that in Carcassonne the Inquisitors had managed to make the prisoners recognize their guilt by not only denying them sleep and food, but also by applying torture. The canons of the Church had expressly forbidden its clerics to use torture (and even to witness it), so to overcome this difficulty, Pope Alexander IV granted special faculties to the Inquisitors so they could absolve each other of these ecclesiastical transgressions.

Before beginning the torture session, the instruments of suffering were shown and explained to the accused: the rack, the seesaw, the hot coals, and the so-called "Spanish boot." Then the Inquisitors would admonish him to make a full confession. If the heretic refused, the henchman stripped him, and the Inquisitors would again beseech him to talk. If he still refused, torment was applied. According to the rules, the accused could only be tortured once; but this was re-interpreted so they could use it "once for each charge in the accusation."

Confirmation was required after every confession obtained in the torture chamber. Generally, the accused was read the statement, and asked if he agreed. Silence signified agreement. If he withdrew the confession, the accused could be handed over to the torturers to "continue with the torture"—not to "repeat it," as they said expressly—implying that the accused had not been tortured enough. Using such methods, the Inquisitors could condemn anybody they wanted.[3]

When a heretic showed remorse after having been condemned, or if he was a perfectus who renounced the heresy, the torment of the *murus* [wall] was inflicted upon him—as a precaution in case he had confessed out of fear of death. It could be *murus largus* or *murus strictus*. At any rate, in both cases the only nourishment was bread and water. The Inquisitors called it the "bread of pain and the water of affliction." The *murus largus* was a relatively benign penalty of prison while the *murus strictus* was comprised of all that human cruelty is capable of imagining. The victim was locked in a tiny cell without windows and chained to the wall by his hands and feet. His food was passed through a small opening built for this purpose. *Murus strictus* was the tomb they ironically called *vade in pacem*: go in peace.

Priestly rules demanded that these jails be as small and dark as possible. The Inquisitors' requirements were satisfied at any cost, and they even managed to invent a crueler prison penalty, which they called *murus strictissimus*. Understandably, the documents of the Inquisition silenced details of the torments of their victims—something that we should be grateful for.

When a heretical perfectus remained obstinately loyal to his faith, he was handed over to the secular arm. If the civil authorities were slow in executing a sentence of death against a heretic, the Church used, without any circumspection, all recourses at its disposal to force them to obey.[4]

According to the Toulouse Inquisitor Bernard Gui, the principles for guiding his colleagues during the exercise of their pious duties were the following: "The goal of the Inquisition is the extermination of the heresy; very well then, this cannot happen if there are heretics, and these cannot be destroyed if those who protect and help them are not destroyed: this can happen only through two ways: converting the heretics to the true faith or handing them over to the secular arm for their cremation."

Before handing a heretic over to the civilian authorities in consonance with canon law, they were asked to apply the punishment in such a way as to avoid *implying* any danger to body and life. This petition was nothing more than a hypocritical dirty trick of the Roman canons, as the words of Saint Thomas Aquinus, written with absolute sincerity, show:

> Under no circumstances is it possible to be indulgent with the heretics. The compassion, full of love of the Church certainly permits that they should be admonished, but in the case that they reveal themselves as obstinate, they have to be handed over to the secular arm so that death gets them out of this world. Isn't this the proof of the infinite love of the Church? For this reason, a repented heretic is always admitted for penitence, and because of this, his life is respected. But if he converts into a relapsed heretic, he could truly accede to penitence for the good of his soul, but he can not save himself from the penalty of death.[5]

The Inquisitors were always very clear: Handing a heretic over to the secular arm meant the death penalty. To avoid profaning their churches, the announcements of the death sentences were never displayed inside their sacred walls; instead they were made public on the main square where the execution pyres were set ablaze and the victims burned to ashes.

The Church considered the incineration of heretics an act of piety of such importance that full indulgences were given to those who brought firewood to the stake. Even more, it warned all Christians that they had the grave obligation to help exterminate the heretics; it taught them to denounce these heretics to the ecclesiastical authorities without any type of consideration, human or divine. No family relation could serve as an excuse: The son had to betray his father; the husband would become an accomplice if he did not hand over his heretical wife for death in the flames.

"The names of all the heretics are not inscribed in the book of life. Their bodies were burned here and their souls are tormented in Hell," a jubilant orthodox chronicler wrote.

The Church wasn't satisfied with letting its power be felt by the living. Its cruel hand also extended to the dead.

As an example of the *condemnation of dead heretics,* we must include what Pope Stephen VII did in 897. The Vicar of Christ had the cadaver of his predecessor, Pope Formosus, dug up in order to condemn him as a heretic; he cut off two fingers from his right hand and had the body thrown in the Tiber. Some compassionate people managed to fish the body of the heretical Holy Father from the waters and buried him again on dry land. The following year, Pope John IX declared the trial of Formosus void, and proclaimed in a synod that nobody could be condemned after death because the accused had to have the possibility of defending himself. Despite this, Pope Sergius III ordered Formosus' body exhumed again in 905. Dressing the corpse in all Papal ornaments, he had it seated on a throne and solemnly condemned again; then they decapitated it, cut another three fingers from its hand, and threw the body in the Tiber. When the remains of the dishonored Holy Father were pulled from the river by some fishermen and taken to Saint Peter's Church, it is said that the images of the saints inclined to them and saluted Formosus with veneration.

Of course, because the decrees of the Curia contradicted each other, the Inquisitors were free to choose those that allowed exhuming the dead whose heresy had only been discovered after their death and treating them as if they were alive. In the end, they burned corpses and scattered their ashes to the four winds. If the civil authorities were reticent to exhume a heretic, the priests threatened to exclude them from the ecclesiastical community, deprive them of the sacraments, and finally, to accuse them of heresy.

One of the first official acts of Pope Innocent III was the publication of the following decree:

> In the nations under our jurisdiction, the assets of the heretics should be confiscated.[6] Regarding other nations, we order those princes and sovereigns to adopt the same measures if they do not wish to see themselves forced to do it by the dispositions of censure of the Church. We equally expect that they should not return their assets to those heretics who have converted, even out of pity with them. In the same way that, according to civil law, the crime of lèse-majesté is punished with death and confiscation of assets, leaving children alive only through grace and pity, those who distance themselves from the faith and blaspheme against the Son of God should be separated from Christ and stripped of their Earthly goods. In fact, isn't it a greater crime to attack Spiritual Majesty than the civil?

This Papal decree was incorporated in canon law. Following the doctrine of Roman law on the crime of lèse-majesté, it postulated that a heretic had lost his right to his assets. This unquenchable thirst for the worldly goods of its unfortunate victims was especially repugnant because it originated in the Church. To a point, its actions would appear to exempt the civilian authorities from guilt; however, little by little, they too became accustomed to confiscating assets—with no less fervor for all that the heretics possessed. Never in history has a more repulsive form of profiteering from the misfortunes of our fellow man ever existed: Following the steps of the Inquisition, these vultures fattened themselves on the misery that they had created.

Thanks to such methods, the income of the Bishopric of Toulouse had grown in such a way that Pope John XXII could create six new bishoprics in 1317. When the Pope died, as one of the chroniclers of the era related, he left a personal fortune of twenty-five million gold florins. There were historians who, basing their work on ingenuity and logic, reduced this sum to one million. They established as a fact that the Pope's annual income was two hundred thousand gold florins, but that half of it, more or less, was destined for his family budget.

A statistic on the activities undertaken by the Toulouse Inquisitor Bernard Gui between 1308 and 1322 helps us understand how the persecution of the heretics could absorb such large sums of money:

> Handed over to the secular arm and burned: 40 people
>
> Remains exhumed and burned: 67 people
>
> Jailed: 300 people
>
> Exhumation of the rests of persons who were previously jailed: 21 people
>
> Condemned to wear crosses: 138 people
>
> Condemned to pilgrimages: 16 people
>
> Banished to the Holy Land: 1 person
>
> At large: 36 people
>
> Total: 619 people

Under Pope John XXII (whose successor Benedict XII cleared the heretics out of the caves of Sabarthès), a method was used that was enthusiastically imitated by the Inquisitors.[7] For reasons unknown, while he was still the son of a small artisan of Cahors, a town to the north of Toulouse, the future pope harbored an insatiable hatred for Hugo Gerold, the bishop of his native town. Once on the Papal throne, John lost no time letting his power be felt. In Avignon, he solemnly removed the unfortunate prelate from all his functions and had him condemned to life in prison. But he still wasn't satisfied. Accusing him of having conspired against the life of the Pope, John had the bishop skinned alive and then thrown into the fire.

Of course, Pope Urban VI had to act in an even more un-Christian way.[8] When six cardinals were suspected of conspiring against him in 1385, he had them arrested and thrown into a pit. The methods used by the Inquisition in its trials were applied against these unfortunate prelates: they were abandoned to hunger, cold, and worms. A confession was obtained from the Bishop of Aquilea under torture that implicated the other five cardinals. Because they never ceased to proclaim their innocence, they too were tortured. The only thing their tormentors could get was the desperate auto-accusation that they were suffering just punishment for the evils that they had inflicted, by order of Pope Urban, on other archbishops, bishops, and prelates. When the Cardinal of Venice's turn came for torture, Pope Urban entrusted its application to a former pirate, whom he had named prior of the Sicilian Order of the Knights of

Saint John. Urban ordered him to continue torturing the Cardinal until he—the Pope—could hear the cries of the victim. The torment lasted from the early hours of the morning until lunchtime.

During the Cardinal's torture, the Holy Father strolled underneath the window of the torture chamber, reciting the breviary aloud so that his voice would remind the torturer of his obligations. But the only thing they could get out of the old and sick Cardinal of Venice was this exclamation: "Christ suffered for us!" The accused remained in custody in their inhuman prison until the day when Carlos de Durazo, the lord of Naples and Hungary, tried to free the Cardinals. Pope Urban fled, but took his victims with him. On the road, the Bishop of Aquilea, weakened by the constant torture, could not keep up with the pace of the forced march. The Pope killed him and left his corpse, unburied, by the roadside. The remaining Cardinals were dragged to Genoa, and in a deplorable state thrown into a repulsive dungeon; their situation was such that the town authorities, moved to compassion, asked for clemency for them. But the Pope remained steadfast. Finally, due to the energetic intervention of Richard II of England, Urban had no other choice than to free the English Cardinal Adam Astom; but the other four princes of the church were never seen again.

Such was the example that those most Christian shepherds, seated on Peter's Holy See, gave their flock. Is it surprising that the Cathars rejected with horror the Church's doctrine and applied Chapter 17 of the Apocalypse to Rome?[9]

> . . . and I saw a woman sitting upon a scarlet-colored Wild Beast,
> full of names of blasphemy, having seven heads and ten horns.
> And the woman was arrayed in purple and scarlet, and decked
> with gold and precious stones and pearls: having a golden cup in
> her hand full of abominations and filthiness of her fornication;
> And upon her forehead a name written, a mystery, "Babylon the
> Great, the Mother of the harlots and the abominations of the
> Earth."
>
> And I saw the woman drunken with the blood of the saints, and
> with the blood of the witnesses of Jesus.

And the woman which thou sawest is that great city which
reigneth over the kings of the Earth.

THE APOCALYPSE, 17:3–7, 18

The night following Ascension Day in 1242, the world was jolted by the news that eleven Inquisitors had been assassinated in Avignonet, a small town on the outskirts of Toulouse.[10]

The exasperation of the people with the congregation of the Holy Office had reached the boiling point. In 1233, the inhabitants of Cordès had killed two Dominicans. The following year, a revolt broke out in Albi when the Inquisitor, Arnaud Catalá, ordered the exhumation of a heretic whom he had condemned. When the workers who were given the task refused to carry out such degrading work, Catalá began to exhume the body with his garden hoe. The indignant inhabitants of Albi pounced on him, shouting, "Kill him! He has no right to live!"

The same year, the fury of the population of Toulouse was unleashed due to the following circumstances: The Bishop and the Dominican friars had solemnly celebrated the canonization of Saint Dominic. At the moment when the Bishop left the Church for the refectory of the Dominican convent where they were going to have their banquet, someone told him that a woman had just received the consolamentum. Immediately, the Bishop, in the company of the prior of the Dominican Order and some friars, set off for the house of the heretic. The friends of the dying woman could only whisper, "The Bishop is coming!" Convinced that she was the heretic, the dying woman confessed to the prince of the Church that she was, and that she wanted to continue being one. Then the Bishop had the dying woman taken from her bed and thrown into a blazing fire where she perished. This done, he returned with the prior and the friars to the refectory to enjoy the banquet that was awaiting them.

In the spring of 1242, a tribunal of the Inquisition arrived in Avignonet, after having sowed terror throughout the region, almost causing its depopulation. This holy tribunal was comprised of two Inquisitors, two Dominican friars, a Franciscan, a prior of the Benedictines, an archdeacon (a troubadour in other times, of whose poetic art only an obscene song has reached us), a helper, a notary, and two ushers. When the arrival of the Inquisitors was announced to the lord of the area, Count Raimon de Alfar urgently dispatched a messenger to Montségur, asking the Sons of Belissena for help.[11] A group of armed knights under the command of Peire-Roger de Mirepoix left the heretical fortress and camped in a forest not far from Avignonet, where they waited for nightfall.

Raimon de Alfar, grandson of the then-Count of Toulouse, received the Inquisitors and invited them to spend the night. They wanted to begin their terrifying judgments over the trembling inhabitants of Avignonet the following morning.

Well into the night, the knights of Montségur—twelve men armed to the teeth—left their forest camp and crept toward the great door of the castle. One of them whispered: "Now they are drinking. . . ."

"Now they are going to bed; they haven't bolted the doors!"

The Inquisitors remained in the main salon of the castle, where they ensconced themselves as if they had a premonition of the danger that was closing in on them. The knights of Montségur, who were joined by the Count of Alfar, twenty-five burghers from Avignonet, and a serf in the service of the Inquisitors, became impatient. They broke down the doors, invaded the salon, and killed the Inquisitors.

As they were returning to Montségur, a Catholic priest who had already learned of the murders gave them shelter in the Castle of Saint Felix.

When the news of the murder of the Inquisitors reached Rome, the College of Cardinals declared that the victims had died as martyrs in the cause of Christ. Pope Pius IX canonized them in 1866, as they had demonstrated their holiness with the performance of multiple miracles.

During the crusades, the promontory of Montségur represented both "Mount Salvatge" and a "Mount Salvat" to the last free knights, the ladies praised in songs by troubadours, and the Cathars who escaped the stake. Over forty years, the towering Pyrenean rock crowned by the "Supreme Temple of the Minne" had challenged the fury of the French invaders and Catholic pilgrims. In 1209, Guy, the brother of Simon de Montfort, wanted to destroy the sacred fortress of Occitania; but when he actually saw the mountain that loses itself in the sky, he gave up on the idea. Later, Raimundo VII, the Count of Toulouse, who had to swear an oath in Notre Dame in Paris to destroy that last nest of heretics, began the siege of the fortress. But he had no interest in seeing the last redoubt of freedom in his native Occitania fall into foreign hands. He even permitted his officers to go up to the castle to attend the sermons of the bonshommes.

Immaculate and free, the holy citadel of Occitania continued to dominate the Provençal plains, where the victorious crusaders sang their *Veni Creator Spiritus* in blazing cities.[12] Gradually, the peasants of the flat-lands began to speak the *langue d'oil*, the language of their new masters, in place of the *langue d'oc*. Only at Montségur, and on the Tabor that protected it, did the last remnants of a civilization that descended from the Greeks, Iberians, and Celts survive, a thorn in the heart of Christian Occitania, which had condemned it to death.

As always, myth and legend have woven their fabric around these severe, fortified rocks, planted in the Tabor since time immemorial. According to Occitan tradition, the "Sons of Gerion" whose flocks were taken by Hercules before he arrived in the Hesperides and Hades constructed Montségur. In the garden of the Hesperides, this favorite of the gods took the golden apples that shone on the chalice of regeneration in the foliage of the tree of life. In Hades, Alcides, similar to the sun, tamed and kidnapped Cerberus, the guard of Hell, because neither death nor Hell could scare this "proto-leader." Could Hercules have brought from the ends of the seas to the children of Gerion (whom the Occitanians saw as their Iberian ancestors) the first good news that death is not awful and that Hell is nothing other than a nightmare as disturbing as life?

Sometimes when the banished knights and Pure Ones in Montségur looked toward the east, they could catch a glimpse of the sea beyond the foggy plains; they would recall Hercules' voyage to Hell because Cape Cerberus was in the "Bebric sea." When knights and their ladies, troubadours, and Cathars, among whom were some of the heroes and ladies we met in the world of the Minne, looked from Montségur to the sea in the east, they knew that Port Vendres was there, the "Port of Venus" where the *Argo,* the ship of the Argonauts, had moored. Among its heroic crew was the mighty Hercules.

Venus is not Artemis; sex is not Eros. It wasn't Venus who reigned invisibly over Occitania. No, it was Artemis, the chaste love that turns the bad into good and makes the good even better. Montségur was not a mountain of sin where the "Venus in the Grail" was to be found. It was the Occitan mountain of the Paraclete, the mountain of the supreme Minne.

Those who received the consolamentum took a first step on the path that leads to the land of light. They may have died to the Earthly world, in which they saw Hell and considered it so. Execution pyres blazed everywhere. In their last sanctuary under the sun, the heretics awaited the "kiss of God," and the Pure Ones in Montségur were about to receive that kiss.

> *Ay Muntsalvaesche, end of our miseries,*
> *That nobody wants to console you!*
>
> WOLFRAM VON ESCHENBACH

Esclarmonde de Foix and Guilhabert de Castres had died. The exact dates are unknown. What is certain is that they did not see the siege of Montségur. The shepherd who on the pathway of the Cathars told me the legend of Montségur, Esclarmonde, the armies of Lucifer, and the Grail knew very well that the "great Esclarmonde," as she is now known in the mountains of the Tabor, did not die at the stake. That was another Esclarmonde: the daughter of Raimon, the lord of the castle of Perelha, a "daughter of Belissena." It was she who took care of the Occitan Mani when the armies of Rome, who swore to destroy the heretical fortress, came up from the plain toward Montségur.

After the murders of the Inquisitors in Avignonet, Hugue de Arcis, seneschal of Carcassonne, Pierre Amelii, Archbishop of Narbonne, and Durand, Bishop of Albi decided to destroy forever that Pyrenean fortress in the hands of the desperadoes, which represented a danger to the new organization of the state and the true faith. They instituted an "armed fraternity" with the aim of carrying out a crusade against Montségur. Their military preparations foresaw a siege of several years.

For their part, the heretics were not inactive. From every region of Occitania, knights and troubadours streamed to the threatened castle. With the consent of the Count of Toulouse, the valiant Bertran Roqua sent a constructor of siege machinery, Bertran de Bacalaira, possibly the same man who had fortified the walls of Montségur at the beginning of the great crusade, to inspect the fortress. From all over came donations of money, supplies, and arms. Throngs flowed to the sermons of the Perfecti, who infused the besieged with valor and put their medical knowledge at the disposal of the defenders.

The siege began in the spring of 1243. The Catholic army established its camp on the crest to the west of the castle's rocks, which is still called *el campis* today. The besiegers surrounded the entire promontory—nobody could enter or leave the castle.

Nevertheless, it appears that the defenders of Montségur had contact with their friends on the plain. For this reason, some historians have concluded that large subterranean galleries may have existed—probably natural caves. Whatever they were, it is certain that one day, Esclarmonde de Alion, niece of Esclarmonde de Foix, sent a Catalan with money and soldiers to the beleaguered fortress. On another occasion, the son of the troubadour Peire Vidal managed to get a message from the Count of Toulouse to the defenders that announced that Emperor Frederick II was coming to their aid, and said, "Resist just another week. . . !"

As he approached Montségur, Peire Vidal's son claimed to have seen a fantastic knight with a purple cape and sapphire-colored gloves. He interpreted this vision as a sign of a favorable outcome, but he was mistaken. He was killed in the first sortie along with the outlaws who were comforted by his news.

The help promised by the Emperor would arrive too late. The night of March 1, 1244—supposedly a Palm Sunday—the Catholics reached the summit. Treasonous shepherds informed some crusaders of the existence of a path on the mountain which climbed from the gorge of Lasset to an advance post and was invisible from the castle. They chose to attack at night, because they were afraid that they would fall into the abyss if they could see the vertiginous heights. They strangled those on guard, and with prearranged signals they communicated to those in the camp that the operation had been successful. An hour later, the fortress was completely surrounded.

The besieged capitulated. In order to avoid a useless spilling of blood, Raimon de Perelha and Peire Roger de Mirepoix declared that they were ready to unconditionally surrender the fortress and all the Cathars in it to the archbishop the next morning, if he would respect the lives of the knights. Pierre Amelii agreed.

Many knights, conscious of the destiny that awaited them, asked the ancient heresiarch bishop, Bertran En Marti, the successor of Guilhabert de Castres, to administer the consolamentum to them before the capitulation, and admit them into the Church of Amor. Nobody thought of fleeing or resorted to the endura; they wanted to be an example to the world of how one should die for his country and his faith. Frequently, Cathar doctrine has been compared—to denigrate it—with the pessimism of Schopenhauer and Nietzsche. Strange pessimism, that can only be compared in the history of humanity with the heroism of the first Christian martyrs! Catharism was no more pessimistic than early Christianity, which it attempted to imitate.

At the start of the day, the castle surrendered to the "armed fraternity." The archbishop of Narbonne demanded that the Perfect Ones renounce their beliefs. Two hundred and five men and women—among them Bertran En Marti and Esclarmonde de Perelha, preferred death in the blazing pyres that Pierre Amelii had prepared on the place that is still called the *camp des crémats,* the field of fires.

The knights were dragged to Carcassonne in heavy chains and thrown in the dungeon under the same tower where, thirty years earlier, Raimon Roger, the Trencavel de Carcassonne, was poisoned, and Raimon de Termès perished so miserably. A few decades later, the Franciscan friar Bernard Délicieux succeeded in getting the last survivors out of that tomb in the Tower of the Inquisition.

Peire-Roger de Mirepoix was the only one who could abandon the castle a free man. He took with him his engineer, doctor, and all the gold and silver that were found there, and headed for Sault, to the house of Esclarmonde de Alion, the niece of the great Esclarmonde, and from there to the castle of Montgaillard, where he died at a very old age. Until his death, Peire-Roger was the secret guide of the outlawed knights of Occitania, knights who found their last refuge and their deaths in the caves of Ornolac.

The night of the fall of Montségur, a fire was seen on the snowy summit of Bidorta. It was not an execution pyre, but a fire of happiness. Four Cathars, of whom three are known to us—Amiel Aicart, Poitevin, and Hugo—were signaling the Perfecti of Montségur, who were about to die, that the Mani was safe.

From the documents of the Inquisitors of Carcassonne, it is surmised that these four Pure Ones, covered in wool blankets, descended on ropes from the summit of the promontory to the bottom of the Lasset gorge to hand the treasure of the heretics to a Son of Belissena, Pons-Arnaud de Castellum Verdunum, in the Sabarthès.

The "treasure of the heretics"?

Since Peire Roger de Mirepoix was given permission to take all the gold and silver with him, what the four intrepid Cathars brought to safety in the caves of the Sabarthès, an area that belonged to the lords of Castellum Verdunum, was certainly not gold or silver.

Amiel Aicart, Poitevin, Hugo and the fourth knight, whose name is unknown, were the grandchildren of those wise Celt Iberians who in other times threw the treasure of Delphi to the bottom of lake Tabor. As Cathars, they would have preferred to take the pathway to the stars together with their brothers in the fire of the *camp des crémats*. As they climbed the pathway of the Cathars that crosses the "valley of enchantment" bordering the lake of the Druids and ascends abruptly toward the Tabor and Bidorta, they must have seen the blazing flames of Montségur to the north. What they were safeguarding was neither gold nor silver; it was the "Desire for Paradise."

The Inquisitors knew full well why the Cathar sanctuary was called the "treasure of the heretics." That is why they set fire to anything that could constitute proof for posterity. They burned everything—even the books, whose life is longer than that of man.

The peasants of the little village of Montségur, a beehive at the foot of the rock upon which the castle sits suspended above the gorge of Lasset, tell the story that on Palm Sunday, when the priest celebrates the Mass, the Tabor rips itself open in a hidden place in the thickness of the woods. That is where the treasure of the heretics can be found. Unfortunate is he who has not left the mountains before the priest intones his *ite missa est*. At those words, the mountain closes, and he who is searching for the treasure will die from the bites of the snakes that guard it.

The peasants of the Tabor have not forgotten that this treasure can only be found when all others are in the church. Despite its power and cruelty, the Inquisition could not erase the memory of what those mountains contemplated seven hundred years ago.

This is how the Grail, the Occitan Mani, was brought to safety in the caves of Ornolac. No tree flowers there, the sun never shines, the nightingale doesn't sing at dawn, and no fish swims beneath the sun. The walls of the cavern are the empire of night and death. Before their exit to the luminous land of light and souls, the last priests of the Church of Amor, the last Pure Ones, had to descend to the Hell of pitiless reality. In the caves of Sabarthès, the Cathars found themselves submerged in a frequent and deeply astral nostalgia. Perhaps it was nothing other than a form of *endura* that led them to make a pilgrimage to Montségur on moonlit nights. In order to reach the stars, it is necessary to die, and in Montségur, death was inexorably waiting for them. The new lord of the castle, Guy de Levis, a comrade in arms and friend of Simon de Montfort, left a guard in the ruins of the heretical fortress and a pack of hounds trained to hunt down the heretics.

By moonlight, the Pure Ones, emaciated and pale, would climb in proud silence through the Forest of Serralunga to the spot where the owl's cry is louder than the wind that resonates in the gorges of the Tabor, that gigantic aeolian harp. From time to time, in forest clearings bathed in moonlight, they took off their berets and pulled out the roll of leather that they carried on their breasts containing the Gospel of the disciple whom the Lord loved. Then they kissed the parchment, knelt down before the moon, and prayed:

". . . Give us today our supernatural bread . . . forgive those who trespass against us."

Shortly thereafter, they continued the march to their deaths. When the dogs pounced on them with foaming mouths and the executioners trapped and beat them, they gazed down to Montségur and then toward the heavens, to the stars, where they would find their brothers. Then they were burned alive.

After the fall of Montségur, the only places left to the outlaws—to the *faydits,* as they were called—were the forests and caves.

The interiors of the mountains and the impenetrable brambles gave them a safe haven. In order to apprehend them, the Inquisitors tried to eliminate all brambles, furze, and thorn bushes. They entrusted this job to Bernard whose nickname was *Espinasser,* which means Thorn Cutter. The legend says that he was hanged by the moon.

In order to root out the heretics from their burrows more easily, the Dominicans set police dogs after them. The faydits were persecuted as savage beasts throughout their native mountains, until they had no alternative other than either to go abroad or, if they wished to die in their homeland, to remain within the solid walls of the spulgas.

The Cathars were steadfast to superhuman levels. They saw how their country was murdered and yet they refused to pick up the sword. Death awaited them on the execution pyre or in the *murus strictus*. Instead of renouncing the Paraclete, an outlawed belief in their world, they accepted their horrible end with a tranquil soul. They were absolutely certain that their desire for Paradise would be realized. The last Occitan knights saw the arrival of their last hour together with the Cathars because they refused to recognize the domination of France. Despite the protection of the robust walls of their spulgas, they were convinced that they had no salvation. And yet they fought until their last breath.[13]

Pope Boniface VIII died on October 12, 1303. In his bull *Unam Sanctam*, he declared that the successors of Peter were the keepers of supreme power, religious and civil, and that every human being must submit to it for the good of his salvation. In two more bulls, by prohibiting the French clergy from paying taxes and giving himself supreme jurisdiction, he converted himself into the irreconcilable enemy of Philippe le Bel [Philip the Fair], the King of France. The king had tried to remedy his financial difficulties by resorting to confiscations and extortions with the collusion of—and against—the clergy. Because this road was now closed to him, his hatred for the Pope knew no limits.[14] After Boniface's death, and with the help of Pope Clement V, who was elected on his and the Inquisition's orders, Philip pressed to have the dead Pope accused of heresy. He managed to find a large number of witnesses—famous clerics, for the most part—who declared under oath that the dead Pope did not believe in the immortality of the soul or in the embodiment of Christ, and that he had shameful and "unnatural" vices. Just a small part of any of these accusations would have sufficed to send any normal accused person to the stake. But this was the only time that the Inquisition used indulgence. It declared the late Pope innocent.

Clement V had been bishop of Comminges and archbishop of Bordeaux. Elected Pope in Lyon at the urging of King Philip, he agreed to stay in France and never set foot on Italian soil. During his Pontificate, the so-called "Babylonian Captivity" began in Avignon and the haughty Order of the Knights Templar was exterminated. One of its founders was a Cathar, who was denounced by a noble and a burgher, both from Béziers, to King Philip, greedy as ever for Templar treasures. The Knights

Templar, far more powerful and rich than many emperors and kings put together, had to watch, on the sadly famous night of October 13, 1307, as their majestic Temple was demolished. In it, according to their accusers, they had worshipped the satanic head of Baphomet in place of the crucifix. It is possible that they too found refuge in the caves of the Pyrenees. Serious clues remain that the white cape of the Templars, on which glittered the eight-pointed red cross, lies together with the black garments and yellow crosses of the Cathars someplace in the shadowy caves of the Sabarthès. The spulgas of Bouan and Ornolac have still not revealed all their secrets.

Written on a stone slab in the fortified Church of the Templars of Luz-Saint-Sauveur (at the entrance to the impressive desert of Gavarni) is this legend: In the crypt, nine Templar skulls can be found; every night of October 13, a voice can be heard in the church that asks, whispering like the wind, "Has the day for the liberation of the Holy Sepulchre arrived?" The nine skulls mumble, "Still not. . . ."

It is said that as he burned at the stake in Paris on an island in the Seine on March 11, 1314 by order of Philip, Jacques de Molay, the Grand Master of the Order, exclaimed: "Pope Clement, unjust judge, within forty days you will be in God's court. And you, Philip, you wicked king within the year. . . ." Forty days later Clement was dead. Eight months later, Philip the Fair no longer lived.

The outrage produced by the murders committed by the Vatican and the Louvre was kept alive in France until well into the eighteenth century. It is related that as the Revolution advanced along the rue Saint-Antoine in Paris, in the direction of the Louvre and Notre Dame, a man dressed in a long tunic started to taunt the priests. Every time his sword pricked one, he exclaimed, "This is for the Albigenses and the Templars!" And when the head of Louis XVI rolled under the guillotine, the same man got up on the scaffold, smeared his fingers in the blood of the unfortunate monarch and shouted, "People of France, I baptize you in the name of Jacques de Molay and liberty!"

At the death of Pope Clement, John XXII occupied Peter's throne in Avignon. John's successor was Benedict XII, who before his election as Holy Father in 1334 was called Jacques Fournier. The son of a baker, he was a native of Saverdun, a small town in the Ariège, in the County of Foix to the north of Pamiers. While still quite young, he entered the convent of the Cistercians at Boulbonne, where the mausoleum of the Counts of Foix is located. All the sons and daughters of the House of Foix found their last resting place there, with the exception of course of Esclarmonde, who had flown to eternal Paradise in the form of a dove.

Jacques was sent by his uncle, the abbot of the monastery of Fontfroide, to Paris to study theology until 1311, when he became abbot of the monastery. Sixteen years later, Pope John XXII named him Bishop of Pamiers, a town where a hundred years earlier Esclarmonde had convoked all the wise men of the Sabarthès in order to decipher the doctrines of Plato and John the Evangelist. As Bishop of Pamiers, Jacques Fournier achieved great success in the pursuit of the heretics: success that would eventually bring him the Papal tiara and the fisherman's ring. But before undertaking the extermination of the heretics of the Sabarthès, he had to form part of the tribunal that judged Bernard Délicieux.

Bernard Délicieux was one of the lectors of the Franciscan convent of Narbonne. He had close contact with the most illustrious minds of his time: for example, with Raimon Llull, the original "Reformer of the World," and with Arnaldo de Vilanova, the private medical officer of the Pope and a tireless seeker of the Philosopher's Stone and the *aurum potabile*. He was a worthy follower of Saint Francis. He was such a Franciscan that he had to share the fate of the Cathars, of whom he became a defender and advocate.

Bernard is one of the most discussed and appreciated personalities of the fourteenth century. In his renunciation of everything worldly, he even sold off his books and went into debt only to help the poor. His Order, which—let us not forget it—opposed the Inquisition of the Dominicans in almost every way, was loyal to him.

Bernard could deliver his speeches against the Dominicans even in the convents of the Franciscans. On one occasion, an Inquisitor, Fulk de Saint George, and twenty-five mounted men arrived at the abbey where Bernard was staying and demanded that he be handed over. The brothers of Saint Francis denied them entrance, began ringing the bells, and from the walls of the convent, started to stone the Dominicans. When they heard the tolling of the bells, the people came in throngs and the Inquisitor was hard pressed to get out alive.

Bernard's fervent eloquence managed to move the burghers of Carcassonne to free those who remained imprisoned in the Tower of the Inquisition's terrible dungeons. Among those who were still alive were the last knights of Montségur, whose records were burned by the Inquisition.

Stimulated by the audacious actions of the Franciscan, other cities of Occitania rebelled against the Inquisitors. When the Dominican Godfrede de Abluses—a cruel man without any scruples—began as Inquisitor in Toulouse, the inhabitants of the city wrote a complaint to the King of France. Out of fear of losing the provinces that he had just conquered, Philip the Fair sent his deputy from Amiens and the Archdeacon de Lisieux to the Midi, with the mission of listening to the complaints of the population and putting a stop to the excesses of the Inquisitors. The deputy had the jails of the Inquisition opened and freed all their prisoners. What is more, he arrested several officials of the Holy Office. The people greeted these measures with enthusiasm, and a real persecution of the Inquisitors began. The disorder was such that Philip had to personally visit Toulouse, where he issued an edict in 1304 that ordered the revision of all the trials carried out by the Inquisition. At the same time, he received Bernard in audience. The Franciscan had the courage to explain to the King that both Saint Peter and Saint Paul would have confessed to being heretics if they had been subjected to the methods of the Inquisitors.

Philip could not totally prohibit the Inquisition in his provinces, because it constituted solid support for his temporal power. Disappointed and annoyed, Bernard went from town to town complaining about the King's lack of action. When Philip saw that the burghers of Carcassonne were seriously contemplating separating from France with the clear intention of putting themselves under the protection of King Ferran of Mallorca, he decided to rescind his edict, and gave the Dominicans new powers. He ordered that heretics should be pursued like savage and dangerous beasts, and demanded the rearrest of all people denounced by the Dominicans.

Terror spread across the country. The Inquisitors treated heretics, real or imagined, with horrible cruelty. If witnesses declared in favor of the accused, there was no inconvenience whatsoever in falsifying the acts. The consuls of Carcassonne were condemned to death. The Toulouse Inquisitor Godfrede de Abluses returned to his position. He began his return to power with the search for the living descendants of those who in their day had been condemned, because in his opinion, the punishment for those crimes should not fall only on those who committed them, but also on their children. The deputy de Amiens was obliged to flee. He went to see the Pope, who threw him out as a heretic. He died, excommunicated, in Italy. Two years after his death, the excommunication was lifted.

Bernard Délicieux belonged to the wing of the Franciscans known as the *spirituals*. Let's go back a bit in time.

Francis of Assisi opposed the arrogance and cruelty of his time with patience and humility. He taught that the supreme pleasure of the soul did not consist in making miracles, curing the sick, expelling demons, resuscitating the dead, or converting the entire world, but in enduring and helping to endure—patiently—any suffering, sickness, injustice, or humiliation. Like the Cathars and the Waldenses, he preached apostolic poverty. As he and his disciples said, Jesus and his Apostles did not possess anything; in this way, perfect Christianity should renounce all property. In 1322, Pope John XXII declared the Franciscan thesis that Christ and the Apostles had never possessed anything as heretical. Those Franciscans who followed the teachings of Saint Francis to the letter were given the name "spirituals." *Amen,* the doctrine of the Order, adopted the apocalyptic ideas of Joachim of Fiore. Before leaving for the Holy Land, King Richard the Lionheart had asked Joachim to explain the meaning of the Apocalypse of Saint John to him. Pope John XXII tried by every means to soften the strict "spiritual" interpretation of Franciscan doctrine regarding poverty and humility. To this effect, he had the spiritualist brothers of Béziers and Narbonne appear before him; their spokesman was Bernard Délicieux. After just beginning the defense of the spirituals, Bernard was accused of undermining the work of the Inquisition and was arrested on the spot. In addition, he was accused of having provoked the death of Pope Benedict XI with black magic and inciting the burghers of Carcassonne to rebellion.

The trial began in 1319, two years after Bernard's detention, and was presided over by the archbishop of Toulouse and Jacques Fournier, the Bishop of Pamiers. Former comrades of Bernard were convoked as witnesses, condemning their friend to death with their testimony to save their own lives. This Franciscan, grown old and totally exhausted by his long stay in prison, was submitted to the most grueling interrogation over two months. On the pretext of saving his soul, they reminded him that under the laws of the Inquisition he was a heretic, and that only a complete confession could save him from the stake. Twice he underwent torture: the first time for high treason, the second for necromancy. The archives of the Inquisition of Carcassonne reveal that despite the tortures—the scribe carefully registered every shout of pain—it was impossible to tear a confession from the old man. But finally, weakened by age and suffering and exhausted by the tortures, the Franciscan brother fell into contradictions, put himself at the mercy of the tribunal, and asked for absolution.

The verdict declared him innocent of the charge of having attempted the assassination of Pope Benedict, but guilty of the rest. His "guilt" was aggravated by not less than seventy false statements uttered during his interrogation. Bernard was condemned to life in prison, on bread and water—in other words *murus strictus*—and was locked away in the Tower of the Inquisition in Carcassonne, where in better times, he had freed the last knights of Montségur. After a few months, a sweet death freed this man, one of the very few who had the courage to openly oppose the Inquisition.

Jacques Fournier denounced fasting, poverty, and chastity as heretical. He had a running love affair with the sister of the poet Petrarch; frequently he was "drunken with wine, and filthy with the liquid that produces sleep." There are chroniclers who say that he was "pot-bellied, and a drunkard."

His brother in profession, Bernard Gui, the Toulouse Inquisitor, had already done a good job in the Sabarthès, publishing in 1309 the following edict:

I, Brother Bernard Guidonis, Dominican and Inquisitor of Toulouse, I offer all those believers in Christ the prize of the crown and eternal life. Come together, children of God, come up with me, fighters for Christ against the enemies of his cross, those corruptors of truth and purity of the Catholic doctrine, against Pierre Autier, the arch-heretic, against his followers and accomplices. I order you in the name of God to persecute, and detain there where you find them those who remain hidden and lie in the darkness. I promise the recompense of God, and a good prize in coin to those who detain the aforesaid, and hand them over to me. Be watchful, pastors, so that the wolves do not devour your lambs. Act with valor, loyal servants of God, so the enemies of the faith cannot flee or escape from us!

Pierre Autier, a notary from Aix-en-Sabarthès, was the leader of the last heretics of Occitania. In his youth, he was not a Cathar, and had a *druda* or lover. With the passing of years, he became an ardent defender of the heretical doctrine, and the leader of the outlaws of the caves of Sabarthès. From there, he undertook missionary travels throughout the Languedoc, and on one occasion in 1295 he escaped the persecution of the Inquisition by fleeing to Lombardy in Italy. Within three years, he was again in the Sabarthès, where he remained hidden for eleven years.

A certain Guillaume Joan presented himself one day to Jacques Fournier to betray the arch-heretic. But two heretics coaxed the traitor to a bridge near Aliat, where they overpowered and gagged him. Then they took him to the mountains, where they forced him to confess and threw him headfirst into the abyss.

When Pierre Autier left his hiding place to visit Castelnaudary, he was arrested, and a year later, in 1310, burned in Toulouse. They did the unspeakable to pry the names and hiding places of his loyal comrades out of him. All efforts to get him to admit and confess the heresy were fruitless. He never pretended to hide his faith; rather he declared it with bravura. And yet, it would appear that the Inquisitor Bernard Gui managed to learn from him the secret of the caves of the Sabarthès, and pass it on to Jacques Fournier in whose parish the mountains of the Ariège were to be found. In later trials, they allude often to the information obtained from Pierre Autier, who had no other course than to reveal the secret of the last Cathars to his torturers.

At the entrance to the Sabarthès, at the doors to the town of Tarascon, you can still see a country house called Jacques Fournier. The bishop of Pamiers directed the war against the heretical troglodytes from there; as long as the caves of Ornolac were not dehereticized, the triumph of the cross was not complete.

The manor of Jacques Fournier rises in the middle of a rocky cone like an eagle's nest that reigned over Calmès and Miramont, the fortresses of the Sons of Belissena of Rabat. These knights remained loyal to

Catharism until their death. Many fell in the defense of Montségur. Still more perished in the Tower of the Inquisition in Carcassonne. Others had to wander their desecrated homeland wearing the yellow cross, symbol of dishonor, on their chest and back. Those who resisted the longest were the lords of Rabat and Castellum Verdunum, now the miserable survivors of the Church of Amor, so powerful in other times.

Jacques Fournier personally indicated to his friars-in-arms where to install their battering rams to force entry into the spulgas. From his manor house in Tarascon, he directed this holy war against those who remained entrenched in the caves.

For more than a century, the Cathars could live in this wild Pyrenean valley without anyone bothering them. They had their huts on the slopes of the mountains, between pines, fig trees, and acacia trees. When danger approached, they lit bonfires on the Soudour, a gigantic plateau near Tarascon that dominates the whole valley, so the smoke could serve as an alarm. Then the heretics took refuge in the caves, which were fatal for anybody who didn't know them. When—for example—the executioners of the Inquisition penetrated the cave of Sacany, before them were six different pathways. Five of them lead in a zigzag to a precipice whose depths nobody to this day has been able to explore. It is possible that more than one henchman's remains rest there after falling in furious pursuit of some Cathar. Once the Inquisitors found the right pathway, the nest of heretics was empty.

In all probability, the smoke signals disappeared from the summit of the Soudour from the moment Jacques Fournier occupied his manor house at its foot. One day, the Inquisitors torched the spulgas, burning all the Cathars who couldn't flee. Jacques Fournier imagined he could become Pope.

A document from 1329 informs us that, after rotting for an eternity in the dungeons of the Inquisition, Pons-Arnaud, the co-lord of Castellum Verdunum, was freed under the condition of wearing the yellow crosses. Falling back into heresy, he was apprehended by the guards of the Dominicans and jailed, dying finally *ab intestato*.

With the death of this Son of Belissena, the caves of the Sabarthès, as remote and inaccessible as they were, could no longer provide security for the heretics. If the walls of the fortified cave of Bouan, the most impressive spulga of the Sabarthès that belonged to the lords of Château

Verdun, could resist until then, now it seemed that without Pons-Arnaud, the walls would explode under the thunderous impacts of the catapults. It seems that the last Cathars fled to the mountains through hidden subterranean chimneys known only to them. From there, they probably emigrated to more hospitable lands, where the sun shone more purely because it was not darkened by the smoke of the execution pyre, and where the stars to which they aspired seemed closer. Before abandoning forever the caves that for so long had given them shelter, that were as free as the wind, one left on the walls some drawings and inscriptions:

A tree of life
A dove, emblem of the God-Spirit.
A fish, symbol of the luminous divinity
Christigrams in Greek and Latin characters
The word Gethsemane

All around, in almost impenetrable places, where a gallery winds itself through chalky rock toward the summits bathed in sunshine, he drew and intertwined the initials "GTS," probably the abbreviation of the word Gethsemane, the garden where Christ was handed over to his enemies.

When one tries to climb these chimneys toward the surface, where freedom exerted its fascination on the Cathars, he will often find his ascent obstructed by walls or impressive stone blocks that the chalk water has converted into impassable stalactites. A Pyrenean legend tells us that the Dominican friars, unable to capture the last Cathars in their inaccessible lair, had them walled off behind these rocks. The mountains of the Sabarthès continue to guard their secrets.

The total disappearance of such an important movement as the Cathars appeared so improbable that it was frequently believed that the *cagots* or "*agots*" were their direct descendants. But these people belonged to the family of gypsies who lived marginalized in the Pyrenees. French Navarre recognized them as citizens with equal rights in 1709, and Spanish Navarre in 1818. This belief affected the *cagots* themselves, who in a request directed to Pope Leo X in 1517, solicited the Holy Father to readmit them to society because the errors of their fathers had long been paid for.

In 1807, several hunters from Suc, a town in the Sabarthès, saw a naked woman on the solitary heights of Montcalm peak, one of the highest summits of the Pyrenees where snow remains throughout the year. Instead of continuing their bear hunt, they tried to trap her, but with no success. Like a chamois, she jumped from rock to rock, running along the edge of incredible cliffs, without any fear that she would fall into the abyss.

The following day, the hunters were reinforced by shepherds from Montcalm, and renewed their chase. Finally they succeeded in capturing the woman alive. They offered her clothes like those worn by women of the region. She tore them to shreds. In the end, they tied her hands, dressed her by force, and took her to the parochial house of Suc where she calmed a bit, looked at her clothes, then fell to her knees and wailed convulsively.

Her face, emaciated and pale, nonetheless showed that in other times she had been very beautiful. Her tall stature and dignified gestures led the townsfolk to conclude that she was of noble lineage. They offered her a room in which to spend the night. The following morning she had disappeared, leaving all her clothes.

A few days later, her presence was detected on one of the snowy summits of Bassiès peak. Winter descended. . . .

With the arrival of springtime, the justice of the peace in Vicdessos headed for the heights of Montcalm, accompanied by policemen. After serious difficulties, they managed to arrest the woman, dressed her again, gave her food, and tried to discover the enigma of her strange existence—they failed. One day, the justice of the peace asked her how it was possible that the bears had not devoured her, to which she replied in the dialect of the valleys, "The bears? They are my friends, they gave me warmth!"

The woman fell ill, so they took her to the hospital in Foix. She escaped again on July 20, but they recaptured her on August 2 in the vicinity of Tarascon, before she could climb back to the Montcalm. They took her back to Foix and locked her in the castle prison, where she died at one in the morning on October 29, 1808. Nostalgia for her mountains killed her.

It has never been possible to resolve the mystery of the "Folle du Montcalm" [The Crazy Woman of Montcalm]. The peasants of those remote valleys wanted to convince me that she was the last descendant of the Cathars.

Six hundred years ago Occitan Catharism died. Its death took place in the caves of Ornolac, the same place that was its cradle for thousands of years.

The Tabor, in other times the Parnassus of Occitania, became an important necropolis, a tomb for one of the most illustrious civilizations of the western world. Perhaps the chalky waters from the springs of the Sabarthès have occluded the place where the mysterious celebration of the Cathar Manisola was held for the last time. Perhaps the last Cathars lie there, dead through endura in defense of the heretical treasure, whose mere contemplation gave their brothers sufficient courage to advance smiling to their deaths and shout in the last moment, as the flames of the pyre began to consume them, "God is Love!" If God is more benevolent and understanding than mankind, shouldn't he concede to them in the Hereafter what they had so ardently desired and pursued with total abstinence, consequential strength, and unparalleled heroism? The divinization of the Spirit—the apotheosis! This is what they wanted. The anxiety of mankind consists in reaching the kingdom of the heavens, which is to say, to live on after death.

What happened to the Grail, the Occitan Mani? According to a Pyrenean legend, the Grail moves farther away from this world, and upward toward the sky, when humanity is no longer worthy of it. Perhaps the Pure Ones of Occitania keep the Grail on one of those stars that circle Montségur like a halo, that Golgotha of Occitania. The Grail symbolized their desire for Paradise, where mankind is the image, not the caricature, of God—an image that is revealed only when you love your fellow man as yourself. Chivalrous knights, wandering poets, poetic priests, and chaste women were in other times the keepers of this symbol.

> *Do not forget of whom they were worthy!*
> *Such scintillating stars scattered them*
> *By nature through infinite space.*
>
> GOETHE

APPENDIX: OBSERVATIONS ON THE THEORETICAL PART

———◆———

SOME TIME AGO, I decided to try to shed light on the relatively obscure relationship between Occitan poetry and mysticism and the mentality of medieval Germany. Only when I had the occasion to test this thesis in Occitania itself did I discover the pathway that led directly from Montségur, Occitania's "Temple of the supreme Minne," to Wildenberg near Amorbach, the location of the castle of Wolfram von Eschenbach— the greatest of all German poets of the Minne. Then I understood that the German and Occitan worlds, so distant and yet at the same time close to each other, could not be fully contemplated in their sublime beauty without recognizing that the mysticism of the Minne had a deep Celtic-Germanic undercurrent.

Catharism was a dualist movement that extended throughout Europe. In order to remain within the boundaries that I set down for this work, I have not dealt with the fact that Cathar sects from the Balkans to Cologne and Toulouse were all organized in a similar fashion in order to be strong in their decisive fight against Rome and Paris, powers that had threatened them for some time. I have also omitted the generalized belief that Occitan Catharism—the Albigenses—was a branch of the Bogomils, or heretical Slavs. In this respect, such an opinion, in no way irrefutable, can be read into any work on Catharism, and above all in the works of Schmidt and Döllinger, and compared with my own thesis. I was very interested in bringing the native element of the Cathars to the forefront of my book, highlighting facts that until now have never been fully brought forward, outlining them with precision and exactness in the area of the link—to my judgment, overdone—with Catharism of Eastern Europe. I wish to expressly underscore this.

The present work could not, and did not pretend to be an exhaustive study of this subject. It is true that it claims to place different aspects within a single perspective. This has conditioned its composition, which is similar to a travel diary through the mountains, castles, caves, and books (more or less ancient)—a structure that will encourage experts to examine the subject material with a magnifying glass.

I am hoping to bring out a second work soon, a continuation of the present one, about Conrad von Marburg, the German Inquisitor. In it, I will refer to the influences of German Catharism on German mysticism into the modern-age (Novalis) Catharism that had thousands of followers in my native land of Hesse and the length of the Rhine, from Cologne to Basel. Some ideas already appear in this work.

I have to thank my teacher in Giessen, Baron von Gall, who first encouraged me to investigate the subject of the heretics. Years passed until circumstances allowed me, in an unexpected way, to travel to the Pyrenees and precisely to Montségur. After a stay of several weeks in the vicinity of that ruined castle, and goaded on by the legend that said that the last Cathars were locked in a cave in the Ariège, I moved to Ornolac in the Sabarthès, where I had the luck to meet as competent and comprehensive a "Trevrizent" as I could ever imagine: the specialist in prehistory, Antonin Gadal, custodian of all the caves of the Sabarthès (with the exception of those found in Niaux and Bédeilhac). Over the years he has been conducting intense and polished research work. Not only did Monsieur Gadal arrange for me to undertake, without any inconvenience, all the expeditions that I felt were necessary in the caves (which are today declared national monuments, and consequently under special rules for their preservation), but he also put his rich library and personal museum at my disposal. He indicated that he intends to publish the results of his investigations sometime soon. Although they are specialized works of prehistory and speleology, they will nevertheless serve as complete support for my affirmations. It is an enormous satisfaction for me to be able to thank Monsieur Gadal here, and pay homage for his disinterested help.

I would be committing the sin of ingratitude if I did not express acknowledgement for my friends in the Pyrenees, who in the most diverse ways pushed forward the birth of my book.

The Countess Pujol-Murat, whose ancestors gave their life in the defense of Montségur for their homeland invaded by the enemy, and who counts among them Hugo De Payens, founder of the Order of the Templars, and, worthy of special mention, the great Esclarmonde de Foix, familiarized me with the heroic past of Montségur. I would not conclude my list of my Occitan friends without mentioning Messrs. Bélissen, Roché, Palauqui, Meslin, and Maupomé, who helped me with great gusto.

Finally I would like to express my sincere gratitude to the people of the Bibliothèque Nationale in Paris and those at the library of the University of Freiburg for their services.

NOTES

———————◆———————

Note: Endnotes preceded by an asterisk (*) have been supplied by the translator and editor Christopher Jones.

Translator's Foreword

1. The Georg Büchner Prize is Germany's most distinguished literary award. It was originally given only to those writers who were born in Hessen; in 1951, it was opened to all German authors. "Kreuz und Gral, Versuch einer Einführung," Nr. 50, *Baseler Nachrichten*, December 10, 1933.
2. *Crusade* has been translated into French, Spanish, Portuguese, and Italian, among other languages. Rahn is also credited as being the prototype for Steven Spielberg's swashbuckling archaeologist Indiana Jones. His books are mentioned as sources in the 1982 bestseller *Holy Blood, Holy Grail* by Michael Baigent, Richard Leigh, and Henry Lincoln, among others.
3. Wolfram von Eschenbach, *Parzival,* translated by A. T. Hatto (New York: Penguin Books, 1980).
4. Robert Graves.
5. *Le livre des sentences de l'Inquisiteur Bernard Gui,* translated and annotated by Annette Palès-Gobillard (Paris: CNRS—Centre National des Recherches Scientifiques).
6. Napoléon Peyrat, *L'Histoire des Albigeois* (Nîmes: Editions Lacour).
7. Paul-Aléxis Ladame, *Quand le laurier reverdira* (Saltkine, 2003). Other works by Ladame include *La quête du Graal* and *Unir l'Europe.*
8. Rahn explains the possible Celtic origins of the legend among the Volcae Tectosages, a tribe that lived in southern France and Germany. What he missed was the fact that this tribe may have been involved in an incident some 600 years before the Christian era, when a comet slammed into the Earth in the area of the Chiemsee in Bavaria that was inhabited by Celtic

tribes. The effects of the explosion were similar to the detonation of an atomic device; however, once the tribes returned, they discovered that the comet had left a special ore that they used to fashion the best swords of antiquity. A real case of a stone that fell from the stars.

Prologue

1. *Parzival*, 827.

2. *"Despite its undeniable religious character, the Church and the clergy never acknowledged the existence of the legend. Not a single writer of the ecclesiastical establishment speaks of the Grail. Although the curious tale of this symbol of the faith could not have passed unnoticed, not one of the numerous works by clerics that have reached us—with the exception of the chronicler Helinand—mentions the name of the Grail. They did not want to mention it. They silenced it, nothing more. Even more than its repudiation by the clergy, what astounds us is that the idea of this precious relic was neither understood nor brought to reality."—Eduard Wechssler, *Gral*, p. 24. In the same work, p. 177, Dr. Wechssler discusses the possible reasons why Guyot's poem was lost.

3. *Walter Map (circa 1140–1210), Archdeacon of Oxford. A Welshman, Walter Map is remembered for *De Nugis Curialium [Courtiers Triflings]* a book of gossip and anecdotes.

4. *Caesarius von Heisterbach (1180–1240), Cistercian, master of novices at the monastery at Heisterbach, and one of the most widely read authors of the thirteenth century. His best-known work is *Dialogus magnus visionum atque miracolorum [Dialogue of Visions and Miracles]*, Libri XII.

5. *Maurice Magre (1877–1941), *Magiciens et illuminés* (Paris: Fasquelle, 1930). Magre, *Magicians, Seers, and Mystics* (New York: E. P. Dutton & Co., 1932), translated by Reginald Merton.

6. *Rahn is referring to his alleged participation in the *Polaire* expedition to southern France in March 1932 that was reported by the southern French newspaper *La Depêche* in several articles. The *Polaires* were a secretive group linked to the Anthroposophical Society; among their most prominent members was writer-poet Maurice Magre.

7. *Joséphin Péladan, *De Parsifal à don Quichotte, le secret des troubadours* (1906).

8. *Franz Kampers, *Das Lichtland der Seelen und der heilige Gral* (1916), p. 78.

PART ONE

Parsifal

1. **Parzival,* Wolfram von Eschenbach, p. 235 (Hatto translation, p. 125). The proper translation of the name "Parsifal" or "Parzival" is disputed. Rahn, in his second book, *Lucifer's Courtiers* (1937), asserts that the name comes from the Persian language and means "Pure Flower" (p. 137).

2. See Peyrat, *Nostradamus* and *Civilisation romaine.* *Physician and astronomer Michel de Nôtredame (1503–1566), better known as Nostradamus, was accused during his lifetime of being a Cathar; see also Claude de Vic and Joseph Vaissètte, *Histoire Générale de Languedoc* (Paris, 1872–1892), Vol. VI, Kampers, Wechssler, *Biographien,* K.A.F. Mahn, Kannegiesser, and others.

3. Re: the troubadour Guilhem de Montanhagol, see Jules Coulet, *Montanhagol* (p. 48 et seq).

4. The didactic poems of troubadours Arnaut de Mareulh and Armanieu des Escas were taken from Peyrat, *Histoire des Albigeois,* Vol. I, pp. 86 and 87.

5. Provençal is the first derivative of the *lingua rustica Latina.* In the Middle Ages it was preferred for poetry. Its name stems from Provence, and it was spoken throughout southern France, above all in the Dauphinat, Languedoc, Auvergne, Poitou, Guyenne, and Gascony as well as in the Spanish regions of Aragon, Catalonia, and Valencia. The basic characteristic of the Occitan language or *langue d'oc* is the word *oc,* which means yes (from the Latin word *hoc*) in juxtaposition to the French *Langue d'oil* (*oil* signifies yes, from the Latin *hoc illud; oui* today).

6. All so-called "protectors" in the biography of Raimon de Miraval were heretics who played an important part in the crusade. Peyrat describes the siege of the castles of Saissac, Cab-Aret, and Penautier with luxuriant detail in *Croisade,* Vol. II. See de Vic and Vaissètte and Guillermo de Tudela, *La Canción de la Cruzada Albigensa.* Bertran de Saissac was the tutor of Raimon-Roger of Carcassonne.

7. Raimon de Miraval's poem was dedicated to Adélaide de Boisseson Lombers, a well-known heretic who preferred the charms of King Pedro of Aragon. Irmingard de Saissac, the sister of Guilhabert de Castres, the patriarch of the heretics, and a "Daughter of Belissena," was celebrated by Raimon as the "Beautiful Albigense." Her infidelity drove the troubadour to the edge of madness. Stéphanie, the "She-Wolf," wasn't any better. During the crusade, Raimon lost his castle to the French. In his novel *Die Dichterin von Carcassonne,* Heyse describes his marriage with "Gaudairenca." See

also *La vie et l'œuvre du troubadour Raimon de Miraval,* Andraud, 1902. Peire d'Auvergne was also known as the "Monk of Montaudon" (de Vic and Vaissètte, Vol. 6, p. 948). He donated the income from his poetry to a convent, the Abbey of Aurillac. Kannegiesser has translated a satire by Peire d'Auvergne called *The Monk* into German, although in reality Peire de Auvergne did not write this play about fifteen troubadours. Raimon's poem is freely translated. Not far from Montségur was Poivert, the summer residence of the Viscountess Adélaide de Carcassonne.

8. See Patzig, *Zur Geschichte der Hermaire* (1891) and Hüffer, *Der Troubadour Guillem von Cabestany* (1869). According to Peyrat (Vol. I, p. 155 et seq), Donna Seremonda was a native of Tarascon, a small town of the Sabarthès. Boccaccio introduced the story of Guilhem de Cabestanh in his *Decameron* (4.9), and Uhland based his famous ballad on it. Petrarca (Petrarch) mentions the troubadour as well in his *Trionfo d'Amore.*

9. Unfortunately, Peyrat does not reveal the source for a different version of the story of Raimon Jordan on p. 153 of Vol. I of his *Histoire des Albigeois,* or *Civilisation Romaine.* Re: Helis and Alix de Montfort, see de Vic and Vaissètte, Vol. VI, p. 558.

10. Re: the discovery of the presumed *"sacro catino"* by the Genoese in the Temple of Hercules in Tyre [which 16th-century legend claims was used by Christ at the Last Supper], see Kampers, p. 85; Wechssler, p. 129; Hertz, pp. 456–457; Birch-Hirschfeld, p. 223. *On the French Emperor Napoléon's orders, the sacred emerald was analyzed in 1806.

11. De Vic and Vaissètte, *Histoire* (especially pp. 161–162); Vaux-Cernay, Ch. IV.

12. From Bertan's *"Guerra me plai."*

13. Re: the origin of the name Papiol, see Peyrat, Vol. I, p. 56. According to K. Mahn in *Biographien,* p. 6, *Papiol was the name of Bertran de Born's juggler.

14. *A mournful poem, elegy.

15. Re: Bertran de Born and Henry of England, see Peyrat, Vol. I, p. 60.

16. *The Third Crusade (1189–1192) was an attempt to reconquer the Holy Land from the forces of Saladin. It is also referred to as the "King's Crusade."

17. The version in prose of the poems of Marcabru and Peirol was taken from Peyrat, Vol. I, p. 193. Also, K. Mahn uses Marcabru's ballad in *Biographien,* p. 15.

18. *Joachim of Flora or "de Fiore" (1132–1202) did not consider himself a prophet. He believed instead that he had the right to interpret biblical prophecies. His writings were compiled under the title *Evangelium aeternum,* and the Franciscan "Spirituals" made good use of them during their confron-

tation with the Papacy. Circa 1254, Gherardino di Borgo San Donnino of the Order of the Minorites wrote an *Introductio ad Evangelium aeternum* in which he accused the Papacy of being a non-spiritual power. The Pope ordered the book confiscated, and the publisher paid for his impudence with fourteen years in prison. See Döllinger, *Der Weissagungsglaube und das Prophetentum in der christliche Zeit* (1880). Re: the links between the song of Alexander the Priest-king and the Grail, see Kampers, p. 105.

19. Wechssler, p. 135: "Arthur was a *dux bellorum* or military leader of the Welsh in their conflicts with the Anglo-Saxons at the end of the fifth and the beginning of the sixth centuries." Also see Hertz.

20. Sources for the chivalric festivities at Beaucaire: Peyrat, Vol. I, p. 236; de Vic and Vaissètte, Vol. VI, p. 60, Baudler, p. 28.

21. Peyrat, Vol. I, p. 239.

22. *Although Richard forgave the man who fired the fatal shot before he died, the assassin was flayed alive and hanged.

23. From Kannegiesser's free translation of Gaucelm Faidit's elegy.

24. The troubadours' poem refers to Raimundo VI. See Lea, Vol. I, p. 146.

25. *Parzival*, p. 235. Achmardi is an emerald green fabric that was exported from the Levant to Western Europe. According to a note by Hatto in his excellent English translation of *Parzival*, although the word is not recognized, it translates as emeraldine or *az-zumurrudi* in Arabic.

26. Peyrat, Vol. I, pp. 22 and 39; de Vic and Vaissètte, Vol. VI.

27. Peyrat, Vol. I, pp. 29 and 265; Garrigou, *Foix*, Vol. I; Louis Palauqui, *Esclarmonde de Foix* (Foix: Lafont de Sentenac, 1911).

28. Re: the Sons of the Moon or Sons of Belissena: Peyrat, Vol. I, pp. 293–296, Vol. II, pp. 15, 17, 118, 197, 258; de Vic and Vaissètte, VI and IX; Witthöft (notes); Garrigou, *Foix*, Vol. I.

29. *Munsalvaesche* or *Munsalvatsche,* as Wolfram calls the Grail Castle, translates in German as *Wildenberg,* the name of the castle that the Graf Wertheim presented to Wolfram von Eschenbach. According to Pannier's prologue to his translation of *Parzival,* Wolfram "believed that the castle of Munsalvaesche was located in the Pyrenees." Re: the lords of Saissac, see Peyrat, Vol. II, pp. 101, 144, 200, 203, 241, etc.

30. See Baudler; Kampers, p. 19; Wechssler, p. 75.

31. See Wechssler, pp. 7, 165; Kampers, pp. 15, 112. Chrétien de Troyes wrote *Li contes del Graal* between 1180 and 1190. It is the oldest version of the story that we have, and it was dedicated to Philip of Flanders. Death surprised the author with pen in hand. "As fascinating as some parts are, compared to Wolfram's *Parzival,* it seems superficial and trivial."—the author.

32. *Parzival,* p. 115; Willehalm, pp. 2–19; Karl Pannier, Vol. I, p. 15.

33. Peyrat, Vol. I, p. 215; Baudler, p. 19.

34. See Titurel, 26, 27. Re: the name Herzeloyde, see Hertz, pp. 469, 478, 529; Wechssler, p. 166.

35. *Parzival,* pp. 140, 235. *Rahn returns to discuss the origins of this name. According to the author, Wolfram based it in *perce* (imperative of "to pierce, cut, or drill") and *bellement.* So in German, Parsifal could be translated as *Schneidgut.* The primitive sense of the name could also be "spring in the valley." See Wechssler, pp. 34, 135; Hertz, pp. 490–492; Kampers, p. 56.

PART TWO

The Grail

1. *Parzival,* p. 235 (Hatto translation, p. 125).

2. Peire Vidal's meeting with the knight named Amor and the lady named Grace is taken from Peyrat, *Histoire des Albigeois,* Vol. I, *Civilisation romaine,* p. 67. According to Pannier's introductory note to his translation of *Parzival,* Peire Vidal shared Wolfram von Eschenbach's concept of the Minne.

3. *Parzival,* pp. 1 and 3 (Hatto translation, p. 15); see also Peyrat, *Histoire des Albigeois,* Vol. I, *Civilisation romaine,* p. 65.

4. *The ancient Zoroastrians.

5. *Antonin Gadal was the first to use the expression "Pathway of the Cathars."

6. *Parzival,* pp. 454–456 (Hatto translation, pp. 233–235). Wolfram uses the word "innocence" in place of "purity." The "Day of the Supreme Minne" refers to Good Friday.

7. The *Gleysos* are located in the vicinity of the spulga (cave) of Ornolac; *during their extensive explorations, Rahn and Antonin Gadal discovered that they are connected through the caves of "the Hermit" and "the Fish."

8. *In 1963, regional publisher Trois Cèdres in Ussat-les-Bains brought out a small book, *Sabarthès,* by G. Zagelow, complete with maps—Karl Rittersbacher.

9. *Parzival,* p. 475 (Hatto translation, p. 242). The Cathars believed that they were celestial spirits who originated in divine substance. Döllinger, *Beiträge zur Sektengeschichte der Mittlealters,* Vol. I, p. 134.

10. Alfred Loisy, *Les mystères païens et les mystères chrétiens* (1914–1918), p. 44.

The Golden Fleece

1. Roscher, *Encyclopedia,* art. "Golden Fleece," calls the Golden Fleece the "Classical Grail."
2. See Reinach, *Orpheus,* pp. 58–59.
3. Re: Ilhomber, see Peyrat, Vol. I, *Civilisation romaine,* p. 127; Abellio, Vol. I, p. xv. Re: the Phoenician settlements in the vicinity of Narbonne, see Movers, II, 2, pp. 644–654. According to Tacitus, *Germania* XLIII, a priest in Germany whose name appears to have been Alcis offered sacrifices to the two divinities, Castor and Pollux, while dressed as a woman. Regarding Orpheus, see Reinach's *Orpheus,* p. 122, and Loisy, Ch. II.
4. Wolfram clearly states that the Grail was a stone. He calls it—erroneously—a *Lapsis exillis,* which is taken from *Lapsis ex coelis;* according to this legend, the "Grâl" fell from Lucifer's crown to Earth during the fall of the angels, and landed directly on Montségur in the Pyrenees. Kampers, p. 86 and his notes at the foot of p. 121. Also see Wechssler, p. 167. Re: the link between the Argonauts and a "cup," see Kampers, p. 72.
5. Kampers, p. 71; "Flegetanis," *Parzival,* p. 454. *According to Wolfram, a Jewish astronomer in Toledo named Flegetanis is the source of the legend of the Grail. Over the ages, many have been intrigued by the character's name, which translates as "familiar with stars" in Persian. Others have identified the character with Thabit ben Gorah, an alchemist who lived in Baghdad between 826 and 901; still others assert that the origin of the name is "Felek Thâni," the guardian of the planet Mercury in Arabic. Surprisingly, Flegetanis is a family name in the Empordà, in the northern Catalonian region of Spain.
6. Kampers, p. 71.
7. The *Ciste Ficorini* is preserved in Rome in the Vatican Museum. See Loisy, p. 67. Re: Pythagoras: *Parzival,* p. 773.

Gwion's Cup

1. Pythagoras of Samos, 580–496 B.C.
2. Dispater: *ab dite patre prognatos* (Caesar, VI, 17).
3. Ptolemy: *Geography,* Vol. II, 10. All sources for the march of the Volcae Tectosages through Greece can be found in de Vic and Vaissètte, *Histoire,* Vols. I and II.
4. Ernest Renan, *La Vie de Jésus,* p. 82. The Manicheans considered both Christ and Manes as prophets who consoled humanity.
5. The head of the Buddha discovered in an Iberian burial chamber is on display in the Museum of Rennes. According to Alexandre de Bernay, two traitors were reponsible for the death of Alexander: Jovispater and Antipater;

Birch-Hirschfeld, *Epische stoffe*, p.21. Peire Vidal also mentions Antipater when he refers to Alexander.

6. Re: Celtic theology, hierarchy, and their God Hesus or Esus in particular, see de Vic and Vaissètte, Vol. I, p. 28, and note 56 (Ammianus Marcellinus).

How the Bard Taliesin Came to the World

1. Re: the legend of Taliesin, see Bosc, *Belisama*, pp. 93 and 107. The Phoenician Hercules was depicted as a dwarf, and was also called Gwion, Ogmi, or Albion, all considered gods. It would appear that the mysterious bards played an important role as guards of the "sacred cup." In Loisy, p. 79, the author describes the extraordinary parallels between the Eleusins and the metamophosis of Gwion.

The Legend of the Bard Cervorix

1. Bosc, p. 122: "The island of the Seine, says Pomponius Mela (III, 6), is renowned as the seat of the oracles of Gaul, whose nine high priestesses have the power to unleash tempests, and winds . . . these Druid women were considered saints because of their chastity." Bosc, p. 56, but also Reinach, *Orpheus*, p. 179. In this respect I would like to call attention to the similarity between the nine muses, the nine priestesses of the Seine, and the seven times nine virgins of the Grail.

The "Pure Ones" and Their Doctrine

1. *Parzival*, p. 463; Astaroth = Astarté; Belcimon = Baal-Schemen or Samin (a Syrian divinity); Beleth = the Chaldean Baal; Radamant = Radamantis; the judge of Avernus = Hell.

2. *"Mosiach" means "descended from King David" in Hebrew; the belief in the coming of the Messiah is fundamental to Judaism.

3. St. Luke, *The Acts and Deeds of the Apostles*, 2:II, 46.

4. Renan, *La Vie de Jésus*, pp. 55, 85, 110; Loisy, p. 251. Also see Peyrat, Vol. I, *Civilisation romaine*, p. xx.

5. Priscillian, Bishop of Avila.

6. Priscillianism was a Gnostic Manichaeism; its cruel extermination—the first time a sentence of death was pronounced against a heresy—provoked a division between the bishops who approved of Priscillian's trial and condemnation, and those like Ambrosio of Milan and Martin de Tours, who opposed it. See Lea, Vol. I, pp. 239–240; Reinach, *Orpheus*, pp. 351 and 383; Peyrat, Vol. I, pp. x, 121, and 286; Vol. II, p. 8. Ref: Babu, *Priscillien et le Priscilliensime*.

7. *In one of the later editions of Rahn's work, Karl Rittersbacher notes that a document, *Liber de duobis principiis,* discovered in Florence in 1939 by Dondaine, is the oldest and most important surviving Cathar document we have. Zoë Oldenbourg proceeds in a different way, publishing Cathar texts—a ritual for example—translated into French, and lets the reader form his own opinion (pp. 382–399).

8. Schmidt, Vol. II, pp. 8 et seq; Döllinger, Vol. I, pp. 132 et seq.

9. Matthew 4:9 and 14:13; Schmidt, Vol. II, p. 16.

10. St. John 1:12 and 13; 3:6; Hebrews 13:14; Schmidt, p. 25.

11. Galatians 3:28; Col. 1:20; Genesis 3:15, 6:2; First Epistle of St. John 3:9; St. John 10:8; Schmidt, Vol. II, p. 21; Döllinger, Vol. I, pp. 144, 147, 165; N. Peyrat, Vol. I, p. 361.

12. *Parzival,* p. 463.

13. Kampers, pp. 103 and 86: "In Merlin's French and Italian prophecies, the *magus* writes of the Babylonian dragon's crown with four precious stones, and something similar that belonged to the mythical Emperor of Orbante, Aurians-Adriano. One of the chapter titles of the Italian prophecy identifies this figure with the Babylonian dragon. By chance, the crown of the lord of Orbante was found in the sea, and a fisherman took the precious stones that adorned it to Emperor Fredrick. In the manner that the passage was written, it is possible to deduce that the stones were the most important part of the crown."

14. Schmidt, Vol. II, p. 72; Döllinger, Vol. I, p. 150; *Dicunt Christum phantasma fuisse non hominem.* Schmidt, Vol. II, p. 38, note 1.

15. Schmidt, Vol. II, p. 36; Döllinger, Vol. I, p. 152; Peyrat, Vol. I, p. 383; *Cum cogitaret Pater meus mittere me in mundum, misit angelum suum ante me, nomine Maria, us acciperet me. Ego autem descendens intravi per auditum, et exivi per auditum.* See Schmidt, Vol. II, p. 41, note 2. Christ is born like Athena from the head: St. Augustine adds (in a treatise attributed to him), *deus per Angelum Loquebatur, et Virgo auribus impraegnabatur.* Ref: Schmidt, Vol. II, p. 41; Peyrat, Vol. I, p. 384.

16. Schmidt, Vol. II, pp. 78, 167, 169; Döllinger, Vol. I, p. 178. For paragraph 3, see Saint Luke, 9:56.

17. Inquisitor and troubadour Isarn was only stating a generally accepted truth when he asserted that no member of the faithful could be converted by the Cathars or Waldenses if he had a good pastor: *Ya no fara crezens heretje ni baudes si agues bon pastor que lur contradisses.* Lea, Vol. I, p. 67.

18. The number of heretical Perfecti was extremely small. During the First Crusade—the glory days of Catharism—their number did not surpass 800.

This is not surprising, given that the Cathar doctrine demanded ascetic practices that could undermine even the most robust constitution. On the other hand, the *credentes* or believers were very numerous. Together with the Waldenses, they topped the number of orthodox Catholic believers, who were eventually reduced to the clergy. Obviously this refers exclusively to the south of France. Regarding the division of Catharism into Perfecti and *credentes;* see 1 Cort. 2:6; Hebrews 5:12–13; Loisy, p. 248; Reinach, *Orpheus,* pp. 104–105. The Cathar faithful were simply called "Christians."

19. The Cathars had their meeting places inside castles, and in the cities as well. Schmidt, Vol. II, p. 11. In Montségur there was an abode *quae erat deputata ad faciendum sermonem* (an entry in a register preserved in Carcassonne dated 1243). Regarding the bendicion, see Schmidt, p. 116; Döllinger, on p. 230. The actual prayer was: *Pater et Filius et Spiritus Sanctus, parcat vobis et dimittat vobis omnia peccata vestra.* A popular Occitan prayer said: *Senhor prega Deu per aquest pecaire, que Deus m'aport a bona fi. . .* to which was answered: *Deus vos benedicat, eus fassa bon Chrestia, eus port a bona fi.* Schmidt, Vol. II, p. 126.

20. Regarding the Cathar's *"particion del pan,"* also called the benediction of the bread, see Schmidt, Vol. II, p. 129. Concerning the dogma of reincarnation, see Reinach, *Orpheus,* p. 422; Hauck, *Transubstantiation.* Finally, in addition to the breaking of bread in primitive Christianity, see for example Loisy, p. 215; *loco vero consecrati panis eucharistie corporis christi, confingunt quedam panem quem appelant panem benedictum seu panem sancte orationis quem in principio mense sue tenendo in anibus secundum ritum suum, benedicunt et frangunt, et distribuunt assistentibus et credentibus suis.* Bernard Gui, p. 12. Also, St. Paul said that the community of the faithful is the "body of Christ": Rom. 12:5; 1a Corint. 12:13. Finally, Schmidt, Vol. I, p. 139 examines the constitution of the "Church of Amor" on p. 139; Döllinger, Vol. I, p. 200; Peyrat, Vol. I, book 6, Ch. 7, pp. 395 et seq.

21. Not all Cathars believed that the Holy Spirit was the Paraclete; according to Psalm 1:14, it was also called the *Spiritus principalis,* to which adoration was given along with the Father and the Son. The Cathars made a distinction between the *Spiritus principalis* and the protecting spirits on one hand, and the "seven spirits" that according to the Apocalypse, 1:4 stand before the throne of God. For the Cathars, one of these seven spirits was the Paraclete. See Döllinger, Vol. I, pp. 137–138, 155 et seq. The predominating belief (found in the Gospel of St. John) was that the Paraclete was identical with the Holy Spirit. See John 14:16 and 26; 15:26; and 16:7 and 13.

22. *The Cathar Manisola was celebrated four times a year, according to a

solar calendar: on the equinoxes in spring and autumn, and at the summer and winter solstices. Three major Cathar castles in Occitania—Montségur, Quéribus, and Cab-Aret—were constructed according to an astronomical plan similar to the pyramids in Egypt. See Fernand Niel, *Les Cathares et Montségur* (Seghers, 1973). According to Rahn's friend, Col. Karl Maria Wiligut, "Mani" is the Old Norse word for "moon"—a clue that could unravel the mystery of the most radical of all Cathar sects, the "Sons of the Moon."

23. Regarding the Cathar consolamentum, see Schmidt, Vol. I, pp. 119, 123; Döllinger, Vol. I, 143, 153, 191, 204; Peyrat, Vol. I, p. 378. *Et confingunt, tanquam simie, (!) quedam alia loco ipsorum, que quasi similia videantur, confingentes loco baptismi facti in qua baptismum alia spiritualem, quem vocant consolamentum Spiritus Sancti quando videlicet recipiunt aliquam personam in sanitate vel infirmitate ad sectam et ordinem suum per impositionem manuum secundum ritum suum execralibem* (!)—Bernard Gui, p. 12. The real purpose of the consolamentum was to stop the transmigration of the soul from one body to another. Re: Cathar beliefs of metempsychosis, the words of St. Peter are especially relevant. Peter referred to spirits that are captured in a prison, which is to say in the human body; he added that Christ preached to the incredulous in the days of Noah (1 Peter 3:19); See Döllinger, Vol. I, p. 143, Schmidt, Vol. II, p. 46.

24. The "Black Mountain" in the Corbières region between Castres and Carcassonne.

25. Schmidt, Vol. II, pp. 83, 94; Peyrat, Vol. I, p. 104. The "habit" can be traced to the *kosti* and *saddarah,* the sacred shirt and dress worn by all Zoroastrian or Mazdaist faithful. The fact that the *Zend* and Brahmans wore them indicates a prehistoric origin, before the dispersion of the Indo-Europeans. In Cathar times, those who wore the habit were considered by the Inquisitors as *haereticus indutus o vestitus,* or "intiates in all the mysteries of the heresy." See Lea, Vol. I, p. 101.

26. Regarding the endura, see Molinier, *Endura,* Schmidt, Vol. II, p. 103; Döllinger, Vol. I, pp. 193, 221, and 225.

27. *A famous plaster death mask of an anonymous young woman who committed suicide by drowning; 1898–1900, plaster; Musée Nationale des Moulages, Paris.

28. Re: Dante's "mountain of purification," see Kampers, p. 62: "the representation—reflection of the Hindu myth—of an inaccessible celestial mountain, where at the foot or on the summit the Garden of Eden could be found, was preserved throughout the Middle Ages."

29. Schmidt, Vol. II, pp. 82, 93; Döllinger, Vol. I, pp. 180–181. Among the first

Christians, there was a strong tendency to explain the apparent injustices of God with metempsychosis. See Lea, Vol. I, pp. 109 and 122.

The Caves of Trevrizent Close to the Fountain Called La Salvaesche

1. Peyrat, Vol. II, p. 78; Lea, Vol. I, pp. 121–122.
2. *Parzival,* p. 452.
3. *Parzival,* p. 459 (Hatto translation, p. 235). Re: Solomon's treasure, see Kampers, pp. 26, 27, 33, 39, 54, 66, 80, 81, 85, 94.
4. Kampers, pp. 15, 28, 34, 42, 43, 62, 71, 90.
5. Re: the Sacred Fish, see Reinach's *Orpheus,* pp. 29–30; *Cultes* II, p. 43; Kampers, pp. 35, 71, 74, 75; Wechssler, p. 130; Renan, p. 238. Unlike the rest of the Cathars, the townfolk of Albi ate fish and drank wine.
6. For specific literature on the Sabarthès, see Garrigou and Antonin Gadal. Peyrat's history of the Albigenses, *Albigeois et l'Inquisition,* is the only work that refers to the death knell of Catharism in the caves of Tarascon. While Garrigou and Gadal (both from Tarascon) discovered traces of the tragedy of the Cathars during their explorations, they mention them only in passing. On the other hand, Peyrat visited only the cave of Lombrives, which he mistook for the spulga Ornolac. In his *Cartullaire de Prouille,* Guiraud dedicates an entire chapter to Lupo de Foix, which is nevertheless very incomplete. See de Vic and Vaissètte, Vols. VI and IX, and Note 46.
7. Re: the *haereticatio* of Esclarmonde, see Peyrat, *Civilisation Romaine,* p. 329; Palauqui, *Esclarmonde de Foix;* Guiraud, *Saint Dominique,* p. 56; Coulet, *Montanhagol,* pp. 28, 97, 103, and 106. Montanhagol's verses probably refer to Esclarmonde de Foix's niece Esclarmonde de Alion, and not the famous Cathar. Today, townsfolk simply refer to "Esclarmonde" without any further elaboration. See Magre, pp. 93–94.

Muntsalvaesche and Montségur

1. Monmur: The obvious correlation between the poems of Huon and the tales of the Grail has been ignored until now.
2. *Parzival,* pp. 250–251, 472, 492, 493, 495, 797, 827.

Repanse de Schoye

1. *Parzival,* p. 235.

PART THREE

The Crusade

1. As Roger, the Bishop of Châlons, asserted in his letter to Wazo, the Prelate of Liège, the Cathars saw the Holy Spirit in their "Mani": *"per sacrilegam manuum impositionem dari Spiritum sanctum mentientes quem non alias Deo missum quam in haeresiarcha suo Mani (quasi nihil aliud sit Manes nisi Spiritus sanctus) fasissime dogmatizarent."* See Schmidt, Vol. II, p. 259, note 1. Peyrat, who changes Manichaeism into Maneism and then designates it "The Church of the Paraclete," speaks of Catharism as a monotheistic Manichaeism. According to the author, Manes was the "messenger of the Mani" or "one who has the Mani." The word "Mani" comes from the *Zend,* the Persian commentary on the Zoroastrian *Avesta,* and (as we have already mentioned) means "spirit," the equivalent of the Latin *mens.* See also Peyrat, Vol. I, pp. xii, 121, and 412.

2. Re: the repudiation of the cross by the Albigenses, see Schmidt, Vol. II, p. 112; Moneta, pp. 112, and 461. The Templar knights also repudiated the cross.

3. Fulk or Folquet in Occitania: Peyrat, Vol. I, p. 311; Lea, Vol. I, p. 148; de Vic and Vaissètte, Vol. VI, p. 243, Vol. VII, p.144; Guiraud, *Dominique,* p. 66. Fulk, St. Dominic, and Simon de Montfort were united in a "pious friendship." See also Dante Alighieri, *La Commedia Divina,* IX, 88; Tudela, Ch. CLXV.

4. Lea, Vol. I, p. 149; de Vic and Vaissètte, Vol. VI, p. 471; Palauqui, *La vérité sur l'Albigéisme,* p. 10. In the city of Toulouse alone, Fulk ordered the execution of 10,000 presumed heretics; Schmidt, Vol. I, pp. 66, 68, 96; Lea, Vol. I, p. 29.

5. Schmidt, Vol. I, pp. 195-196. Already in the era of St. Bernard de Clairvaux, almost all knights of the Midi—*fere omnes milites*—were heretics. Guiraud, *Dominique,* p. 23.

6. Lea, Vol. I, pp. 40, 142; Schmidt, Vol. I, p. 192. On p. 70, Vossler writes: "From an ethical and political perspective, Cardinal put himself so decidedly on the side of the persecuted Albigenses, and above all with the Counts of Toulouse with his quatrains, that he can be considered without any doubt the author of the second part of the epic poem of the Crusade against the Albigenses."

7. Lea, Vol. I, pp. 15, 16, and 18; Schmidt, Vol. I, p. 335; Doat, XXV, folio II. Re: the Waldenses, see above all Jas, Moneta, and Bernard Gui; Vaux-Cernay says of them in Ch. II they were *"longe minus perversi"* than the Cathars.

8. *Bernard Gui, né Guidonis, Dominican monk and French bishop (1261–1331), wrote the *Practica Inquisitionis Heretice Pravitatis [The Conduct of the Inquisition of Heretical Depravity]* (1307–1323), better known as the *Inquisitor's Manual*. Recently Annette Palès-Gobillard translated *Le livre des sentences de l'Inquisiteur Bernard Gui* into French (CNRS Editions). The fanatical Inquisitor Gui appeared as a character in Umberto Eco's 1983 novel *The Name of the Rose* (also a 1986 film). Also see David de Augsburg's *De inquisitione haeretocorum*, p. 206, Mollat (prologue to Gui), p. xxxix, and finally Lea, Vol. I, pp. 35, 93, and 95.

9. Re: the Council of Tours: Peyrat, Vol. I, pp. 123 and 160. Around this time, the slave Niketas appeared as the Pope-heretic. See Peyrat, Vol. I, Ch. IV and V; Döllinger, Vol. I, p. 122; de Vic and Vaissètte, Vol. VI, pp. 2 and 3; Schmidt, Vol. I, p. 73.

10. Re: the discussion at Lombers, see Peyrat, Vol. I, p. 127; Schmidt, Vol. I, p. 70. Re: Peire Morand: Peyrat, Vol. I, p. 161; Schmidt, Vol. I, p. 76; Lea, Vol. I, p. 135; de Vic and Vaissètte, Vol. VI, p. 3.

11. Re: the supposed orthodoxy of the House of Trencavel, see de Vic and Vaissètte, Vol. VI, p. 155.

12. *Pope Alexander III (1105–1181, r. 1159–1181).

13. Re: Cardinal Albano and his "crusade," see Peyrat, Vol. I, pp. 165, 171; Schmidt, Vol. I, p. 83; Lea, Vol. I, p. 137. On p. 176, Peyrat writes: "As Albano headed for Gascony, all the inhabitants of the plains fled to the mountains accompanied by Esclarmonde de Foix and her troubadours, Arnaut Daniel, Peire Vidal, and the intrepid Marcabru."

14. Re: Innocent III, see Achille Luchaire, *Innocent III,* and in particular Vol. II (1906); Peyrat, Vol. I, pp. 251, 286; Lea, Vol. I, p. 149.

15. Schmidt, Vol. I, pp. 197, 205; Lea, Vol. I, p. 197; Guilhem de Puylaurens, *Guilelmus de Podio Laurentii chronica*, p. 671; Vaux-Cernay, pp. 559, 560.

16. Also known as Arnaud Amaury or Amalric (?–1225). For a biography of Arnaud de Cîteaux, see Peyrat, Vol. I, pp. 291, 315. Also see Schmidt, Vol. I, p. 210; Lea, Vol. I, pp. 156, 157; de Vic and Vaissèette, Vol. VI, pp. 245–246.

17. Peyrat described the conference of Pamiers in detail in Vol. I, book IV. See Schmidt, Vol. I, p. 213; Vaux-Cernay, Ch. VI; Palauqui, *Esclarmonde de Foix,* p. 21; de Vic and Vaissètte, Vol. I, p. 250; Puylaurens, Ch. VIII (672). The Count of Foix, Raimon Roger, authorized the conference. His wife Philippa and (as we know) his sister Esclarmonde were both Cathars. His second sister Cecilia, the wife of Roger Comminges, was a Waldense—the only case that we have of an Occitan noble belonging to this sect, which is

surprising because they were basically composed of farmers and artisans. In the Council of the Lateran of 1215, Fulk of Marseille accused the Count of Toulouse of heresy: see Tudela, Ch. CXLV.

18. Mirepoix and Montségur: Peyrat, Vol. I, p. 303 etc; Palauqui, *Esclarmonde de Foix*, p. 19. Schmidt, Vol. I, pp. 215, 234; Doat, XXIV, folios 217 and 240; XXII, folios 168 and 216; Tudela, verses 3260 et seq; Guiraud, *Cartullaire*, p. CCL. The foundation of the first Dominican convent, Notre Dame de Prouille, near Fanjeaux: Guiraud, *Cartullaire* and *Saint Dominique*; de Vic and Vaissètte, Vol. VI, p. 252; Peyrat, Vol. II, p.131; Schmidt, Vol. I, p. 216; Luchaire, Vol. II, p. 99. According to Peyrat and Palauqui, Bertrand de la Baccalaria reconstructed Montségur. In pagan times, a sanctuary dedicated to Abellio stood close to another venerating Belissena.

19. "Blessed" Pierre de Castelnau was killed on January 15, 1208. To this day, the Papal legate's assassin has never been identified. Tudela asserts that the murderer was a shield bearer of the Count of Toulouse who wanted to avenge the insults to his lord.

20. Re: the Papal Encyclica of Leo XIII, see Lea, Vol. I, pp. 169, 170; Schmidt, Vol. I, pp. 221, 228; Louis Palauqui, *Esclarmonde de Foix*, pp. 22–24.

21. Tudela, p. 175 (Verse 342 et seq). Apart from Raimon-Roger, Raimon Roger de Foix, and the Sons of Belissena, the most powerful protectors of the Cathars at the beginning of the crusade against the Albigenses were Gaston VI, Count of Béarn, Gérard VI, Count of Armagnac, and Bernard VI, Count of Comminges. There were no heretics in the domains of Guilhem VI, Count of Montpellier. See Schmidt, Vol. I, p. 196. Re: the siege of Béziers: Tudela, Ch. XVI et seq; Vaux-Cernay, XVI; Peyrat, Vol. II, p. 40; Schmidt, Vol. I, p. 228; de Vic and Vaissètte, Vol. VI, p. 288. Caesarius von Heisterbach, Book V, Ch. 21. According to one chronicler, 60,000 persons perished; Heisterbach puts the figure closer to 100,000. *Que nols pot grandir crotz* (Tudela, verse 495): "Nothing could save them, not the cross, the altar or the crucifix. Those madmen and sneaky ruffians slit the throats of priests, women, and children. Not one, I believe, was left alive; shall God receive them in his Glory!" Tudela continues, "I do not believe that since the time of the Saracens, such a bestial killing has been decided upon and carried out. The booty that the French obtained was enormously large. If those ruffians and crooks had not appeared with their King, all the inhabitants of Béziers would have been rich for the rest of their lives."

22. Re: the siege of Carcassonne: Tudela, Ch. XXVI et seq; Vaux-Cernay; Guillaume de Puylaurens, Ch. XIV; Peyrat, Vol. II, p. 48; Schmidt, Vol. I, p. 230; Lea, Vol. I, p. 174; de Vic and Vaissètte, Vol. VI, p. 291. Caesarius von

Heisterbach calls the town *pulchravallis*. The *Veni Creator Spiritus* was the official hymn of the crusade against the Albigenses, and so became the leitmotiv of all the atrocities committed by the Vatican and Royal Paris against the "Church of the Paraclete." *Messa lor cantata:* Tudela, verse 768.

23. Re: the death of Raimon Roger Trencavel: See de Vic and Vaissètte, Vol. VI, p. 313. Raimon Roger was less than thirty years of age when he died. The year of his birth is given as 1185. His mother, Adélaide de Burlats, had died in 1199. Raimon Roger's wife, Inès de Montpellier, fled to Foix with her only son, Raimon Trencavel (b. 1207) before the arrival of the crusaders; see de Vic and Vaissètte, Peyrat, and above all Tudela, p. 181, note 1. Shortly after the death of her husband, Inès left her parents in Foix and went over to the enemy.

24. Lea, Vol. I, p. 178; Peyrat, Vol. II, Books VIII and X (Ch. VI); Schmidt, Vol. I, p. 233.

25. Minerve: Lea, Vol. I, p. 181; Schmidt, Vol. I, p. 242; Peyrat, Vol. II, p. 157; Tudela vv 1071; Vaux-Cernay, Ch. XXXVII; de Vic and Vaissètte, Ch. LXXXVII. Termès: Peyrat, Vol. II, p. 184; Schmidt, Vol. I, p. 243; as well as the sources given for Minerve; Tudela, Ch. LVI; de Vic and Vaissètte, Vol. VI, Ch. XCIII. *Raimon de Termès' son Olivier became an expert in siege warfare. After serving in the Catalonian army, he converted to Catholicism and died in the Holy Land.

26. Lea, Vol. I, p. 184; Peyrat, Vol. II, p. 184; Schmidt, Vol. I, p. 244; de Vic and Vaissètte, Vol. VI.

27. Lavaur: Peyrat, Vol. I, pp. 325 and 337; Vol. II, p. 204; Schmidt, Vol. I, pp. 247–248; Vaux Cernay, Ch. XLIX; Tudela, Ch. LXVIII; de Vic and Vaissètte, Vol. VI, Ch. CII, CIII, CVIII; Guillaume de Puylaurens, Ch. XVI. *Estiers dama Girauda:* "Donna Geralda was thrown into a well. (The Crusaders) covered her with stones. Supreme mockery and derision, because nobody in this world—you can take this for certain—ever left her home without receiving hospitality." Tudela, vv 1557 et seq. *Dominal etiam castri, quae erat soror Aimerici et haeretica pesima, in puteum projectam Comes lapidibus obrui fecit; innumerabiles, etiam haereticos peregrini nostri cum ingenti gaudo combuserunt.* Vaux Cernay, end of Ch. LII.

28. Re: Innocent III: see Schmidt, Vol. I, p. 244, Note 1.

29. Lea, Vol. I, pp. 174, 190; Schmidt, Vol. I, p. 255; Peyrat, Vol. II, book XI. Re: the death of Simon de Montfort: Peyrat, Vol. II, pp. 68, 410; Schmidt, Vol. I, p. 270; Lea, Vol. I, p. 208; Puylaurens, Ch. XXVIII-XXX; Vaux-Cernay, Ch. LXXXIII et seq. Re: the death of Raimundo VI: Purlaurens, Ch. XXXIV; de Vic and Vaissètte, Vol. VI, book XXV.

30. Re: the end of the third part, see Lea, Vol. I, p. 227; Schmidt, Vol. I, p. 283; de Vic and Vaissètte, Vol. VI, books XXV.

31. The poem by Bernard Sicard has been taken from Peyrat, *l'Histoire des Albigeois*.

PART FOUR

The Apotheosis of the Grail

1. Domingo de Guzman: Peyrat, Vol. I, p. 316; Guiraud, *Saint Dominique*; Dante Alighieri, *La Commedia Divina* (Heaven) XII. Tomas de Malvenda: Guiraud, p. 40; Lea, Vol. I, pp. 335, 337, 368, 411, 459, 487. The "model interrogation" was taken from Bernard Gui, Vol. I, p. 64, and Lea, Vol. I, p. 459. Also see David von Augsburg, pp. 229–232.

2. Re: the oath of Joan Teisseire: Lea, Vol. I, pp. 107–108. Re: flagellation: Lea, Vol. I, p. 519; Cauzons, Vol. II, p. 299. Re: pilgrimages: Lea, Vol. I, p. 520; Cauzins, Vol. II, p. 295; Mollat, *Manuel*, LVI. Re: wearing the crosses: Lea, p. 523; Doat, XXXI, 57; Cauzons, Vol. II, p. 227.

3. Re: Torture: Lea, Vol. I, pp. 470, 477; Doat, XXXI, 57; Cauzons, Vol. II, p. 227.

4. Re: murus: Schmidt, Vol. II, p. 196; Cauzons, Vol. II, p. 367; Lea, Vol. I, p. 544, Vol. II, p. 36. Re: death by fire and the "secular arm": Lea, Vol. I, pp. 249, 597; Cauzons, Vol. II, pp. 381, 401. The Inquisitors believed that they could justify death by burning at the stake with the Gospel According to St. John 15:6. Re: condemnation of dead heretics: Lea, Vol. I, pp. 259, 501, 566, 619. Cauzons believes that the phenomenon is based in 1 Kings 13:2 and 2 Kings 23:16. See Cauzons, Vol. II, p. 360. Re: Pope Stephen VII, see Lea, Vol. I, p. 259.

5. St. Thomas Aquinas (circa 1225–1274), "doctor angelicus," a Dominican.

6. Re: confiscation of assets: Lea, Vol. I, p. 560; Cauzons, Vol. II, p. 318.

7. Pope John XXII: born Jacques Duèse in 1245.

8. Pope Urban VI (1318–1389, r. 1378–1389), born Bartolomeo Prignano, provoked the Great Schism; he died in Rome from the injuries caused by a fall from his mule.

9. Lea, Vol. I, pp. 623–625; Ch. XVII of the Apocalypse says: *Item, duas configunt esse ecclesias, unam benignam quam dicunt esse sectam suam, eamque esse asserunt ecclesiam Jhesu Christi; aliam vero ecclesiam vocant malignam, quam dicunt esse Romanem ecclesiam eamque impudenter appellant matrem fornicationum, Babilonem magnam meretricem et basilicam dyaboli et Sathanae synagogam*; Bernard Gui, Vol. I, p. 10; Döllinger, Vol. I, p. 189.

10. The murder of Inquisitors in Avignonet: de Vic and Vaissètte, Vol. VI, p. 738; Puylaurens, Ch. XLV; Lea, Vol. II, p. 37; Doat, VVII, 107, XXIV, 160; Peyrat, *Les Albigeois et l'Inquisition,* Vol. II, p. 304; Schmidt, Vol. I, p. 320.

11. *Raimon de Alfar, Alfaro, or Alfier, was part of a family of Navarran knights in the service of Count Raimundo of Toulouse; it is rumored that Raimon, Ferran, and Hugo or Huc were among the four knights who evacuated the Grail from Montségur. All escaped from Montségur and at least one joined the army of James I of Aragon (aka Jaume "el Conquistador") during the seventh crusade to the Holy Land; see Gauthier Langlois, *Olivier de Termès.*

12. Montségur: de Vic and Vaissètte, Vol. VI, pp. 766–769; Puylaurens, Ch. XLVI; Catel, *Histoire des Comtes de Toulouse,* p. 162; Doat, XXII, 202, 204, 210, 214, 216–217, 224, 228, 37; XXIV, 68, 76, 80, 160, 168, 172, 181, 182, 198; Peyrat, *Croisade,* p. 359; *Les Albigeois et l'Inquisition,* Vol. II, pp. 299, 315, 324; Palauqui, *Esclarmonde de Foix,* p. 31; *Albigéisme,* pp. 10–11; Magre, p. 88; Duclos, Vol. II, Ch. I. Also see Gaussen, Garrigou (*Foix*) Gadal.

13. Lea, Vol. II, p. 105; Magre and the oral tradition. Re: Jacques Fourner, Bernard Délicieux, and Pierre Autier: Jakob, *Studien über Papst Benedikt XII;* de Vic and Vaissètte, *Histoire,* Vol. IX, p. 86, 229, 258, 260, 277, and 333, 389–392, 445; Lea, Vol. I, p. 297, Vol. II, pp. 80, 93, 107, 475; Peyrat, Lavisse, Haureau, Vid.

14. *Some say that Philip had Boniface beaten so badly that the Pontiff died.

BIBLIOGRAPHY

Alighieri, Dante. *La Divina Commedia.*

Biese, Alfred. *Deutsche Literaturgeschichte.* 17th ed. 1921.

Birch-Hirschfeld, Adolf. *Uber die den provençalischen Troubadours des XII und XIII Jahrhunderts bekannten epischen Stoffe.* 1878.

Brinkmeir, Eduard. *Die provençalischen Troubadours.* 1882.

De Vic, Dom Claude & Vaisette, Dom Joseph. *Histoire générale de Languedoc* (Privat, Toulouse ed.). 1872–1905.

Hoepfner, T. *Die Heiligen in der christlichen Kunst.* Leipzig: Breitkopf Und Härtel, 1893.

Kampers, Franz. *Das Lichtland der Seelen und der heilige Gral* (Göres Gesellschaft). 1916.

Karpeles, Gustav. *Allgemeine Geschichte der Literatur.* 1891.

Lavisse, Ernest. *Histoire de France.* Paris: Armand Colin et Cie, 1911.

Lea, Henry Charles. *Geschichte der Inquisition im Mittelalter.* 1905ff.

Lenau, Nicolaus. *Werke* (Deutsche Bibliogr. Instituts, Leipzig ed.).

Magre, Maurice. *Magiciens et Illuminés.* Paris: Bibliotheque-Charpentier, 1930.

Petrarca. *Trionfi* (Critical edition from Appel: Die Triumphe Petraracas). 1901–1902.

Peyrat, Napoléon. *Histoire des Albigeois.* Vol. I: Civilisation romaine; Vol. II: La Croisade. 1880

———. *Histoire des Albigeois.* Vol. I–III: Les Albigeois et l'Inquisition. 1870.

Reinach, Salomon. *Orpheus.* Paris, 1905.

Wechssler. Eduard. *Die Sage von heiligen Gral in ihrer Entwicklung bis auf Richard Wagners Parsifal.* Halle, 1898.

Wolfram von Eschenbach. *Parzival* (A. Leitzmann, Altdeustche Textbibliotek XII ed.). 1902.

The Birth of Romanesque Culture

Bérard, Victor. *La Méditerranée phénicienne* (annales de géographie). 1895–1896.

Bertrand, Alexandre. *Archéologique celtique et gauloise.* 1889.

Bosch Gimpera, Pedro. *Los antiguos Iberos y su origen* (Conference held on March 22, 1927 and published in *Conferencias dadas en el centro de inter-cambio intelectual Germano-español*). 1928.

Bouché de Cluny, J.B. *Les Bardes.* 1844.

Cartailhac, Emile. *l'Or gaulois* (Revue d'Anthropologie). 1899.

Clerc. *Histoire de Marseille dans l'Antiquité.* 1900.

De Vic, Dom Claude & Vaisette, Dom Joseph. *Histoire générale de Languedoc* (Privat, Toulouse ed.). 1872–1905.

Garrigou, Adolphe. *Ibérie et les Ibères.* 1884.

Herzog, A. *Gallia Narbonensis historia.* Leipzig, 1864.

Humboldt, Wilhelm von. *Prüfung der Untersuchungen über die Urbewohner Hispaniens vermittels der vaskischen Sprache.* 1821.

Jones-Williams, Owen. *The Myvyrian Archaeology Of Wales.* 1862.

Jung, Julius. *Die romanischen Landschaften des römischen Reiches.* 1881.

Lavisse, Ernest. *Histoire de France.* 1911.

Movers, Franz Karl. *Die Phönizier.* 1840–1856.

Napoléon III. *Histoire de Jules César.* 1866.

Peyrat, Napoléon. *Histoire des Albigeois.* Vol. I: Civilisation romaine; Vol. II: La Croisade. 1880

———. *Histoire des Albigeois.* Vol. I–III: Les Albigeois et l'Inquisition. 1870.

Phillips. *Die Wohnsitz der Kelten auf der pyrenäischen Halbinsel.* 1872.

Thierry, Amedée Simon Dominique. *Histoire des Gaulois.* 1877.

Wilke, Georg. *Kulturbeziehungen zwischen Indien, Orient und Europa.* 1923.

Druidism and Related Theogonies, until Manichaeism

Anrich, Gusatav. *Das antike Mysterienwesen.* 1894. 1904.

D'Arbois, M. *Les druides.* 1906.

Aubé, B. *Histoire des pesécutions.* Didier & Cie, 1875–1885.

Babut, Ernest Charles. *Priscillien et le Priscillianisme.* Paris, 1909.

Bachofen, Johann Jakob. *Der Mythos von Orient und Occident—Urreligionen und antike Symbole.*

Bardenheyer. *Geschichte der altchristlichen Literatur.* 1903.

Barth. *Uber der Druiden der Kelten.* 1826.

Baur, Ferdinand Christian. *Das manichäische Religionssyteme.* 1831.

Beausobre, Issac de. *Histoire critique de Manichée et du manichéisme.* 1734.

Beauvais, E. *L'Elysée transatlantique et l'Eden occidental* (Revue de l'histoire des religions). 1883.

Bertrand, Alexandre. *La Religion des Gaulois*. 1897.

Boissier, Gaston. *La fin du Paganisme*. 1891.

Boltz, August. *Der Apollomythus*. 1894.

Bosc, Ernest. *Belisama*. 1910.

Bouché-Leclerc, André. *L'Intolérance religieuse et la politique*. Paris: Flammarion, 1911.

Bühler, George. *The Laws of Manu*. Oxford, 1886.

Cumont, Franz. *Cosmogonie manichéene*. 1908.

Cumont, Gehrich. *Die orientalischen Religionen*. 1910.

Darmesteter, James. *Ormazd und Ahriman*. 1876.

Decharme, Paul. *Mythologie de la Grèce Antique*. Paris: Garnier, 1886

Déchelette, Joseph. *Manuel d'archéologie préhistorique et celtique*. 1908.

Delitsch, Friedrich. *Das babyl. Weltschöpfungsepos*. 1896.

De Vic, Dom Claude & Vaisette, Dom Joseph. *Histoire générale de Languedoc* (Privat, Toulouse ed.). 1872–1905.

Dobschütz, Ernest von. *Die urchristlichen Gemeinden*. Leipzing, 1902.

Duschesne. *Origines du culte chrétien*. 1925.

Flügel, Gustav Leberecht. *Mani, seine Lehren und seine Schriften*. Leipzing, 1862.

Grimm, Jacob. *Deutsche Mythologie*. 4th ed. 1875–1878.

Gruppe, Otto. *Griechische culte und Mythen*. 1887.

——. *Griechische Mythologie*. 1906.

Hahn, J.G.V. *Mythologische Parallelen*. Jena: Mauke, 1859.

Harnack, Adolf. *Lehrbuch der Dogmengeschichte*. 4th ed. 1910.

——. *Die Mission und Ausbreitung des Christentums in den ersten drei Jahrhunderten*. 1902.

Hauck-Herzog. *Realenzyklopädie für protestanische Theologie und Kirche*. 1877. sq. Art; Gnostizismus, Marcion, Priscillianus, etc.

Hirt, Hermann. *Die Indogermanen*. 1905.

Huggler, Max. *Mythologie der altchristl. Kunst*. Strassburg: JH ed. Heitz (Heitz &. Mündel) 1929.

Kessler, K. *Mani. Forschungen über die manichäische Religion*. Berlin, 1889.

Kittel, Rudolph. *Die hellenistische Mysterienreligion und das alte Testament*. 1924.

Lavisse, Ernest. *Histoire de France*. 1911.

Le Blant, Edmund Frederic. *Les persécuteurs et les martyrs*. Paris, 1893.

Leisegang, Hans. *Gnosis*. Leipzig: Kroner, 1924.

Loisy, Alfred. *Les mystères païens*. 1930.

Martigny, Joseph Alexander. *Dictionnaire des antiquités chrétiennes*. Paris, 1865.

Martin, Dom Jacques. *La religion des Gaulois*. 1727.

Maury, Louis Ferdinand Alfred. *La magie et l'astrologie dans l'Antiquité et au Moyen Age*. Paris: Didier & Cie, 1860.

Menzel, Wolfgang. *Vorchristliche Unsterblichkeitslehre*. Leipzing, 1870.

Milloué, Dr. Leon de. *Métempsychose et ascéticisme*. 1901.

Mogk, Eugen. *Germanische Mythologie*. Berlin: Mayer & Müller, 1906.

Paton, Lucy Allen. *Studies in the Fairy Mythology of Arthurian Romance*. Boston: Ginn & Company, 1903.

Paul. *Das Druidentum* (Jahrbücher für klass. Philologie). 1892.

Peyrat, Napoléon. *Histoire des Albigeois*. Vol. I: Civilisation romaine; Vol. II: La Croisade. 1880.

———. *Histoire des Albigeois*. Vol. I–III: Les Albigeois et l'Inquisition. 1870.

Pokorny, Julius. *Der Ursprung des Druidentums* (Mitteilungen der Weiner anthropol. Gesellschaft). Vienna, 1908.

Reclus, Elisée. *L'Homme et la Terre*. Paris: Libraire universelle, 1905.

Reinach, Salomon. *Cultes, mythes et religions*. 1904–1912.

Reitzenstein, Richard. *Hellenistische Mysterienreligionen*. Leipzing, 1904. 1910.

———. *Die vorgeschichte der christl. Taufe*. 1929.

Renan, Ernest. *La vie de Jésus*. 1863.

Réville, Albert. *Vigilance*. 1902.

Reynaud, Jean. *L'esprit de la Gaule*. Paris: Furne, 1866.

Rochat, Ernest. *Essai sur Mani et sa doctrine*. Geneva, 1897.

Rohdes, Erwin. *Psyche*. 1903.

Roscher, Wilhelm H. *Ausführliches Lexikon der griech. und röm. Mythologie*. Leipzig, 1884.

Sili Italici Punica (Editor Ludovicus Bauer). 1840.

Söderblom, Nathan. *La Vie future d'après le mazdéisme*. Paris, 1901.

Steffen, Albert. *Mani. Uber sein Leben und seine Lehre*. 1930.

Steiner, Rudolf. *Wendepunkte des Geisteslebens*. 1927.

Stender, J. *Die Argonautorum expeditione*. 1874.

Steuding, Hermann. *Griechische und römische Mythologie*. Leipzig, 1905.

Stoll, Heinrich Alexander. *Die Götter und Heroen des griechischen Altertums*. 7th ed. 1885.

Stoop, Emile. *La Diffusion du manichéisme dans l'Empire romain*. Gand 1909.

Vater. *Die Argonautenzug.* 1848.

Volkmann, Richard Emile. *Leben, Schriften und Philosophie des Plutarch.* 1873.

Wilamowitz-Möllendorf, Ulrich von. *Der Glauben der Hellenen.* 1931.

The Poetry of the Troubadours

Anglade, Joseph. *Anthologie des troubadours.* Paris: De Boccard, 1927.

———. *Histoire sommaire de la littérature au Moyen Age.* Paris: De Boccard, 1921.

———. *Les Troubadours.* Paris: Librairie Armand Colin, 1922.

Bartsch, Karl. *Chrestomathie provençale.* Berlin: Wiegandt & Schotte, 1904. 6th ed.

Baudler, A. *Guiot von Provins.* Halle, 1902.

Birch-Hirschfeld, Adolf. *Uber die den provençalischen Troubadours des XII und XIII Jahrhunderts bekannten epischen Stoffe.* 1878.

Brinkmeir, Eduard. *Die provençalischen Troubadours.* 1882.

Coulet, Jules. *Le troubadour Guilhem de Montanhagol* (Privat, Toulouse ed.). 1898.

De Vic, Dom Claude & Vaisette, Dom Joseph. *Histoire générale de Languedoc* (Privat, Toulouse ed.). 1872–1905.

Diez, Friedrich. *Die Poesie der Troubadours.* 1883.

———. *Leben und Werke der Troubadours.* 1882.

Fauriel, Claude. *Histoire littéraire des troubadours.* 1802.

Gautier, Léon. *La chevalerie.* 3rd ed. P. Welter, 1895.

Kannegiesser, Karl Friedrich Ludwig. *Gedichte der Troubadoure im Versmass der Urschrift übersetzt.* 1852.

Lavisse, Ernest. *Histoire de France.* 1911.

Mahn, Carl August Friedrich. *Gedichte der Troubadours in provenzalischer Sprache.* 1864.

———. *Biographien der Troubadours in provenzalischer Sprache.* 1883.

Meyer, Fritz. *Die Stände ihr Leben und Treiben dargestellt nach den altfranz. Artus und Abenteuerromanen* (Ausg. U. Abh. Ans D. Gebiete d. roman. Phil. LXXXIX). 1892.

Michelet, Joseph. *Les poètes gascons du Gers.* Auch: Th. Bouquet, 1904.

Millot, Abbé Claude-Françoise-Xavier. *Histoire littéraire des troubadours.* 1802.

Nostradamus, Jehan de. *Les vies des plus célèbres poètes provençaux.* 1575. 1913.

Peyrat, Napoléon. *Histoire des Albigeois.* Vol. I: Civilisation romaine; Vol. II: La Croisade. 1880

————. *Histoire des Albigeois.* Vol. I–III: Les Albigeois et l'Inquisition. 1870.

Suchier, Hermann. *Geschichte der französichen Literatur.* 1900.

Villemain, Abel-François. *Tableau de la littérature au Moyen Age.* 1840.

Vossler, Karl. *Peire Cardenal, ein Satiriker aus d. Zeitalter der Albigenser Kriege* (compiled by the Bavarian Academy of Sciences). 1916.

Wechssler, Eduard. *Die Sage von heiligen Gral in ihrer Entwicklung bis auf Richard Wagners Parsifal.* 1898.

Witthöft. *Sirventes joglaresc. Ein Blick auf das altfranzösische Spielmannsleben* (Ausg. U. Abh. Aus d. Gebiete d. roman. Phil. LXXXVIII). 1891.

The Albigenses and their Doctrine

Benoist, I. *Histoire des Albigeois.* 1691.

Clédat, Léon. *Le Nouveau Testament traduit au XIIIeme siècle en langue provençale, suivi d'un rituel cathare.* 1887.

De Vic, Dom Claude & Vaisette, Dom Joseph. *Histoire générale de Languedoc* (Privat, Toulouse ed.). 1872–1905.

Döllinger, Johann Joseph Ignaz von. *Beiträge zur Sektengeschichte des Mittelalters.* 1890.

Douais, Abbé Célestin. *Les Albigeois, leur origine.* Paris: Didier et Cie, 1879.

Dulaurier, Edouard. *Les Albigeois ou les cathares du midi de la France* (Cabinet historique XXVI). 1880.

Füszlin. *Kirchen und Ketzerhistorie der mittleren Zeit.* 1772.

Gieseler, Johann Karl Ludwig. *Lehrbuch der Kirchengeschichte.* 1844.

Guiraud, Jean. *Cartulaire de Notre Dame de Prouille* (Préface sur l'albigéisme au XIIIeme siècle). 1907.

Hahn, J.G. *Geschichte der neu-Manchéischen Ketzer.* 1845.

Jas. *Disputatio academica de Valdensium secta ab Albigensibus bene distinguenda.* 1834.

Lavisse, Ernest. *Histoire de France.* 1911.

Lea, Henry Charles. *Geschichte der Inquisition im Mittelalter.* 1905ff.

Magre, Maurice. *Magiciens et Illuminés.* 1930.

Maitland, Rev. Samuel Roffey. *Facts and Documents illustrative of the history, doctrine, and rites of the ancient Albigenses and Waldenses.* London, 1838.

Manuel de l'Inquisiteur Bernard Gui (Mollat ed.). 1926.

Molinier, Charles. *L'Endura, coutume religieuse des derniers sectaires albigeois* (Annales de la Faculté des lèttres de Bordeaux III). 1881.

Moneta of Cremona. *Adversus Catharos et Waldenses.* libri V. 1743.

Palauqui, Louis. *La verité sur l'Albigéisme.* Bordeaux: H. Alzieu, 1932.

Peyrat, Napoléon. *Histoire des Albigeois*. Vol. I: Civilisation romaine; Vol. II: La Croisade. 1880

————. *Histoire des Albigeois*. Vol. I–III: Les Albigeois et l'Inquisition. 1870.

Schmidt, Charles. *Histoire et doctrine de la secte des cathares ou albigeois*. 1849.

Vidal, J. M. *Doctrine et morale des derniers ministres albigeois* (Revue des questions historiques, LXXXV). 1909.

Walch, Christian Wilhelm Franz. *Entwurf einer vollständigen Ketzergeschichte*. 1766.

Parsifal and the Grail

Baist, Gottfried. *Parzival und der Gral*. Freiberg, 1909.

Bartsch, Karl. *Die eigennamne in Wolframs Parzival und Triturel*. 1875 (in Germanische Studien II).

Baudler, A. *Guiot von Provins*. 1902.

Benziger, Karl J. *Parzival*. 1914.

Beslais, A. *Le légende de Perceval le Gaullois*. 1904.

Biese, Alfred. *Deutsche Literaturgeschichte*. 17th ed. 1921.

Birch-Hirschfeld, Adolf. *Die Sage vom Gral und Ihre Entwicklung und dichterische Ausbildung in Frankreich und Deutschland im XII, und XIII Jahrhundert*. 1877.

Duchesne, Louis. *La légende de sainte Marie-Madeleine* (Annales du Midi). 1892–1893.

Fisher, Lizette Andrews. *The Mystic vision in the Grail Legend and the Divine Comedy*. New York: Columbia University Press, 1917.

Golther, Wolfgang. *Parsifal und der Gral in deutscher Sage des Mittelalters und der Neuzeit*. Leipzig: Xenian Verlag, 1908.

Griffith, Reginald Harvey. *Sir Perceval of Galles*. Chicago: Chicago University Press, 1911.

Hagen, Paul. *Der Gral*. Strassburg, 1900.

Heinrich, Guillaume Alfred. *Le Parcival de Wolfram d'Eschenbach et la légende du Saint-Graal*. Paris, 1855.

Heinzel, Richard. *Uber Wolframs von Eschenbach Parzival* (compiled by the Imperial Academy of Sciences, Vienna. Phil.-hist. Kl. 130). 1893.

————. *Uber der Französischen Gralromane* (ibid.). 1892.

Hertz, W. *Parzival*. Stuttgart: JG Cotta, 1898.

Historia dos Cavaleiros do Santo Graal. 1887.

Hoffmann, Walther. *Die Quellen des Perceval*. Halle an der Saale, 1905.

Iselin, Ludwig E. *Der mörgenlandishe Ursprung der Grallegende*. Halle an der Saale, 1909.

Kampers, Franz. *Das Lichtland der Seelen und der heiligen Gral* (2d Görres Gesellschaft). 1916.

Karpeles, Gustav. *Allgemeine Geschichte der Literatur*. 1891.

Küpp, Otto. *Die unmittlebaren Quellen des Parzival Wolfram von Eschenbach* (Zeitschr. f. d. Phil. XVII). 1885.

Lang. *Die Sage von heiligen Gral*. 1862.

Manteyer, Georges. *Les légendes saintes de Provence* (Mélanges d'histoire et d'archéologie de l'Ecole de Rome). 1897.

Martigny, Joseph Alexander. *Dictionnaire des antiquités chrétiennes*. 1865.

Martin, Ernst. *Zur Gralsage*. Strassburg, 1880.

Morin, Dom G. *Saint-Lazare et Saint-Maximin* (Mémoires de la Société des antiquaires de France). 1897.

Palgen, Rudolph. *Der Stein der Weisen* (Etudes des sources de Parsifal). Breslau: Trewendt &. Granier, 1922.

Paris. *Perceval et la légende du Saint-Graal*. 1883.

San Marte (pen name for Albert Schulz). *Leben und Dichten Wolframs von Eschenbach*. Magdeburg, 1887.

———. *Parzivalstudien* I–III. 1861–1862.

———. *Sein oder Nichtsein des Guiot von Provence*. 1883. [in the magazine, Zeitschr. f. d. Philologie XV].

———. *Uber die Eigennamen im Parzival des Wolfram von Eschenbach*. 1887.

Sterzenbach. *Ursprung und Entwicklung der Sage von heiligen Gral*. 1908.

Strucks, Carsten. *Der junge Parzival*. 1910.

Sühling, Freidrich. *Die Taube als religiöses Symbol im christl. Altertum*. Freiberg, 1930.

Wechssler, Eduard. *Die Sage von heiligen Gral in ihrer Entwicklung bis auf Richard Wagners Parsifal*. 1898.

Weston, Jesse L. *The Legend of Sir Perceval. Studies upon its origin*. London: David Nutt, 1909.

Huon de Bordeaux

Graf. *I complimenti della Chason d'Huon de Bordeaux*. 1878.

Guessard, F. & Grandmaison C. (eds). *Les anciens poètes de la France*, vol. V, *Huon de Bordeaux*. Paris, 1860.

Schäfer, Hermann. *Uber die Pariser Hss. 1451 und 22555 der Huon de Bordeaux Sage*. Marburg, 1892.

Voretzsch, Carl. *Die Kompositionen des Huon von Bordeaux*. Halle, 1900.

Esclarmonde et Montségur

Coulet, Jules. *Le troubadour Guilhem Montanhagol*. Toulouse, 1898.

Gaussen, Louis. *Montségur roche tragique*. 1905.

Palauqu, Louis. *Esclarmonde de Foix*. 1911.

Peladan, Josephin. *Le secret des troubadours*. Paris: Sansot et Cie ed., 1906.

Sabarthès

Castillon (d'Aspet). *Histoire du comté de Foix*. Toulouse, 1852.

Gadal, Antonin. *Ussat-les-Bains*. Editions de La Rose-Croix d'Or.

Garrigou, Adolphe. *Etudes sur l'ancien pays de Foix*. 1846.

———. *Sabar*. 1849.

Vidal, Abbé J. M. *Doctrine et morale des derniers ministres albigeois* (Revue des questions historiques LXXXV). 1909.

———. *Tribunal de l'Inquisition de Pamiers*. Toulouse, 1906.

The Albigensian Crusade

Barreau-Darragon. *Histoire des croisades contre les Albigeois*. 1843.

Chanson de la croisade contre les Albigeois (Begun by Guillermo de Tudela and continued by an anonymous poet). Paul Meyer ed. 1875.

Guilelmus de Podio Laurentii Chronica super historia negotii Francorum adversus Albigenses (Duchesne, Scriptores historiae Franciae V). 1649.

Heisterbach, Caesar von. *De miraculis et visionibus sui temporis seu dialogus miraculorum*. 1850.

Julia, Henri. *Histoire de Béziers*. Paris: Maillet, 1845.

Langlois, Gauthier. *Histoire des croisades contre les Albigeois*. 1703.

Luchaire, Achille. *Innocent III*. Vol. II: *La croisade des Albigeois*. Paris, 1905.

Marturé, B. A. *Histoire des comtes de Toulouse*. Castres: Auger, 1827.

Petri Vallium Sarnaii Monachi Albigensis (Guèbin-Lyon ed.). 1926.

Sismondi, Jean-Claude. *Die Kreuzzüge gegen die Albigenser*. 1829.

Walch, Christian Wilhelm Franz. *Entwurf einer vollständigen Ketzergeschichte*. 1766.

Works already cited, however indispensable:

De Vic, Dom Claude & Vaisette, Dom Joseph. *Histoire générale de Languedoc* (Privat, Toulouse ed.). 1872–1905.

Lavisse, Ernest. *Histoire de France*. 1911.

Lea, Henry Charles. *Geschichte der Inquisition im Mittelalter*. 1905ff.

Magre, Maurice. *Magiciens et Illuminés*. 1930.

Peyrat, Napoléon. *Histoire des Albigeois*. Vol. I: Civilisation romaine; Vol. II: La Croisade. 1880

———. *Histoire des Albigeois*. Vol. I–III: Les Albigeois et l'Inquisition. 1870.

Schmidt, Charles. *Histoire et doctrine de la secte des cathares ou albigeois*. 1849.

Vossler, Karl. *Peire Cardenal, ein Satiriker aus d. Zeitalter der Albigenser Kriege* (compiled by the Bavarian Academy of Sciences). 1916.

The Inquisition

Augsburg, David von. *Tractatus de inquisitione haereticorum* (compiled by the historical section of the Royal Bavarian Academy of Science). 1876.

Cauzons, Thomas. *Histoire de l'Inquisition en France*. 1909.

Comba, Emilio. *Histoire des Vaudois*. Paris, Lausanne, Florence, 1901.

De Vic, Dom Claude & Vaisette, Dom Joseph. *Histoire générale de Languedoc* (Privat, Toulouse ed.). 1872–1905.

Doat, Jan. *Copies des registres de l'Inquisition d'Albi, Carcassonne, Toulouse, Narbonne, etc* (compiled on the orders of the Minister Colbert under the direction of Jan Doat—a series of 258 mss. at the Bibliothèque Nationale de France, Paris).

Douasis. *Documents pour servir à l'histoire de l'Inquisition dans le Languedoc*. 1900

———. *L'Inquisition ses origines, sa procédure*. 1906.

Gmelin, Julius. *Schuld oder Unschuld des Templarordens*. Stuuttgart, 1893.

Gui, Bernardo. *Manuel de l'Inquisiteur* (Mollat ed.). 1926.

Guiraud, Jean. *Cartullaire de Notre Dame de Prouille* (Préface sur l'albigéisme au XIIIeme siècle). 1907.

Guiraud, Jean. *Saint Dominique*. 1923.

Haller, Johannes. *Papsttum und Kirchenreform*. Vol. I, Berlin,1903.

Hauréau, (Jean) Barthélemy. *Bérnard Délicieux et l'Inquisition dans le Langue-doc*. 1877.

Havel. *L'Héresie et le bras séculier au Moyen Age jusqu'au XIIIeme siècle* (Bibl. de l'Ecole des Chartes XLI). 1880.

Jakob, Karl. *Studien über Papst Benedikt XII*. 1910.

Lacordaire, Jean Baptiste Henri. *Vie de saint Dominique*. 1840.

Lea, Henry Charles. *Geschichte der Inquisition im Mittelalter*. 1905ff.

Limborch, Philippus van. *Historia Inquisitionis cui subjungitur Liber senten-tiarum Inquisitionis Tholosanae ab anno 1307 ad annum 1324*. 1692.

Michelet, Jules. *Procès des Templiers* (Collection des documents inédits sur l'histoire de France). 1841.

Molinier, Charles. *L'Hérésie et la persécution au XIme siècle* (Revue des Pyrénées VI). 1894.

———. *L'Inquisition dans le midi de la France.* Paris, 1880.

Mollat, Guillaume. *Les papes d'Avignon.* Paris: Librairie Lecoffre, 1924.

Müller, Karl. *Die Waldenser und ihre einzelnen Gruppen.* 1886.

Peyrat, Napoléon. *Histoire des Albigeois.* Vol. I: Civilisation romaine; Vol. II: La Croisade. 1880

———. *Histoire des Albigeois.* Vol. I–III: Les Albigeois et l'Inquisition. 1870.

Schmidt, Charles. *Histoire et doctrine de la secte des cathares ou albigeois.* 1849.

Tanon, C.L. *Histoire des tribunaux de l'Inquisition dans le Languedoc.* 1893. 1900.

Tuberville, Arthur S. *Medieval Heresy and the Inquisition.* 1920.

Verlaque, V. *Jean XXII, sa vie et ses oeuvres.* Paris, 1883.

Vidal, Abbé J.M. *Bullaire de l'Inquisition française au XIVe siècle et jusqu'à la fin du Grand Schisme.* 1913.

———. *Le tribunal de l'Inquisition de Pamiers.* 1906.

Vossler, Karl. Peire Cardenal, ein Satiriker aus d. Zeitalter der Albigenser Kriege (compiled by the Bavarian Academy of Sciences). 1916.

TRANSLATOR'S BIBLIOGRAPHY

English Titles

Baigent, Michael, Richard Leigh, and Henry Lincoln. *Holy Blood, Holy Grail.* London: Jonathan Cape, 1982.

Biedermann, Hans. *Dictionary of Symbolism: Cultural Icons and the Meanings behind Them.* Trans. by James Hulbert. New York: Meridian Books, 1994.

Bulwer-Lytton, Edward. *The Coming Race.* London: George Routledge and Sons, 1871. Reprinted by Sutton, 1995.

Burkat, Paul. *Island Erforscht.* 1936.

Eschenbach, Wolfram von. *Parzival.* Trans. by Arthur Thomas Hatto. London: Penguin Books, 1980.

Evola, Julius Caesar. *Introduction to Magic.* Rochester, Vermont: Inner Traditions, 2001.

———. *Men Among the Ruins.* Rochester, Vermont: Inner Traditions, 2002.

———. *The Mystery of the Grail.* Rochester, Vermont: Inner Traditions, 1996.

———. *Revolt Against the Modern World.* Rochester, Vermont: Inner Traditions, 1995.

Freelander, Alan. *The Hammer of the Inquisitor, Brother Bernard Délicieux and the Struggle against the Inquisition in the XIVth century.* Leiden, Netherlands: Brill Academic, 1999.

Kurlansky, Mark. *The Basque History of the World*. New York: Vintage, 2000.

Lea, Henry-Charles. *A History of the Inquisition of the Middle Ages*. 3 volumes. New York, 1888.

Milington, Barry (ed.). *The Wagner Compendium*. London: Thames and Hudson, 2001.

Pennick, Nigel. *The History of Pagan Europe*. New York: Routledge, 1995.

Non-English Titles

Angebert, Jean and Michel. *Hitler et la Tradition Cathare*. Robert Laffont ed. Paris, 1971.

Bandino, Mario. *Il Mito che Uccide*. Longanesi, 2004.

Benoist, Alain de. *Les Translations d'Europe*. Editions du Labrynthe, 1996.

Boron, Robert de. *Le saint-Graal, ou Joseph d'Arimathie*. 3 volumes. Le Mans: Moyer, 1878.

Burkat, Paul. *Island Erforscht*. 1936.

Conte, Paul. *Le Graal et Montségur*. Auch: Impr F Cocharaux, 1952.

Evola, Julius Caesar. *Julius Evola nei documenti segreti dell'Ahnenerbe, a cura de B. Zoratto*. Fondazione Evola.

Fiebag, Johannes and Peter. *Die Entdeckung des Grals*. Goldman Verlag, 1989.

Gadal, Antonin. *Sur le chemin du saint-Graal*. Rozekruis ed. Haarlem, Netherlands: Pers., 1991.

Gui, Bernard. *Le livre des sentences de l'inquisiteur Bernard Gui* (1308–1323). Texte edité, traduit et annoté par Annette Pales Gobillard. CNRS. 2 tomes. Paris, 2004.

Hervas, Ramon. *Jesus, o el gran secreto de la Iglesia*. Barcelona: Ediciones Robinbook, 2004.

Kater, Michael. *Das Ahnenerbe der SS*. 1935–1945. R. Oldenburg, 1974.

Ladame, Paul-Aléxis. *Quand le laurier reverdira*. Geneva: Slatkine, 2002.

Lange, Hans-Juergen. *Otto Rahn und die Suche nach dem Gral*. Engerda: Arun-Verlag, 1999.

Loisy, Alfred. *Les mystères païens et les mystères chrétiens*, Paris, 1914–18.

Magre, Maurice. *Lucifer*. Paris: Fasquelle, 1929.

———. *Magiciens et illuminés*. Paris: Fasquelle, 1930.

———. *Le sang de Toulouse*. Paris: Fasquelle, 1931.

———. *Le trésor des Albigeois*. Paris: Fasquelle, 1938.

Nelli, René. *Ecritures cathares*. Planète, 1968.

Niel, Fernand. *Les Cathares de Montségur*. Paris: Seghers, 1973.

————. *Montségur, la montagne inspirée*. Paris: La Colombe, 1952.

Pauwels, Louis and Jacques Bergier. *Le Matin des Magiciens*. Poche, 1972.

Peladin, Joséphin. *Le secret des troubadours—de Parsifal à Don Quichotte*. Sansot et Cie. ed. Paris, 1906.

Peyrat, Napoléon. *Histoire des Albigeois*. 1500 pages; *Histoire des Albigeois*, Volume I, *Civilisation romaine*, and Vol. II, *La Croisade*. A second series appeared with vols. I–III, *Les Albigeois et l'Inquisition*.

————. *L'Histoire des Albigeois*. Lacour-Ollé ed. Nîmes, 1998.

Rachet, Guy. *La Bible, myths et réalités, La Bible et l'histoire d'Israël*. Paris: Editions du Rocher, 2004.

————. *Les Matins de la France*. Paris: Bartillat, 1999.

Renan, Ernest. *La vie de Jésus*. Schönhofs Foreign Books, 1974.

Roché, Déodat. *L'Eglise romaine et les cathares albigeois*. Cahiers d'Etudes Cahiers, 1969.

Troyes, Chrétien de Troyes. *Perceval et le Gaullois ou li contes du Graal*. Trans. by L. Foulet. Paris: Cent Romans Français, 1947.

INDEX

Abluses, Godfrede de, 182–83
achmardi, 25, 197
The Acts and Deeds of the Apostles (Luke), 72
Adélaide. *See* Boisseson Lombers, Adélaide de
Ahura Mazda, 64–65
Albano, Cardinal, 206
Albi, 121
Albigenses, ix, xx–xxi, 78, 119, 123, 131, 190–91
   See also Crusade, Albigensian
The Albigenses (Lenau), 75–76, 81–82, 86, 116, 148, 149, 155
Albion, 67, 200
Alexander III, Pope, 121, 123, 206
Alfar, Raimon de, 172
Alfonso the Chaste, 10–12, 37–38
Améric, 33
Amor, 86–87
Amor-Eros, 43–44
Apocalypse of Saint John, The, 72
Apocalypse to Rome, 170–71
Apollo, 55, 57–58, 58, 69, 97
Aragon, Pedro de, 150–51
Argonauts, 55–56
Arianism, 122
Arthur, King, 20, 197
assets, confiscation of, 168, 209
Astarté-Artemis-Diana, 105–6

astrologers, 66, 92
Autier, Pierre, 185
Auvergne, Piere de, 7–8, 196
Avignonet, 171

Baal, 54–55
Babylonian dragon's crown, 79, 201
baptism, 87
Barbarossa, Frederick, 18
bards, 66
Bebrices, 54
Belissena, 105
Benrath, Henry. *See* Rausch, Albert H.
Bernard, Roger I (Count of Foix), 30
Béziers, 132–34
"Black Mountain," 203
boats, 97
Boisseson Lombers, Adélaide de, 34–35, 37–39, 122–24, 195
Boniface VIII, Pope, 179
bonshommes, 91
Born, Bertran de (Viscount of Hautefort), 6, 13–15, 18, 20–21, 22–24
Buddhism, xxi, 65, 86, 115
Burlats, Adélaide de, 21

Cabestanh, Guilhem de, 8–9
Carcassonne, 26
carnal love, 80, 106–7, 112, 120

Castell Roselló, Raimundo del, 8–9
Castelnau, Pierre de, 128, 129
Catharism, 115
Cathar Manisola, 86–87, 202–3
Cathars, xx–xxi
  debates, 121, 126
  descendants, 187–89
  doctrines, 74–95, 201
  literature, 74–76
  pathway of the Pure Ones, 47, 60,
   198
Celt Iberian
  theogony, 64
  tribes, 45, 61–64
Cervorix, 68–69
chastity, 112
chivalry, 4–10, 117
Christian religion, 70–73
Church, corruption in the, 118–19
Church of Amor, 84–92, 111–12
  See also Cathars
The Church of the Paraclete, 205
Ciste Ficorini, 199
Cistercian order, 129
Citeaux, Arnaud de, 125, 129–30,
  137, 138, 206
Clairvaux, Henri de, 123
Clement V, Pope, 179–80
Conrad, Prince of Tyre. See
  Montferrat, Marquis of
consolamentum, 87–92, 99–100,
  171, 174, 203
Consolamentum Spiritus Sancti, 87
Constance (wife of Saint-Gilles), 12
Conti, Lotario de', 124
Council of the Lateran, Third, 123
Council of Tours, 121
cross
  repudiation of, 115–16, 205
  symbol of God, 57
  wearing as punishment, 164, 209
Crotona, 59

crown, Babylonian dragon's, 79, 201
Crusade, Albigensian, 123, 129–54
Crusade, Second (1147–1148), 11
Crusade, Third (King's Crusade),
  15–16, 19–20, 196
Crusade Against the Grail (Rahn), vii

death, 50–51, 64, 89–92
debates, 121, 126
Délicieux, Bernard, 181–84, 183
Delphi, 62–63
devil, 76–77, 83
Die Albigenser, viii
  See also The Albigenses (Lenau)
Dispater, 60, 199
Döllinger, Ignaz von, x
Domingo, 157–58
Dominican Order, 158–59
dove, symbol of, 106, 108–9
Drudjodemana (House of Lies), 65
Druids, 59–61, 66, 68, 73–74, 105,
  200
dualism, 65–66, 76, 82–83, 115
Dyaus pitar, 65

ecclesiastical power, contempt for,
  119
Eleonore of Poitiers, 12
endura, 89, 203
Epistle to the Romans, 78
Escas, Amaniu des, 5–6
Eschenbach, Wolfram von, vii–viii,
  35–37, 44–45
  quotes, xix, 32, 35, 40, 47, 48,
   49, 78, 93–96, 102–3, 104–5,
   106–7, 108, 111, 194
Esclarmonde. See Foix, Esclarmonde
  de
Eucharist, 85–86, 120

Faidit, Gaucelm, 23–24, 197
faydits, 178

field of fires, 176

The First Walpurgis Night (Goethe), 73–74

fish, symbol of, 97–98, 204

flagellation, 163–64, 209

Flandres, Mathilde de, 131

Foix, Castle of, 29–30, 110

Foix, Esclarmonde de, 30, 99–100, 106–7, 108–10, 115, 126, 174, 204, 206

Foix, Lupo de, 99

Formosus, Pope, 167

fountain of youth, 97

Fountane la Salvaesche, 93–100

Fournier, Jacques, 180–81, 183–86

Francis of Assisi, 183

Frisé, Adolf, xii

Fulk of Neuilly-sur-Marne, 22, 116, 205

Gadal, Antonin, xi, 191

Gall, Baron von, 191

Genesis dogma, 45

Georg Büchner Prize, vii, 193

Geralda, Donna, 33–34, 146–47

Gerold, Hugo, 169

Gethsemane, 187

Gleysos, 48, 198

Golden Fleece, 56, 66, 97, 106

Good Friday, 198

Grail, xiv, xix, 47, 56, 94–112, 115, 177, 189, 193–94, 199

Graveillaude, 134–35

Graves, Robert, 193

Gui, Bernard, ix, 184–85, 206

Guyot, xix, 194

Gwion, 67, 200

"habit," the, 88, 203

Heisterbach, Caesarius von, xx, 194

hell, 200

Henry II, 12–13, 14–15

Hercules, Tomb of, 52–53, 55

hermitages, 48

Herodotus, 54

Himmler, Heinrich, xii–xiii

Hindus, 115

Holy Spirit, xi, 86, 115, 202, 205

House of Anjou, 12–13

House of Aragon, 10–11

Huon de Bordeaux, 101

Hursio, 11

Hyperboreans, 57

immortality, 59–60

Inconnue de la Seine, 89–92

India of Toulouse, 11–12, 15

Innocent III, Pope, 22, 118, 125, 147–48, 168, 206

Inquest, proceedings model, 159–63

Inquisition, 158–89

Inquisitors, assassination of, 171, 210

Inquisitor's Manual, The (Gui), ix, 119–21, 193

Iranian Mazdaist doctrine, 64

the island of the Seine, 68, 200

Jehovah, 77–78

Jerez de la Frontera, 95

Jesus of Nazareth, 70

Jewish populations, 28

Joachim of Flora (de Fiore), 18–19, 196–97

John, Gospel of, 48, 77, 80, 81, 82, 86, 88, 91, 112, 209

John XXII, Pope, 168–69, 209

Jordan, Raimon, 9–10

Judgment Day, 65

Jupiter, 65

Kampers, Franz, xxii, 194

Kant, Immanuel, 50

knights, 4–10

knights of Montségur, 172

Knights Templar, 179–80
Kyot, xix, 35

Lac des Druides. See Lake of Trout
Ladame, Paul-Aléxis, xi, 193
Lake of Trout, 60–61
Lapis exillis, 199
   See also Grail
Las Navas de Tolosa, 150
La Tour, Michel de, 6–8
Lavaur, 145–46
Lavaur, castle of, 33–34
Lazarus, 111
Lenau, Nikolaus, viii
   See also The Albigenses (Lenau)
Leo XIII, 131–32
leys d'amors, 3–10, 112
L'Histoire des Albigeois (Peyrat), ix, 193
Liber de duobis principiis, 201
life-fertility, 64
Lille y Gimoez, Jordan de, 100, 109
Lombrives cave, 51–53, 55
Lord's Prayer, 85, 120
love
   carnal love, 80, 106–7, 112, 120
   laws of the Minne, 3–10
Lucifer, 49–50, 77–81, 106, 112
Lucifer's Court, a Journey to Europe's Good Spirits (Rahn), xii–xiii
Luke, 72, 200

Magdalena, Maria, 111
Magdalene, Church of the, 27
Magre, Maurice, xxi, 194
Mani, viii, xiv, 86, 115, 205
Maouran, Pèire, 122
Map, Walter, xx, 194
Marcabru, Troubadour, 16
Mareulh, Arnaut de, 5–6, 38–39, 195

Marjevols, Bernard Sicard de, 153–54
matrimony, 112
Matthew, gospel, 126
Mazdaist theogony, 65
meat, consumption of, 88, 93, 120, 204
Melkart, 54
Merlin's prophecies, 201
Messiah, 70–71, 200
metempsychosis, xxi
Minne, 3–10, 38–39, 45, 84–92, 111–12
Minnedienst, 4
Minne singers, 36
Miravalh, Raimon de, 6–7, 25–26, 195–96
Mirepoix, Peire-Roger, 176–77
Mitilene, Alkaios de, 58
Monmur, 102–3
Montanhagol, Guilhelm, 4, 195
Montferrat, Marquis of, 17–18
Montfort, Simon de, 141–42, 145–46, 152
Montségur, xxi, 47, 60, 105–7, 108–11, 172–76, 191–92
Mosaic Law, 78
Moses, 78
Mount of Transfiguration. *See* Tabor
Munsalvaesche, 32, 197
Muntsalvaesche, 96, 104–7

Narbonne, 27–28
naturalism, 72
Nostradamus, 195

oak trees, sacred, 3, 26, 56, 66, 106
Oberon, 102–3
Occitan Cathars, 74–75, 81–92
   See also Cathars
Occitania, 21–22, 28, 45, 117–19, 190

Occitan knighthood, 4–10
Ogmi, 67, 200
Ornolac, 177

paleness, 94
Pamiers conference, 126–27, 206
papal brutality, vii–ix, 167–71,
    179–80
Papiol, 196
Paraclete, 173
Parnassus of Occitania, 111
Parsifal (Eschenbach), viii, xix,
    35–40, 44, 193, 195
Path of the Pure Ones, 47, 60, 198
Peirol, 17
Péladan, Joséphin, xxi, 194
Perfect Ones, 84–92, 176, 201–2
    See also Cathars
Peyrat, Napoléon, ix–x, 195, 196,
    197, 198, 204, 205, 206
Philip of France, 19–20
Philip the Fair, 179–80, 182
Philosopher's Stone, 56
Phocians, 54, 55
Phoecaea, 55
Phoenicians, 54
pilgrimages, 164, 209
Pirène, Tomb of, 53
planh, 14, 196
Plantagenets, 12–13, 21
    See also Richard the Lionheart
Polaires, 194
Priscillianism, 74–75, 200
protectors, 6, 195
Provençal, 6, 195
Provins, Guyot de, 34
Pure Ones, 45, 47, 60, 82–92,
    108–12, 178
    See also Cathars; Path of the Pure
    Ones
purgatory, 120
Pythagoras, 59, 69, 199

Rahn, Otto, vii–xv
Raimon Drut, 29, 33, 99
Raimon-Roger, 132, 135–36, 139,
    208
Raimundo V, 24–25, 26
Raimundo VI, 124–25, 130–31,
    141–42, 152, 197
Raimundo VII, 152–53, 172–73
Rausch, Albert H., vii
Renan, Ernest, x
resurrection, 71
Richard the Lionheart, 14, 18–20,
    22–24
Rittersbacher, Karl, vii

Sabarthès caves, 48, 63, 93–100,
    186–87
Sacconi, Rainier, 124
sacro catino, 196
Saint-Gilles, Raimundo de, 11–12
Saissac, Ermengarde de, 32
Saladin, Sultan, 15–16, 18–19, 22
Saosyat, 65
Schoye, Repanse de, 107, 109–10
Semitic migration, 54
Seremonda, Donna, 8, 196
Seven heavens, 78
She-Wolf (Stéphanie), 32–33, 195
snake that bites its tail, 109
Solomon's Treasure, 95
Sons of the Moon (Belissena), 30–31,
    197, 203
spirituals, 183
spulgas, 98–99
suicide, 89–92
Swan Knight, 104
swastikas, 65

Table of the Hebrews, 95
Tabor, 46–47, 108–11, 177, 189
Taillefer, Roger, 28–29, 122–24
Taliesin, 67, 200

Termès, Raimon de, 142–43
Third Reich, xi–xii
Thomas Aquinus, 166, 209
torture, 164–65
Toulouse, 121–23, 171
Toulouse, Count of, 24–25, 128–31,
   130, 144
   See also Raimundo V; Raimundo
   VI; Raimundo VII
transmigration, 87, 91–92
"treasure of the heretics," 177
Trencavel, 26
Trencavel, Raimon de, 26–27, 28
Trevrizent, 93–100
troubadours, 4–10, 45, 74, 105, 112
Troyes, Chrétien de, 35–36, 197

Urban VI, Pope, 169–70, 209

vates, 66
vegetarianism, 88, 93, 120, 204
Veldenaer, 104
Vidal, Peire, 32, 43–44, 198
Vigeois, Prior de, 21
virgins, 107
Vision of Gregory the Great, 97
Volcae Tectosages, 61–63

Waldenses, xx, 119–21
Waldo, Peter, xx, 119
Water of Regeneration, 67
weavers, xx, 91

Zeus patar, 65
Zoroastrians, 198